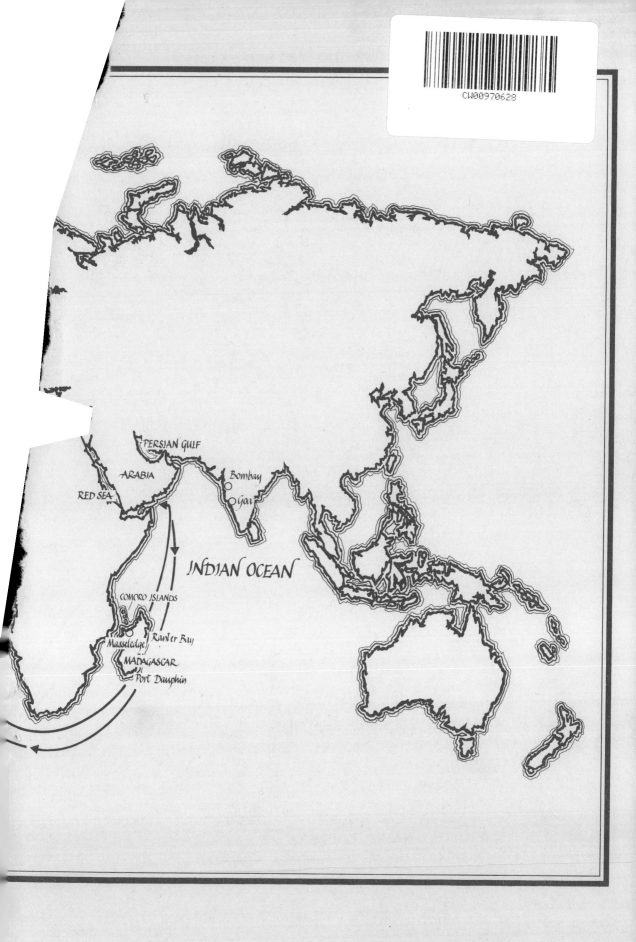

PERSIAN GULF

ARABIA

Bombay

RED SEA

Goa

INDIAN OCEAN

COMORO ISLANDS

Masselidge

Ranter Bay

MADAGASCAR

Port Dauphin

OUTCASTS OF THE SEA

Edward Lucie-Smith

OUTCASTS OF THE SEA

Pirates and Piracy

PADDINGTON
PRESS LTD
NEW YORK & LONDON

22

Library of Congress Cataloging in Publication Data

Lucie-Smith, Edward.
   Outcasts of the sea.

   Bibliography: p.
   Includes index.
   1. Pirates.   I. Title.
G535.L8   910'.453   77-20813
ISBN 0-448-22617-0

Printed in England by BAS Printers Limited, Over Wallop, Hampshire
Bound in England by R. J. Acford Limited, Chichester, Sussex
Designed by Patricia Pillay

IN THE UNITED STATES
PADDINGTON PRESS
Distributed by
GROSSET & DUNLAP

IN THE UNITED KINGDOM
PADDINGTON PRESS LTD.

IN CANADA
Distributed by
RANDOM HOUSE OF CANADA LTD.

IN SOUTHERN AFRICA
Distributed by
ERNEST STANTON (PUBLISHERS) (PTY) LTD.

Contents

Introduction

THE PIRATE HAS LONG been a figure of fascination to stay-at-home romantics, and the fascination is justified not only by the extraordinary adventures, many perfectly authentic, which are related by the principal pirate historians, but by the notion that the pirate himself is the type of the outcast, the man who has opted out of society. But, while there is certainly truth in the idea that the pirate is a kind of self-appointed Ishmael, it is also necessary to understand the circumstances which made piracy a tempting mode of existence, and a viable alternative to a life lived under the rule of law. It was not only that men have always been covetous, violent and greedy; and that, at times when the rule of law was weak upon land, it was natural that it should be almost non-existent at sea. It was also that the European nations built up, from the fourteenth century onward, a system of licensed reprisal for maritime wrongs which in times of war enabled seamen to take the law into their own hands. Piracy, from that time onward, was always a branch of privateering. It is not too much to say that a pirate was created when a privateer over-stepped the bounds of what was considered permissible. The moment when this was most likely to happen came at the conclusion of a long war, a period during which privateering had had the opportunity to take root as a form of maritime industry blessed by the very authorities who now, at the conclusion of peace, withdrew their sanction from it without making any provision for the employment of either the ships or the men which had been thus occupied.

So it is that the three great ages of piracy were: first, the early seventeenth century, when Elizabethan privateering was brought to an end by a new policy of peace with Spain; secondly, the early eighteenth century, especially after the general settlement brought about by the Peace of Utrecht in 1713; and thirdly, the two decades following the conclusion of the Napoleonic Wars in 1815. No sensible history of piracy can fail to take privateering into account, and that is why it plays such a prominent role in this book.

The other point which a survey of this kind must attempt to deal with is the pirate's semi-legendary status, the hold which he has established over the imaginations of mankind. The outcast escaped into fiction and established a new kingdom for himself, and lived there more vigorously and colorfully than ever in reality. No book on piracy can ignore this legendary dimension, which continues to influence our attitude to the facts, and to govern our responses to them. It is for this reason that my first chapter concerns itself with an analysis of literature rather than with history, as it is fiction in this instance which paradoxically directs us to the places where the real truth is to be found.

BRITISH MUSEUM

1
The Image of the Pirate

THE DEFINITION OF PIRACY is quite simple. It would be difficult to put it more plainly and concretely than it was put by Sir Charles Hedges, Judge of the Admiralty, at the trial of Joseph Dawson and others for piracy, at the Old Bailey in 1696:

> Now piracy is only a term for sea-robbery, piracy being a robbery committed within the jurisdiction of the Admiralty. If any man shall be assaulted within that jurisdiction and his ship or goods violently taken away without legal authority, this is robbery and piracy. If the mariners of any ship shall violently dispossess the master, and afterwards carry away the ship itself or any of the goods, or tackle, apparel or furniture, in any place where the Lord Admiral hath, or pretends to have jurisdiction, this is also robbery and piracy.

Granted that piracy is really no more than robbery at sea, how did the crime come to acquire the aura of sinister glamor that still clings to it, an aura which sets the pirate apart from other and more commonplace malefactors? Here is something which has a particular lure for men's imaginations, a source of deep-rooted and powerful fantasy. To some extent, these fantasies seem always to have existed. In the *Odyssey*, the swineherd Eumaeus tells how he was captured as a child by Phoenician

8

pirates, thanks to the treachery of his nursemaid, and then sold into slavery. In the much later *Aethiopica*, a Greek romance written in the third century A.D., the hapless lovers Theagenes and Chariclea are captured by pirates in a scene which resembles many to be found in far more recent novels. Equally familiar is the mechanism whereby they escape their captors. Trachinus, the pirate chief who desires the heroine, is robbed of her by dissension among his own crew, one of whom claims that the girl is his by right since he was the first to board the captive vessel.

But it is not until we reach the English and American literature of the past three centuries that we find anything resembling a continuous tradition of stories about pirates—stories which make sense in terms of the psychological needs of the societies that produced them. The development of the pirate tale goes hand in hand with the development of the novel, and it, too, must be regarded as the product of the social and economic factors which turned the novel into a separate and recognizable literary genre. In particular, the pirate tale, like the novel in general, is the product of the bourgeois imagination. One of its most important functions is to provide a safety valve against the pressures put on the individual by the demands of bourgeois morality.

In fiction there are pirates who are heroes, pirates who are villains, and occasionally pirates who are a combination of the two. But they are always larger than life. Even the most apparently sober and naturalistic fiction gives them a mythical dimension. The key fantasies are those of unrestrained liberty and power—compensations for what the prudent bourgeois can never achieve, however successful he is materially. The pirate is attractive to the reader not only because he acknowledges no constraints but because, in fantasy at least, he rises to incredible heights of power with only his own talents to help him. But he pays an appropriate price. He is self-sufficient, but he is also outcast, satanically alluring because he separates himself from the existing community, with all its compromises and hypocrisies, and creates his own world, at the price of declaring unconditonal warfare on the rest of mankind. Though the pirate is by this very definition an altogether exceptional being, he is also, paradoxically, a symbol of equality, a leveller either by inadvertence or design.

We first meet the fictional pirate, in the form in which I have been describing him, in the novels of Daniel Defoe and his imitators. Defoe's *Captain Singleton*, which is an elaboration of a supposedly factual pamphlet that he had once written about the notorious Captain Avery, the most celebrated pirate of the early eighteenth century, shows the genre at the beginning of its development. Typically, Defoe does his uttermost to convince the reader that the fictional character is no invention, but a being who actually existed—he blurs the line between what is truly reported and what is created as much as he can. Typically, too, he makes Singleton a matter-of-fact kind of man, an entrepreneur whose attitudes are little different from those of his colleagues, though these may be engaged in a more legitimate line of business. The blurring of the line between fact and fiction is accompanied by an equally deliberate blurring of the line between right and wrong. For the greater part of his career, Singleton is accompanied by a friend—the Quaker William. As a Quaker, William is officially a representative of puritan morality. Yet at any moment of crisis it is always he who provides Singleton with the excuse for continuing with his nefarious career. Defoe is aware of the irony, but he does not force this upon the reader. Indeed, *Captain Singleton* often seems like a cleverly baited trap, designed to demonstrate that conventional standards of morality are necessarily flimsy when confronted with the antagonists the story provides—liberty and the profit motive.

Other novels of the period, again usually presented as fact rather than fiction, are less subtly ambiguous. The pirate takes the villain's part, and is often employed as part of the picaresque mechanism, as an agent of violent change in the hero's fortunes. This is true, for example, of William Rufus Chetwood's *Captain Falconer* (1720), a direct imitation of Defoe both in style and in narrative method; and it is also true of John Barnard's *History of the Strange Adventures and Signal Deliverances of Mr. Philip Ashton* (Boston, 1735). This early example of American literature confronts us with a number of problems we shall meet again when discussing pirate sources. Though experts on the early eighteenth century novel usually treat it as fiction, and point to its manifest derivation from *Robinson Crusoe*, the British Library continues to catalogue it as fact. And there is plenty of evidence that Philip Ashton existed, and that he really was seized by the pirate captain Edward Low in Massachusetts Bay in 1722. His name, and those of other men concerned, were printed in the *Boston News-Letter* of July 9 that year. We know that he was born in 1702 in Marblehead, and that he had two wives and six children in the course of his life. But there is also evidence that Ashton's story has been considerably modified to fit the pattern of already popular fictional models.

Perhaps because piracy was an absolutely contemporary crime at the time when they were written, this first batch of pirate novels is considerably more restrained in its treatment of the theme than what was to come later. The nearest we get to the blood and thunder of nineteenth-century authors is on the stage, in a play called *The Successful Pyrate*, by Charles Johnson (1713). This seems to be the earliest dramatic work which takes a pirate for its central figure, though it is not the first in which pirates appear. Thomas Dekker's *If This be not a Good Play, The Devil is in It* (1612) contains token appearances from John Ward and Captain Dansiker, two famous seamen-renegades to the states of Barbary. The dramatist shows them as sinister figures of fun. The improbably named Arvigarus (a version of the ubiquitous Avery) is a different matter, a self-made king in Madagascar, ready to spout the noblest sentiments whenever occasion offers. Referring to his crew, he declaims:

> Have they not rang'd the Globe to serve my Cause;
> With me they made a Circle round this World,
> Disdain'd Relation, Country, Friendship, Fame,
> They toil'd, they bled, they burnt, they froze, they starv'd,
> Each element and all Mankind their Foe,
> Familiar to their Eyes saw horrid Death,
> In every Climate and in every Shape,
> When, in this Isle our shatter'd Barks found Rest,
> With universal Voice they call'd me King.

This is already the heroic outcast who makes frequent appearances in both the plays and the novels of the nineteenth century.

Pirate fiction languished in the latter part of the eighteenth century, as piracy itself was stamped out. The book which gave renewed impetus to the vogue, and indeed reinvented the genre almost completely, was Walter Scott's *The Pirate*. This enjoyed such a huge success with the public that in 1822 there were no less than three different versions of it being played on the London stage.

What Scott had done, as he perhaps consciously realized, was to tap a potent vein of folk-memory and folk-fantasy. In an appendix to the text he describes a meeting with an ancient "seller of winds" who lived at the village of Stromness in the Orkneys, and who claimed to have known John Gow the pirate—the subject, like Avery, of one of Defoe's pirate pamphlets. This meeting seems to have supplied the initial inspiration for the book.

The pirate of Scott's title, Captain Cleveland, is, as the old witch Norna describes him, "bold, haughty, and undaunted, unrestrained by principle, and having only in its room a wild sense of indomitable pride, which such men call honour." He is therefore the very type of the new kind of pirate-

These covers for early nineteenth-century music illustrate the Byronic cult of the pirate and its impact on the English theater.
HALL AND MCWILLIAM

hero, touched with the light and shadow of the Romantic Movement. The tale in which he appears, a farrago of spells, secret passages and long-lost sons, is equally typical of the direction pirate fiction was now to take, as it loosened its roots in reality and set out instead to create archetypes which fulfilled the demands of uninstructed popular fantasy.

One of the most convincing indices of the popularity of pirate stories with the nineteenth-century public is supplied by the list of play titles in the sixth volume of Allardyce Nicoll's classic *History of the English Drama, 1660–1900.* Here we find not only *The Pirate* (a title used by no less than eight different dramatic authors between 1800 and 1889) but all of the following, and quite a number more: *The Wizard Skiff, or the Pirate Boy* (1831); *Ocean Born, or the Pirate Father* (1852); *Battle of the Heart, or the Pirate Merchant* (1865); *The Pirate Minister* (1844); *Seven Capes, or the Pirate of Algiers* (1808); *The Pirate of Genoa* (1828); *The Island of Silver Store or the Pirate of the Caribbees* (1858); *The Devil's Ship and the Pirates of the Charmed Life* (1829). The words "buccaneer" and "corsair" were also popular in play titles.

What seems to have happened, thanks to Scott and his imitators, such as B. F. Judah, whose novel *The Buccaneers* appeared in 1827, was that pirate tales became a special department of the already established "gothic" tradition of romantic storytelling which started with Horace Walpole's *Mysteries of Udolpho*, and which continued to flourish until at least the middle of the nineteenth century. The special status, and special flavor, of gothic fiction can be compared to the position enjoyed by science fiction in the literary market today. Typical "pirate gothic" titles are *Captain Kyd, or the Wizard of the Sea* (1838), and *The Death Ship, or the Pirate's Bride and Maniac of the Sea* (1846). Pirate stories rapidly established a firm hold in the juvenile market with the work of Reid and Kingston, and that of Ballantyne.

Not all pirate literature after Scott was lacking in quality, however. It was American authors who helped to fashion that special branch of storytelling, the tale of pirate treasure. Amongst the earliest specimens are Edgar Allan Poe's "The Gold Bug" and Washington Irving's "The Guests from Gibbet Island." Later, Harriet Beecher Stowe was to attempt the same theme, with her "Captain Kidd's Money," published in *Oldtown Fireside Stories*. These treasure tales also belong to the gothic genre, since they nearly always contain some reference to the supernatural, though some authors (Poe is an example) tend to sidestep the issue by supplying a rational explanation for things which at first seemed entirely uncanny and inexplicable.

Like Sir Walter Scott on his visit to the Orkneys, Poe and, particularly, Washington Irving found a vein of folklore to draw upon. The activities of pirates in the early eighteenth century off the eastern seaboard of North America left their mark on the collective memory. And the mark was the deeper because what the pirates did could be yoked to one of the most persistent of all human fantasies. The idea of untold riches buried in the earth, waiting for the destined finder, has such an appeal to the unconscious that we find treasure-tales in almost all cultures. It is therefore not surprising to find that there is a persistent belief that the pirates of bygone days left behind them gigantic sources of hidden wealth, though eyewitness accounts generally represent them as being, like all adventurers, spendthrift and heedless with their money. The book which triumphantly synthesizes many aspects of the pirate myth, and in which buried treasure plays a leading part, is Robert Louis Stevenson's *Treasure Island*. Like Defoe's *Robinson Crusoe*, this has been relegated to the level of a children's classic; and, again like Defoe's story, it has become the pretext for plays and films which are quite frankly directed at a juvenile audience.

The horror movie and the pirate movie were sometimes combined (a continuation of a nineteenth-century convention): Christopher Lee in The Devil-Ship Pirates.
RONALD GRANT

These adaptations do less than justice to the subtlety of Stevenson's conception.

Treasure Island treats piracy at one remove. Indeed, it handles the pirate myth itself with a certain irony. When, in the first pages, the old sea captain arrives to install himself at that lonely seaside inn, the "Admiral Benbow":

> His stories were what frightened people worst of all. Dreadful stories they were; about hanging, and walking the plank, and storms at sea, and the Dry Tortugas, and wild deeds and places on the Spanish Main.

Yet the pirates the captain speaks of turn out to be real enough, and they supply the story not only with the mainspring of its plot, but with its most memorable characters. Blind Pew, who appears so briefly, is a wonderful personification of pure evil. But the most memorable characterization, and the making of *Treasure Island*, is that of the one-legged Long John Silver.

Silver, like Pew, has a moral nature whose ugliness is symbolized by

*Many actors have portrayed Stevenson's Long John Silver on stage and
screen. One, inevitably, was Orson Welles.*
RONALD GRANT

disabilities acquired in the pursuit of his piratical profession, but his
plausible joviality takes the reader in just as it takes in the boy who is
Stevenson's narrator. The way in which the boy is pulled this way and that
by Silver's flattery reflects the fluctuating nature of our own attitudes
towards the material Stevenson is using. And it is a stroke of genius to
permit Silver to survive unpunished, and to let him at last abscond with a
small share of the loot. By allowing Silver to live, and by rubbing in the fact
of his ambiguity, Stevenson shows how well he understands our deeper
feelings.

The literary tradition of piracy has continued into the twentieth
century. A number of gifted writers have attempted the genre, among
them the French surrealist Pierre MacOrlan, whose brief novel *Le Chant de
l'équipage* (1920) is a deliberate homage to Stevenson, and John Steinbeck,
whose *Cup of Gold* (1937) is a fictional life of Sir Henry Morgan. No one
could describe *Cup of Gold* as one of Steinbeck's major works, but it is
interesting to see that this supposedly realistic writer felt compelled to pay
homage to the gothic or supernatural element in the tradition he was using.

Before he sets off from Wales to make his fortune and lose his soul in the Indies, the young Harry Morgan has an interview with the wizard Merlin (a Welshman like himself), who foretells what will become of him.

On the whole, it is the writers of unashamedly popular fiction who have been most eager to quarry the pirate vein. In the twenties and thirties the pirate tale gradually shed its old-fashioned gothic appurtenances, but remained a specialized branch of storytelling. It was, perhaps, a cut above the pulp western that flourished at the same period, but was subject, like the western, to rigorous rules which had nothing to do with the disorder of real life. The most expert practitioner was undoubtedly Rafael Sabatini, whose buccaneer romances won him an immense following. It is hard to give a better description of one of these stories than the publisher's blurb that accompanies *The Black Swan* (1932), one of the best known of Sabatini's books:

> Rafael Sabatini . . . sweeps you, from his first words, into another world of thrilling adventure—a world of pirates and buccaneers, of challenge upon the high seas, of blood lust and brute strength pitted against gay courage. There are ships asking to be raided; there are murderous men waiting to leap upon their prey; and there is the fair Priscilla, wooed by a man who counts her heart above all plunder on the mighty main.

A recent article in *Time*, which scrutinized the current revival in Sabatini's reputation, pointed out that the Sabatini hero is a quite distinctive figure. He is a gentleman who has taken to piracy because he nurses some terrible secret of past misfortune, and the complications of the plot hang not only on the superior resourcefulness that good breeding brings with it, but on the hero's feelings of unworthiness when confronted with the transcendent, and rather icy, virtue of the heroine. Sabatini, though often careless, can be a fine descriptive writer, and he manipulates the sea-terms of the seventeenth and eighteenth centuries in a convincing way.

It was his books, and others like them, which inspired the long series of pirate movies made in Hollywood from the late twenties to the early fifties. It is not quite dead yet—an attempt was made to revive it with the unsuccessful *Swashbuckler* (*The Scarlet Buccaneer* in the United Kingdom), which was released in 1976. One of the earliest and most naively spectacular of these pirate epics was *The Black Pirate* (1926), a silent movie starring Douglas Fairbanks Snr. Here the director concentrated on stunts which would show off his athletic leading man to the best advantage. The

Douglas Fairbanks in The Black Pirate, *the most famous of the pirate silents.*
RONALD GRANT

best remembered of these shows Fairbanks descending from crowtop to maindeck by the simple expedient of planting his knife in the middle of a spread sail, and using this alone to break his fall. In fact, the trick was done by means of a concealed counterweight.

The long run of Sabatini films included silent versions of *The Sea Hawk*, with Milton Sills, in 1924, and *Captain Blood*, with J. Walter Kerrigan, in the same year. The later remakes of these titles are, however, better remembered today. The remake of *Captain Blood* in 1935, directed by Michael Curtiz, made a star of Erroll Flynn. *The Sea Hawk*, with the same star and the same director, was made in 1940, and epitomized the spectacular possibilities of the pirate film. It was followed in 1942 by an adaptation of *The Black Swan* starring Tyrone Power.

For many people (those old enough to remember them) it is these films which epitomize what piracy was about. In fact, as the rest of this book will demonstrate, the truth was usually very different. But we need not think that, by simply exchanging the fictions described above for the classic pirate source-books, we shall immediately arrive at a correct picture. It is a

17

Sabatini's novels were an inspiration for music as well as films.
HALL AND MCWILLIAM

peculiarity of the subject that the sources are corrupted, not only by the natural wish of criminals to conceal the facts about their activities, but by the degree of bias to be found in the contemporary chroniclers. There are two books in particular which have been responsible for creating the historical, as opposed to the fictional, image of the pirate. Both have the advantage of being immensely readable; and both have the disadvantage that they are difficult to check against documentary sources.

The earlier of the two is A. O. Exquemelin's *History of the Buccaneers of America*. This was first published in Dutch in 1678, and enjoyed immense success throughout Europe. There were editions in German (1679), Spanish (1681), English (1684) and French (1686). In each version the text tended to be modified to suit the tastes of the intended audience. Meanwhile, the author's own identity was until recently uncertain. It used to be thought that he was one Hendrick Barentzoon Smeeks, a surgeon and apothecary living in Zwolle, but it has since been discovered that an Alexandre Olivier Exquemelin really existed. Born about 1645, he was a native of Harfleur in France, and, on his return from buccaneering in the

The Sea Hawk, *in the Errol Flynn talking version (1940), illustrates the lavishness of Hollywood movies during this epoch.*
RONALD GRANT

West Indies he settled in Holland, probably because he was a Huguenot. He went to Tortuga, the principal buccaneer stronghold of the period, in about 1666, having entered the service of the French West India Company, and stayed on the island for three years. Later he sailed with the buccaneers themselves. After overseeing the publication of his book, he once again crossed the Atlantic, and was present at the attack on Cartagena in 1697.

Though Exquemelin seems genuinely to have been an eyewitness of the events he describes, he is a prejudiced and not always accurate historian. In addition to this, he was, as much as Sabatini at a different epoch, consciously engaged in writing for a popular audience. Nevertheless, he supplies details which exist nowhere else, and his influence has been enormous. It has been said of him that "perhaps no book of the seventeenth century in any language was ever the parent of so many imitations and the source of so many fictions. . . ." But one can go further than this. It is Exquemelin who supplies the framework for our understanding of the buccaneering episode in West Indian history, and his prejudices are so closely interwoven with our perception of the facts that it is impossible to separate the one from the other.

Intellectually speaking, however, it is Captain Johnson's *General History of the Pirates* which has had a more profound and lasting influence on the European mind. The book was first published in 1724, and there was a second and considerably enlarged edition in the same year, a third the year following and a fourth in 1726. In 1725 Dutch and German editions appeared, and within two years of publication there was a French translation as well. The authorship of "Captain Johnson's" work has been the subject of much debate and investigation. One thing seems certain: the book is not by the Charles Johnson who wrote *The Successful Pyrate*. The consensus of scholarly opinion now is that the *General History* is a late production of Daniel Defoe.

Defoe is one of the most fascinating and most elusive of English authors. Trying to determine just what he did and did not write is a task which has occupied investigators for many years. But this is not the only problem. As we have already seen from *Captain Singleton*, Defoe is adept not only at concealing his own identity but at counterfeiting the truth. Sir Leslie Stephen, with Victorian forthrightness, credited him with "the most amazing talent on record for telling lies." A modern authority speaks of his "genius for parquetry, piecing together bits from everywhere in new designs." The *Journal of the Plague Year* is a celebrated and typical example of his ability to produce an effect of utter verisimilitude in what is, at least technically, a work of fiction. Any historical work written by Defoe is therefore automatically suspect.

But if Defoe was a liar, *The General History of the Pirates* is nevertheless an important book both for its contents and its tone. It reflects both the man who wrote it and the age in which it was written, and does so more intensely than most works of narrative history. It can be examined on a number of different levels. The first of these concerns the question of its reliability. A close examination of the text does indeed do something to redeem Defoe's reputation for truthfulness, and certainly demonstrates his gift for conscientious research. Not only is it clear that the author had access to many sources which are now lost, but on those occasions where it is possible to check what he says, against trial records, government records and other "objective" material, it is evident that he reports accurately. The text is conspicuously fuller where Defoe had special resources at his disposal. For instance, one of Defoe's relatives by marriage participated in the trial of the surviving members of Bart Roberts's crew at Cape Coast Castle in March 1722, and the account of this pirate and his associates is

Captain Kidd was inevitably the subject of many movies. Two which starred Charles Laughton were the straightforward Captain Kidd *and the utterly improbable* Abbot and Costello Meet Captain Kidd.
RONALD GRANT

therefore quite logically the longest in the book and includes a summary of the trial proceedings. Defoe, who was a merchant and entrepreneur as well as a writer, was also at one period in his life a ship-owner. The *General History of the Pirates* shows that he retained his maritime connections and was able to make good use of them.

Those parts of the book which are invented rather than factual seem to fall into two categories. The first set of inventions is easy to detect. It consists of the long passages in direct speech, and the lively exchanges of dialogue. These can be thought of as approximations to what was actually said, which have been cast into this form for the sake of vividness. But we have to realize that they also serve another function, since they act as a convenient vehicle for the author's own ideas and opinions. Nevertheless, it would be risky to say that these are the only fictional passages. There is also the question of Captain Misson and of his associate, the priest Carraccioli.

Many pirate historians have no trouble in swallowing both Misson and his pirate republic of Libertalia, a settlement where every man had equal rights, and none was permitted to be rich and none poor. On the other hand, those who have examined the *General History* not so much because they are interested in pirates but because they are interested in Defoe and his ideas have tended to see both Misson and his republic as typical inventions of their author. They point out first that it is difficult to find any proof of Misson's existence outside Defoe's own pages (the fact that he and Carraccioli are the only foreign pirates in the book certainly adds to their elusiveness), and secondly that the episode itself serves an important balancing function in the design of the work as a whole.

The characteristic which is easily missed on a first reading of the *General History* is that which is most important about it: far from being a mere collection of anecdotes about maritime crime and criminals, it expresses a whole philosophy and view of society. As an author of his own special type, Defoe was always exceptionally sensitive to currents of popular feeling and popular opinion. In choosing to write a book about pirates he acted in response to a demand which he was certain existed. The correctness of his judgment was proved by the immediate success of the work. Clearly piracy was very much in the news in the first quarter of the eighteenth century, and, equally clearly, the figure of the pirate had already achieved legendary status in the public mind. Part of Defoe's purpose was to supply a want by giving fuller and more accurate information about pirates than had hitherto been available. In this sense, he was undertaking what is apparently a work of demythologization, and correcting the errors of his own earlier pamphlets about Gow and Avery. The brisk, humdrum style he uses, larded with excerpts from documents and trial records, is meant to confirm the impression that his purpose is to let a flood of light into a hitherto murky corner of contemporary history.

Yet to some extent at least he uses the pirate as a stalking horse. The *General History* contains a number of statements about the nature of society and the rights of property which were put into the mouths of the pirates themselves. Captain Bellamy declares, to the master of a ship he has just taken:

> I am a free prince, and I have as much authority to make war on the whole world as he who has a hundred sail of ships at sea, and an army of 100,000 men in the field, and this my conscience tells me. But there is no arguing with snivelling puppies, who allow superiors to kick them about deck at pleasure and pin their faith upon a pimp of a parson, a squab, who neither practices nor believes what he puts upon the chuckleheaded fools he preaches to.

Bellamy also speaks scornfully of those "who will submit to be governed by laws which rich men have made for their own security, for the cowardly whelps have not the courage otherwise to defend what they got by their knavery."

The complexity of the book springs in part from the care which Defoe takes to balance not only one character, but one point of view, against another. The psychopathic Blackbeard and the brutal Low (who cut off a captive's lips, broiled them before his face, and made him eat them) are contrasted with the idealistic Misson. Defoe gives the impression that he thinks democracy is the purest and most natural form of government, and he implicitly contrasts the instinctive egalitarianism of the pirates with the evils and corruptions of contemporary England. He even goes so far as to endow Libertalia with features borrowed from Sir Thomas More's *Utopia*. Yet he cannot bring himself to condone the complete breach with traditional moral and legal systems that the free life of the pirate implies. For him, the outcasts of the sea must inevitably slide towards the mindless cruelty which is the consequence of their devotion to purely material ends.

It is here that we seem to make a transition between what Defoe consciously thought and the unconscious pressures and prejudices which give their tone to his book. Defoe's own personal fascination with piracy is well established. In addition to the *General History* he produced the pamphlets about Gow and Avery which have already been mentioned, and largely rewrote and reshaped the material in Robert Drury's *Journal*,

Charles Boyer and Yul Brynner also had a go at the pirate genre in The Buccaneer, *directed by Cecil B. de Mille.*

the classic account of Madagascar in the pirate period. Piracy appears in seven of his major works of fiction: *Robinson Crusoe, Parts I and II*; *Captain Singleton*; *Moll Flanders*; *Colonel Jacque*; *A New Voyage Round the World*; and *The Four Years' Voyages of Captain George Roberts*. So in responding to the popular demand, he was also evidently responding to a need in himself.

Defoe belonged to the new class of "projectors" or, as we should call them, company promoters who emerged in London from 1680 onward in response to a marked quickening in the pulse of trade. Had he been more fortunate in that profession, he would never have felt the need to become more than an occasional writer. In many ways his thinking is typical of the group from which he came, the more so as many of its members were Dissenters, just as he was. A man of Defoe's type could not help sensing a parallel between pirate activity and his own economic ambitions. To his imagination such activity must have seemed an extension, thrilling because so logical, of the economic imperialism in which he too had participated.

At the same time, the figure of the pirate represented not only a social and material, but even a psychic threat to the world Defoe inhabited. He embodied an aggressive denial of the values of interdependence and social unity, supported by Dissent as well as by established religion, in which Defoe and the rest of the English mercantile middle class had been brought up. Defoe, like his audience, was still partially oriented by the old Christian frame of reference but was becoming uneasily aware that the world was steering by new stars. Though in theory he believed in *jure divino*—that Reason was the one monarch ruling by divine right—he instinctively tilted the balance against pirate society because it was too crudely "reasonable" for comfort. Writers ever since have done the same. They revel in the bizarre and exaggerated scale of many of the personages they describe, but it is not really their cruelties which Defoe and subsequent historians hold against the pirates. Their aim is to prove, not that wickedness must inevitably be punished, but that total and secular democracy (which many of them, including Defoe himself, find admirable in theory) leads inevitably to total chaos. The pirate community is an acceptable subject for an entertaining and colorful book because, when closely examined as a political institution, it is found to be self-destructive and therefore harmless.

The *General History* has been thus minutely discussed, not only because it is as much a work of literature as the novels which are also surveyed in this chapter, but because Defoe's brilliance has given a special character to piracy. Though in fact his book only covers one facet of a vast subject, it has dominated historical thinking about it for more than two centuries, much as Gibbon's *Decline and Fall* has continued to dominate thinking about the history of the Roman Empire. Nearly all subsequent accounts, even those dealing with material unused by Defoe or even unknown to him, perpetuate his point of view with all its inherent contradictions. The present volume, though its boundaries extend a very long way beyond what Defoe attempted to treat (though the text itself is much briefer) must still be regarded as essentially a critique of what the *General History* has to say. Like its great predecessor, it assumes that the pirate can only be defined by examining his social relationships—with other pirates, with those whom he robs, those who protect and profit from him, and those who attempt to suppress him. Society is the mirror in which we see this anti-social figure full-length.

But there is a further dimension which I have attempted to add. Defoe contributes to the pirate's mythical status without realizing what he is doing. Novelists, playwrights and film-makers have added to the myth, but without feeling any particular responsibility for the truth. This new outline history recognizes that the myth itself has become encapsulated in the subject. It is as much part of the "facts" as Morgan's sack of Panama. Here, if anywhere, we must examine the past in the light of what man's imagination has made of it.

2
Before the New World

I T IS PROBABLE THAT piracy has existed as long as seamanship. As soon as men learned to build boats, and to cross even short stretches of water in them, other men were making plans to attack and rob them. The pattern of piratical attack evolved step by step with the evolution of naval science. The earliest mariners had no navigational aids. They stuck to the coast, avoiding the open water whenever possible, and they beached their boats at night. The pirate, therefore, needed little cunning and less equipment. His plan was to attack the trading vessel when it was helpless, and drawn up on shore. A fight at sea was the exception rather than the rule. But as the situation altered, the pirate we now think of came into being.

As far as the ancient world is concerned, the area where we have the most information about piracy is the Mediterranean. The Greeks learned to be seamen very early, and some authorities would claim that they were sailors before they were recognizably Greek. The Minoan kings of Crete ruled over a maritime empire. Despite this, the Greek relationship with the sea was always one of love-hate. One of the great terrors for a Greek was to die far from his own kindred, and to be denied the customary funeral rites. Such a denial would leave his restless ghost to wander forever, unable to escape the trammels of mortality. It might come about through drowning, but another possibility was being taken as a slave.

The frequent references to pirates and piracy in Greek literature make it plain that the profession was well established in the Bronze Age, and continued to flourish thereafter. They also call our attention to another point. Pirates were not only robbers but, more specifically, slavers. Human merchandise was the most valuable, as indeed it continued to be in Mediterranean waters until at least the beginning of the nineteenth century. In the Greek world, each community tended to set its hand against every other. A free man, snatched from the city to which he belonged, might expect to find himself reduced to the status of a chattel. When Tyrrenhian pirates seized the god Dionysius, and tied him to the mast of their vessel, their object was to sell him as a slave. But, as we are told in the Seventh Homeric Hymn, the bonds fell off the captive, a vine grew up the mast and, seized with madness, the pirates themselves plunged into the sea, where they were transformed into dolphins. The subject is sometimes shown on Greek cups, appropriately enough, since Dionysius is the god of wine.

Greek pirates being keelhauled. From an engraving after a Greek vase.
BRITISH LIBRARY

It can be seen from the references to piracy and pirates in the Greek historians that patterns were soon established which are to be found repeated much later and in a very different context. Certain isolated groups of islands became notorious as nests of pirates—the Lipari islands became a headquarters for Rhodian and Cnidean filibusters from 580 B.C. onward.

It can also be seen that, as soon as a range of different types of ship

29

became available, the pirates had a decided preference for some rather than others. The boats they liked were swift, maneuverable, but above all versatile. One type of Greek ship that had a definite association with piracy was the *hemiola*, a smallish vessel with a bank and a half of oars, a feature which must have given it a good turn of speed. A ship of this sort is shown on a late archaic Greek vase in the British Museum, together with one of the heavy, round-bottomed cargo-carriers which would have been its natural prey. Another favorite pirate craft was the *myoparo*, an extremely versatile vessel with room to stow cargo, a mast and oars.

A hemiola *(right) attacking a merchantman (left). Greek black-figure cup, late sixteenth century B.C.*
BRITISH MUSEUM

In the ancient Mediterranean world, piracy always tended to flourish when control of the seas was contested or divided. In particular, an ambitious ruler would be inclined to give countenance to pirates if they helped him in his enterprises (we shall meet the phenomenon again in the England of Elizabeth). During the years that followed Alexander the Great's death, at a time when various successor kings were struggling fiercely for his heritage, pirates were enrolled in the fleets of Demetrius Poliorcetes, who in thanksgiving for a naval triumph erected the Victory of Samothrace which is now in the Louvre. A little later King Mithradates, the enemy of Rome, made use of Cilician pirates to harry his opponents.

The Civil Wars which led to the birth of the Empire allowed much scope for pirate activity. Perhaps the most famous story concerning pirates of this epoch is the one which is to be found in slightly different versions in Plutarch and Suetonius, and which concerns the early career of Julius Caesar.

The year was 78 B.C. Caesar, who had impeccably aristocratic connections, had nevertheless been a supporter of Marius, the leader of the "popular" party. After the triumph of Sulla, Marius' opponent, he was lucky not to be proscribed. Caesar withdrew from politics and from Rome, and was on his way to study rhetoric in Rhodes. While his ship was sailing

Demetrius Poliorcetes (left), king of Macedon, and Mithradates the Great (right), king of Pontus. Both used pirates as allies in their naval campaigns.
BRITISH MUSEUM

past the island of Pharmacusa, off the coast of Caria, it was captured by the pirates who then swarmed in those seas. Their business was mainly in ransoms, and they were pleased to find a rich Roman on board. Twenty talents was the ransom suggested; Caesar told his captors he was worth at least fifty. The pirates took him at his word, and the bulk of his attendants were sent off to raise the money. Caesar was left in the pirates' camp with two valets and his personal physician. The money was slow to come in, and he remained there for the space of nearly forty days.

During this time, Caesar spent his days in physical exercise, often in competition with his captors, and in writing verse and orations. These he read to his companions, who did not much care for them. When the pirates made too much noise and disturbed his rest, he sent to tell them to be quiet; and he promised them that, once he was set free, he would hunt them down and crucify them. His captors naturally regarded this as a joke.

When the ransom money finally arrived, Caesar was sent to Miletus, where the cash was handed over in exchange for his freedom. He

31

Coin portraits of Julius Caesar (left)
and Sextus Pompeius (right).
BRITISH MUSEUM

immediately borrowed four war galleys and some soldiers, attacked the pirate camp while the pirates were still celebrating their good fortune, and captured nearly all of them. The Roman praetor in charge of the area was reluctant to see sentence carried out, probably because he himself had a profitable relationship with this particular band (a pattern to be repeated centuries later in the West Indies and in the American colonies). Caesar circumvented him, and had all of the captives killed. The leaders were crucified as he had promised, but, out of gratitude for their hospitality, he had their throats cut before they were nailed to the cross.

Private arrangements between pirate bands and the Roman authorities were certainly not unknown at this period. Verres, the corrupt governor of Sicily denounced by Cicero in some of his most famous speeches, seems to have entered into such bargains from time to time. In any case, he was reluctant to spend money to quell the pirate menace. When his forces did capture a pirate ship—one such, off Megara, was so full of silver plate, silver coin, woven stuffs and handsome captives that it was unable to get away—Verres took possession of the loot, and the original owners never saw their property again.

The climax of piratical activity during the Civil Wars came with the career of Sextus Pompeius, the son of Pompey the Great. Sextus, unable to establish himself firmly on land, created a sea power which seriously threatened the triumvirs—Antony, Octavian and Lepidus. Shakespeare makes him one of the important secondary characters in *Antony and Cleopatra*. In Shakespeare, and indeed in Shakespeare's source, Sextus shows himself to be more honorable than most robbers. When the three triumvirs are trying to conclude a treaty with him, and are feasting aboard his vessel, one of his henchmen proposes that he should cut the cable. Sextus refuses:

> Ah, this thou shouldst have done,
> And not have spoke on't! In me 'tis villainy;
> In thee't had been good service.

His disgusted follower allows himself an aside:

> I'll never follow thy pall'd fortunes more.
> Who seeks and will not take, when once 'tis offer'd,
> Shall never find it more.

In fact, Sextus, after concluding a treaty with the triumvirs, fell out with them for a second time, and was finally defeated in a naval battle in the straits of Sicily.

Even under the Empire, there was sporadic pirate activity, and we find records of pirates in remote corners of the Roman world. For example, an inscription found on the island of Leuce at the mouth of the Danube tells of their presence in the Black Sea in imperial times. So long as the Empire still held together, the emperors remained very concerned about the safety and freedom of the seas, if only because Rome itself was so dependent on grain supplies shipped from outside Italy, and any interruption of these meant immediate trouble with the spoilt and restless populace.

The glimpses we get of piratical activity in the ancient Mediterranean do not amount to coherent or continuous history. For that it is necessary to go northward, and to move on at least as far as the Dark Ages. It has often been claimed, both in their own time and since, that the Vikings were pirates. The churchmen who suffered from their depredations certainly applied the term "pirate" to them, borrowed from the Latin. But it is doubtful if, in that context, it has any meaning. There was as yet no sea law, and no law upon the sea, save that which the individual could enforce with his own strength and his own weapons, and the situation was to continue for centuries to come.

Viking superiority at sea consisted in their tribal coherence and in their skill both as shipwrights and seamen. They built wonderful ships and handled them superbly well. Their raids upon England, Ireland and continental Europe represent only part of their activity; there was, in addition, their early commerce with the East. It is significant that, in early Viking hoards, the vast majority of the silver coins found come from the

The Roman grain fleet. A sarcophagus from Ostia.

Muslim world, and were struck by rulers such as the Umayyad and Abbasid caliphs who ruled in Baghdad.

The Vikings' activities in Europe itself have been divided by the Swedish scholar Fritz Askelberg into four different categories: first, individual raids, which can loosely be called "piratical"; second, political expeditions; third, colonizing ventures; and fourth, commercial penetration. Obviously there were not fixed barriers between these types of activity—they blended into one another.

Where England and Ireland were concerned, the destructive Viking raids upon monasteries began in 793, with an attack upon Lindisfarne. *The Anglo-Saxon Chronicle* gives a good idea of its devastating psychological effect:

> In this year terrible portents appeared in Northumbria, and miserably frightened the inhabitants: these were exceptional flashes of lightning, and fiery dragons were seen flying in the air, and soon a great famine, and after that in the same year the harrying of the heathen miserably destroyed God's church in Lindisfarne by rapine and slaughter.

In 794, there was a raid on Wearmouth monastery, and then in the year following one upon Iona. The raids were at their height between about 834 and about 930, and the aims of the various bands differed to some extent according to their own origins in Scandinavia. The Norwegians who made the earliest attacks showed a disposition to settle as well as to plunder. Norway was experiencing a rapid growth of population, and at the same time many of its inhabitants were growing restive at the constant expansion of royal power. The Danes, who did not begin their raids until forty years

A Roman merchantman, second century B.C. Ships of this kind formed the grain fleets that the emperors tried to protect at all costs.
SCIENCE MUSEUM

after the Norwegians, seem at first to have been raiders pure and simple. They behaved in the North Sea as they were accustomed to behave in the Baltic. But by Canute's day they were mustering fleets so large and magnificent that they were clearly no longer pirates but a mighty nation on the move:

> So great, also was the ornamentation of the ships that the eyes of the beholders were dazzled, and to those looking from afar they seemed of flame rather than wood. For if at any time the sun cast the splendor of its rays among them, the flashing of arms shone in one place, and in another the flame of suspended shields. Gold shone on the prows, silver also flashed on the variously shaped ships. So great, in fact, was the magnificence of the fleet, that if its lord had desired to conquer any people, the ships alone would have terrified the enemy, before the warriors whom they carried joined battle at all.

Conditions in the Baltic involved raids on a smaller and less organized

35

A Viking ship.
SCIENCE MUSEUM

scale and can be illustrated from the *Life of St. Ansgar*, written by his disciple Rimbert. Ansgar was born in the year 801, and trained as a monk at the monastery of Corbie, near Amiens. Transferring to Germany, he became involved in the effort to convert the pagan Danes and Swedes to Christianity. His biographer gives a vivid description of how the saint and a companion, making their way across the Baltic to the important Swedish trading town of Birka, which was on an island in Lake Malar, were set upon and robbed by sea-raiders:

> The merchants with whom they were traveling defended themselves successfully, but eventually they were conquered and overcome by the pirates, who took from them their ships and all they possessed, while they themselves barely escaped on foot to land. They lost here

the royal gifts which they should have delivered there, together with all their other possessions, save only what they were able to take and carry with them as they left the ship. They were plundered, moreover, of nearly forty books which they had accumulated for the service of God.

Long after the migratory impulse of the Vikings was spent the seas remained unsafe for travelers. Once out of sight of land, it was every man for himself. Until the very end of the fifteenth century, small distinction was made between pirate and merchant, and shipmasters often adopted one or the other role at will. Chaucer well characterized the type in his portrait of the Shipman in the Prologue to the *Canterbury Tales*:

> Few were the rules his tender conscience kept,
> If, when he fought, the enemy vessel sank,
> He sent his prisoners home; they walked the plank . . .
> The barge he owned was called the *Maudelayne*.

In the early part of the Middle Ages, independent pirate chiefs could often accumulate considerable power. It was an English pirate called Goderic, operating in the Mediterranean, who in 1102 successfully piloted Baldwin, King of Jerusalem, into Jaffa past the Egyptian blockade. A little later, in the thirteenth century, two men made considerable reputations for themselves in English waters. One was William March, son of the Justiciar in Ireland and married to the niece of the Archbishop of Dublin. Thanks to these connections, he obtained a post at the court of Henry III, but in 1235 he killed a king's messenger in Westminster Palace, thus committing the crime of *lèse majesté*. Outlawed, he fled to Lundy Island, which was to be for many years a pirate hide-out, and proceeded to raid shipping in the Bristol Channel for the next seven years, making a living by kidnapping and ransoming merchants. In 1238 he even went so far as to send an emissary to try to assassinate the king in his palace at Woodstock. The nuisance he caused became so intolerable that a successful assault was made on Lundy on a misty day in 1242.

Another, and even more celebrated, thirteenth-century outlaw was Eustace the Monk. Eustace is a well-established historical figure—he appears in the chronicle of Matthew Paris, and we know from other sources that at the height of his career he had a house "rich and well-built" in London, and that he had placed his daughter in the ultra-fashionable convent of Wilton Abbey. But he is also the hero of a French verse-romance which gives many picturesque, if apocryphal, details of his career.

37

Medieval pirates attack in the Baltic.
BRITISH LIBRARY

The younger son of a petty noble from Boulogne, Eustace was once in a
monastery (hence his nickname), but was later recalled to the secular life.
His adventures began when he fell out with his overlord, the Count of
Boulogne. After many escapades and hairbreadth escapes from his enemies
on land, he took to the sea and turned pirate as an ally of King John against
the French king. For seven years he was an auxiliary in the English royal
service, basing himself upon the Channel Islands, where he at one time
held Sark. In 1214, when the English barons rebelled against John,
Eustace the Monk changed sides and allied himself to Louis (the later
Louis VII) who, somewhat against the wishes of his father Philip
Augustus, was trying to seize England for himself. Thanks to Eustace's
help, Louis had at one time a fleet of nearly 900 ships. But this change of
masters brought the pirate no luck. He was in the van of an attempted
French invasion in the year 1217, and his fleet was routed off Sandwich on
St. Bartholomew's Day. His own ship, called "the great ship of Bayonne,"
is reported to have been hampered by being packed with soldiers and
freighted with a huge seige machine. After his defeat Eustace was captured
and executed at sea, having offered no less than 10,000 marks for his life—
an indication of the wealth he had accumulated.

Despite the existence of men like William March and Eustace the Monk,
the thirteenth century did see some developments in law, in shipbuilding

38

The punishment of pirates in the Baltic.
BRITISH LIBRARY

and in social organization which were eventually to bring about a
significant increase in safety at sea, and to lead to a more exact definition of
piracy. But it was to be a slow process. In the English law the most
significant event was the issue of the first privateers' commissions in 1243.
These gave seamen who were not employees of the crown a licence to wage
war in the king's name, and to recover from his and their enemies
compensation for supposed injuries. But they only provided the cover of
legality for a situation which was for the moment not susceptible to change.
It was not until the next century, for example, that new courts were
created to deal with pirate offences. In 1414 English law at last made
piracy into high treason though in 1435, at a time of chronically weak rule,
the act was suspended and there was an immediate outbreak of maritime
lawlessness.

The big change in shipbuilding was an increase in cargo capacity, which
gave an added importance to maritime trade and thus an additional
impulse towards regulating it and making it safer. Some time just before
1200 a new type of ship was invented, called the cog. It is uncertain
whether these ships were first constructed in the Hanse towns—a league of
German free cities which had banded together for the protection of maritime trade—or in the Low Countries. An account of the departure from
Cologne in 1188 of four great ships carrying crusaders to the Holy Land

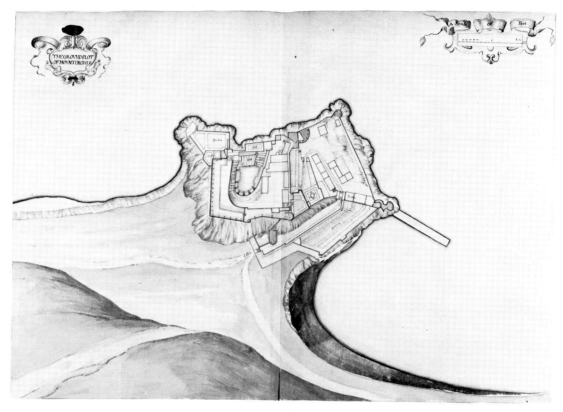

The castle of Mont Orgeuil, built partly as a bastion against pirate attacks on the Channel Islands in the Middle Ages.

seems to be one of the earliest mentions of them. The cog was a ship about ninety feet long and twenty feet broad, clinker-built and much deeper in draft than the Viking ships had been. It drew up to ten feet of water. The keel and sternpost were rectilinear, and some time after 1200 ships of this type began to be equipped with sternpost and rudder rather than with a steering oar. Cogs could carry up to 200 metric tons of cargo. Later, in the fourteenth century, another type of cargo-carrier was introduced, broader and flat-bottomed, the "barge" of Chaucer's poem, otherwise known as the hulk. Bulk cargo was at last a thoroughly economic proposition— provided, that is, the risks of voyaging could be somewhat reduced.

A third factor was the way in which trading seaports began to band themselves together into mutual-protection associations. In England, the Cinque Ports of the south coast, such as Rye, Winchelsea and Sandwich, formed a maritime league which became a force to be reckoned with, though it is typical of the time that their conduct was as much aggresive as it was defensive. Some historians have seen them as being themselves little

An English cog. The Hanse ships were of the same type.
SCIENCE MUSEUM

more than nests of pirates, the better equipped for their activities because they were answerable to no court in the kingdom except their own Shepway Court. In the conflict between Henry III and his barons (1264–6), they took the side of Simon de Montfort against the king, and installed Simon's son as their Warden. Thanks to their raids, all maritime trade came to a halt for two years along the east coast of England. After Montfort was defeated at Evesham, his son escaped to Winchelsea and continued the struggle by sea. When the Cinque Ports at last made their submission to the future Edward I, he was careful to treat them very leniently. And when Edward came to the throne, he found they had by no means lost their appetite for combat of whatever kind: in 1297 the king landed at Sluys, with the help of a fleet drawn from many parts of the kingdom. As soon as his troops were ashore, the ships of the Cinque Ports turned on those which came from Yarmouth, and burned seventeen of them. Another twelve were looted, and 165 men were killed.

More important than the Cinque Ports on the European stage was the

A ship of the Cinque Ports.
SCIENCE MUSEUM

Hanseatic League. The cog and the hulk are ship types intimately associated with the cities that belonged to this organization. One of the chief was Lübeck, on the Baltic, founded in 1143 and refounded on a slightly different site in 1158–9. In 1226 its growing importance was recognized when it was granted an imperial charter and became an imperial city, independent of any overlord. About 1230 Lübeck allied itself to the neighbouring city of Hamburg (whose maritime outlet was not, however, to the Baltic but to the North Sea). Other cities such as Rostock joined in and just over a century later the first general Hanseatic diet took place.

One of the fiercest trials the League underwent was its prolonged conflict with the Vitalienbrüder in the fourteenth and early fifteenth centuries. The pirates of the Baltic, who had continued to flourish long after the decline of the Vikings and the conversion of Scandinavia to

An early view of Lübeck, one of the most important Hanse towns.
BRITISH MUSEUM

Christianity, found a new patron in the house of Mecklenburg, one member of which was elected king of Sweden. Chosen in 1364, Albert of Mecklenburg was deposed and imprisoned in 1389, when his great rival Margaret of Sweden supplanted him on the throne. But Stockholm itself stood firm for the Mecklenburg cause, and the pirates made it their business to succour the beleaguered town, earning themselves the name of Vitalienbrüder, or Victualling Brothers, in the process. Their success went much further than this: they captured Bornholm and Visby in Sweden, and Åbo and Viborg in Finland. In 1393 they took and plundered Bergen, which was then the most important town in Norway, and the next year they sacked Malmö. The price of herring rose to three times its previous level in Prussia, and ten times in Frankfurt. In 1397, however, Margaret of Sweden succeeded in imposing the Union of Kalmar, which united the three Scandinavian kingdoms under her great-nephew, Eric of Pomerania. Visby was recaptured, and the Vitalienbrüder were driven from the Baltic. But they were by no means finished. Now calling themselves the Likedeeler, or Fair Dividers, they transferred their activities to the North Sea, basing themselves on east Frisia as the Danish Vikings had done before them. The most famous name associated with this phase of their activity is that of Klaus Störtebeker. Like Eustace the Monk, Störtebeker is a semi-legendary figure, as are his associates Gödeke, Michels and

43

Klaus Störtebeker.
LONDON LIBRARY

Wigbold, once a professor at Rostock. Störtebeker is said to have been a nobleman of Verden, who turned pirate after living a scapegrace life on land. Under the influence of his Frisian wife, he was particularly brutal to those he captured, but some of those he took were allowed to keep their lives in return for joining his crew. When a candidate of this kind presented himself, a vast jug or "beker" of wine was brought, and the man was required to prove himself by downing it at a single draught. It was from this ceremony that Störtebeker is said to have taken his name. One of the fascinating things about the Vitalienbrüder in this period of their existence is that, from our imperfect knowledge of them, they seem to have been very like the buccaneers in the West Indies during the seventeenth century. Here too we find an egalitarian community with its own customs, its own ferocious independence and contempt for outsiders.

Those who suffered most from the Frisian pirates were the Hanse merchants, who were the biggest ship-owners in the area, and it was the League which eventually brought Störtebeker and his associates to book. In 1402 they were defeated in a battle at the mouth of the Elbe by the

44

A late sixteenth-century view of the Hanse town of Rostock.

Hanse admiral Simon of Utrecht. Störtebeker was captured aboard his ship the *Mad Dog*, and he and eighty companions were afterwards executed in the market-place at Hamburg by the city executioner, Master Rosenfeld. When an alderman commiserated with Rosenfeld on the severity of the day's work, the latter replied that he was still fresh enough to slice off the heads of the whole town council!

Throughout the Middle Ages, the constant warfare between England and France provided an excuse for piracies of all kinds. Indeed, it was often difficult to draw the dividing line between acts of war and simple acts of robbery. The Flemings and the English were equally ready to fight one another at sea. Documents of 1311 and 1312, for instance, establish that between 1297 and the year immediately preceding that of the inquiry the Flemish herring fishers lost 400 men, ships and other goods to the value of 4,000 livres, and over 1,700 livres worth of herring to English raiders. In 1345, the Hispano-Flemish wine fleet was captured by corsairs from Bayonne, and Edward III of England took the profit.

In particular, the sea remained the refuge of those who had suffered

45

ABOVE: *the kind of ship used by the Vitalienbrüder and their opponents.*
BRITISH LIBRARY

RIGHT: *an early sixteenth-century map of the Baltic and Scandinavia.*
BRITISH LIBRARY

misfortune upon land. This was the case, for example, with the first recorded female pirate, a Breton noblewoman called Jeanne de Belleville. Her husband, accused of betraying the French cause during the war of succession which raged in Britanny during the mid-fourteenth century, was taken to Paris and beheaded, and his head displayed as a warning on the ramparts of the ducal capital at Nantes. The widow hurried there with her children, and made them swear to avenge their father. She then raised a small army, sacked a number of castles, and finally, when forced to flee, took to the sea with a squadron of three ships and proceeded to harry the commerce of the opposite party. We are told that she herself was always the first to board an opponent's vessel. She is remembered now not only for her own deeds but because her son, Olivier de Clisson, eventually became Constable of France. It was he who ended the war for the succession to the duchy by defeating and killing the French candidate, Charles of Blois, at the battle of Auray in 1364. So his mother's vengeance was at last complete.

ISLĀDIA

BIARMIA

FINMARCHIA
SCRIC
FINIA

TRONDANES
LAPPIA
TORNIA
LACVS ALBVS

HALOGIA
BOTNIA
OCCIDĒTALIS
BOTNIA
ORIENTALIS
80

FAROGIA
CARELIA

NIDROSIA
IEMPTHIA

NILANDIA

HETLADIA
ANGERMĀNIA

MIDDELPADIA
TAVESTHA

HELSINGIA
FINLADIA
MOSCOVI
PS

TILEMARCHIA
SVETIA
GESTRICIA
70

DALIA
VERMELADIA
HOLMIA

NORVEGIA
VELADIA
ALANDIA

MOTES
FERRI
ESTHIA

NERICIA

SCARIS
60
RIGA

SCOTIA
GOTHI
OCCIDETAI
135 TERRITO
RIA VETER
ORIE
TALE

GOTLADIA
LIVONIA

SCONI
GIA
ELANDA

TAGLIA

DANIA
CVRETES
55

HOLSACI
MEMEL

FRISIA
VITTA

HOLLADIA
ALBI
30
MAGNO
POLIA
POMERAIA
PRVSSIA
VISTVLA
50
GRAD 9.
LOGITV

47

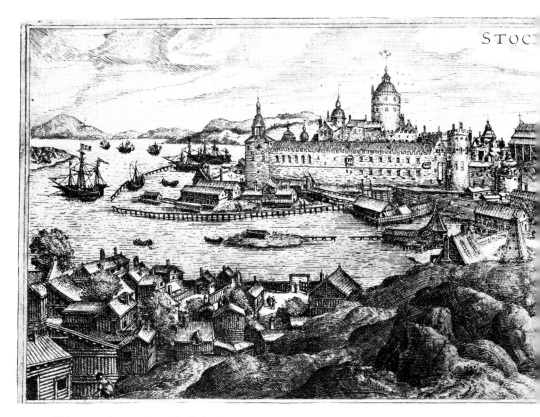

This seventeenth-century view of Stockholm still gives a good idea of what the city looked like in the days of the Vitalienbrüder.

Some medieval pirates, however, managed to pursue their trade and yet remain solid and respected citizens of their native towns. This was particularly true of England—the English were apparently adept, even in those days, at maintaining a double standard of morality. In the reign of Edward III, the Cornish port of Fowey was famous for the "Fowey Gallants" who raided the Normandy coast. They were not averse to fighting their own countrymen as well, and on one occasion were the victors in a sharp skirmish with the Cinque Ports men of Winchelsea and Rye. We are told that they gave the latter "so rough an entertainment as their welcome that they were glad to depart without bidding farewell."

The fifteenth century showed little change in the situation at sea, though there was an increasing tendency to try to repress piracy by means of legislation. This failed, since the laws, once enacted, remained unenforceable. But an increasing mass of documentation, legal, commercial and diplomatic, does give us a great deal more specific information about sea robbery and its effects. In England, piracy was a profession which could be

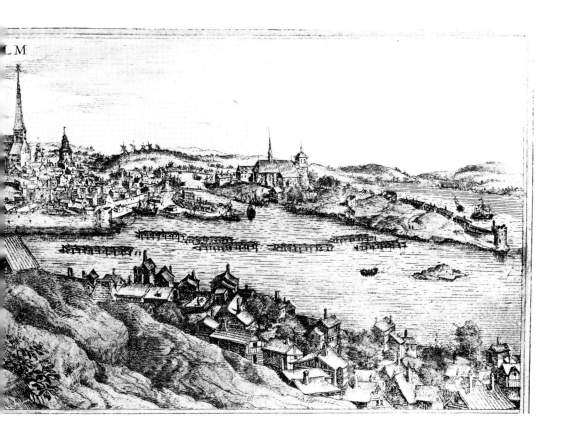

practiced by more or less anybody, and which left not the slightest stain upon a man's honor. Great noblemen indulged in it when this was convenient to them. Richard Beauchamp, Earl of Warwick, later to be Joan of Arc's jailer at Rouen, made a pilgrimage to the Holy Land as a young man (despite his treatment of Joan, he was reputed by his contemporaries to be exceptionally pious). From the *Beauchamp Pageant*, which is the pictorial record of his life, we learn that his ships attacked whom they liked in foreign waters. Later, Lord Grey of Powis led an attack from the decks of his own ship upon a Hanse merchantman anchored in Portsmouth harbor, plundered her, and retired to Poole laden with booty.

More typically, the successful freebooter came from a little lower down in the social scale, and was a prosperous and well-connected bourgeois. Perhaps the most celebrated fifteenth-century Englishman of this type was Harry Pay of Poole, called "Arripay" by the Spaniards. Though he took many prizes off the Breton coast, Pay's real speciality was raiding Spain. He burned both Gijon and Finisterre, and carried off the crucifix from the

ABOVE: *Hamburg, where Störtebeker was executed.*
BRITISH MUSEUM
LEFT: *Richard Beauchamp, Earl of Warwick, committing piracy on his travels. From the* Beauchamp Pageant.
BRITISH LIBRARY

greatly venerated shrine of Santa Maria de Finisterre. In 1402 he took the Spanish ship *Marie* of Bilbao, with a huge treasure aboard her. Eventually the Spaniards found Pay's activities too much to bear, and in 1406 they mounted a revenge raid against Poole when the pirate and his ships were absent. They burned the town, crippling its then considerable commercial importance, and killed Pay's brother.

Pay's impudent resourcefulness was worthy of some of his buccaneering successors. Once, for example, he was captured by a French ship, but escaped from his captors, turned the tables, and took their vessel. He then sailed it, still under French colors, with his own and another English ship in tow, up the Seine as if returning from a successful expedition. Having created havoc with the French shipping he found at anchor, he turned safely home. He ended his days respectably as water-bailiff of Calais.

In the late fifteenth century it was the ships of Venice which perhaps suffered most heavily from piratical attack. Not the English alone, but all the seafaring nations of Europe seemed to regard the rich vessels of the republic as fair game, and maritime losses due to piracy played a significant role in the Venetian decline. These attacks could take many forms. In 1491, for instance, we find a report in the Venetian diplomatic

A Flemish carrack, 1480. Such a ship would have been a rich prize for pirates.
SCIENCE MUSEUM

papers that English ships, under the pretext of trade, were in the habit of going to Candia in Crete for wines. On their way back they would capture and plunder Venetian ships. The English government took Venetian complaints about this so seriously that in 1498 it forbade English ships to go to Candia at all.

The most tempting targets were the rich Flanders galleys, which the Venetian state dispatched every year to trade with the Low Countries. In 1485 Venetian commerce suffered a major disaster when the four Flanders galleys under Bartolomeo Minio were attacked and taken after a twenty-four-hour battle off Cape St. Vincent by a fleet of nine vessels flying the

French flag and commanded by one Colombo, alias Nicolo Griego, who seems to have been a Gascon. Over 400 Venetians were killed, and the captured ships were taken to Lisbon. Colombo then stowed his booty and made off for Honfleur. The Venetians were not at war with France at the time, and naturally they made strong representations to the government of Anne de Beaujeu, then acting as regent for her brother Charles VIII. But thanks to the strong resistance put up by the men of Honfleur, very little of what had been taken was ever recovered.

Ten years later there was an even bolder, though less damaging, attack on the annual Flanders fleet. On this occasion some Frenchmen sailed up Southampton Water and raided the Venetian ships which happened to be lying at anchor there. They seized the commander, and also the Venetian consul in England, and made them pay a ransom of 550 ducats each. Altogether, it is not surprising to learn that insurance and other charges rose so high that in the late fifteenth century it was actually cheaper to send goods from London to Venice by the overland route up the Rhine and across the Alps than it was to do so by sea.

It must seem at first, as we pass from the fifteenth to the early sixteenth century, that conditions do not really change so very much—that the risks faced by peaceful mariners and the opportunities offered to sea-rovers remained the same and that so too did the relationship between the pirate and his own community, which for the most part gave him all the approval and support it could muster. The fifteenth-century "pirate," like his predecessors, might be a robber but he was very seldom an outcast. In the eyes of those who surrounded him, and often in the eyes of his own government (despite increasingly draconian legislation) his sins were venial ones. But two developments were to change the situation completely. In the first place there was the discovery of the sea-route to India, followed by Columbus's discovery of the Americas, which put immense power and wealth into the hands of Spain and Portugal and at the same time expanded the horizons of all Europeans. And in the second place came the rise of Protestantism. This was to exercise a very definite influence upon the history of the overseas empires which offered the pirate new opportunities to ply his trade, and would often, in addition, offer a religious justification for piratical conduct.

3
Mediterranean Corsairs

BEFORE SPEAKING OF THE gradual evolution of the pirate in the West Indies and in the Indian Ocean, until he achieves the form described and immortalized by Defoe in the *General History*, it is necessary to return to the closed world of the Mediterranean. In the great inland sea piracy never ceased to exist, either before the coming of the Turks or after it. The unfortunate trader could expect, just as he might elsewhere, to find himself set upon at any moment, by an enemy of almost any nationality. In his *True Travels*, *Adventures and Observations*, published in 1630, the Englishman Captain John Smith describes with some relish a sea-fight between a Breton ship which had taken him aboard, and a great argosy of Venice. And he smacks his lips over what happened when the Venetian vessel was at last forced to surrender:

> The silks, velvets, cloth of gold and tissue, piastres, sequins and sultanies, which is gold and silver, that they unloaded in four-and-twenty hours was wonderful. Whereof having sufficient, and tired with toil, they cast her off with her company . . .

There is evidence, in Venetian maritime records of the period 1592–1604, that at this period the republic's shipping was under attack from Maltese, Florentines, Englishmen, Dutchmen and Spaniards, as well

A fifteenth-century Mediterranean pilgrim galley—a rich capture for slavers.
SCIENCE MUSEUM

as from the Turks and from the Dalmatian Uskoks. They feared the
English and Spanish, as well as the Dalmatians, as much as they did their
Turkish enemies. The English, indeed, had a particularly ingenious system
for committing piracy in the course of their own trading voyages. They
made their victims sign declarations saying either that nothing had been
taken or that what had been taken was the property of a nation with whom
England was at war.

But the English were at any rate less fanatical and dangerous than the

55

Uskoks. Based on Segna, near Fiume, these were Christian brigands who had successfully resisted the Turks, and who did much damage to Venetian commerce in the course of the sixteenth and seventeenth centuries, though they probably never numbered a force of more than five hundred men. They used small, shallow-draught galleys called *fuste*, and depended on the impetus with which they attacked. Though nominally Catholics, the Uskoks made piracy itself into a kind of religion; their priests held that it was a pious duty to plunder Venetian ships, because the latter carried Muslim goods. In 1601 a Venetian spy saw the people of Segna crawling on their knees from the harborside to their numerous churches to give thanks for what he called "their uninterrupted robberies and murders." The Venetian treated the Uskoks not as civilized men but as vermin, to be exterminated by any means, and used to display their severed heads in front of St. Mark's.

Basically, however, piracy in the Mediterranean took on a special character because of the tireless raids of Muslims upon Christians, and vice-versa. The religious difference sanctioned hostilities which acquired an institutional character, and made the corsairing activities of the two sides very different from anything which would normally be recognized as true piracy. For one thing, those who engaged in it had the full support of the laws and institutions of the communities to which they belonged. The official protagonists in this long-drawn-out struggle were the Barbary states of North Africa on the one hand, and the Knights of St. John of Jerusalem on the other.

The Barbary states were independent maritime fiefdoms, technically dependent on the Turkish Sultan, but in fact paying little attention to him. They had ports in the Mediterranean—Tripoli, Tunis and Algiers—but also on the Atlantic coast of Africa. They had been active at sea from the fourteenth century onward.

The Knights of St. John were a crusading military order, which had originally been formed to defend Jerusalem and to succor pilgrims to the Holy Land. When Palestine was lost, they withdrew to Rhodes, and waged war on Turkish commerce. But the loss of this island to the Sultan at the beginning of the sixteenth century forced them to withdraw westward to Malta, and here they established a strongly fortified base which commanded the most important sea-routes between Europe and the Levant. It was the move to Malta which gave the war of corsairs its strangely institutional status, though the true pattern of activity did not become apparent for some time.

In the early 1500s, it was the Spaniards, not the Muslims, who were on

A knight of St. John, by Francesco Francia, early sixteenth century.
NATIONAL GALLERY

A late medieval plan of Rhodes, original headquarters of the Knights of St. John.
BRITISH LIBRARY

the offensive in North Africa, since the crusading impulse which had driven the Moors from Spain was not yet spent. In 1509 they captured Oran, Bougie and Tripoli with little loss, though they failed at Djerba in 1510 and again in 1511. The resistance to the Spanish offensive was led by two Turkish adventurers, scions of a Greek convert family in Mitylene, Aruj and Kheir-ed-din, usually called by their Christian opponents the brothers Barbarossa. They were recognized by Christian and Turk alike as being amongst the most talented seamen of their time. Kheir-ed-din was a particularly outstanding personality—cultivated, fluent in languages (he spoke Turkish, Arabic, Greek, French, Spanish and Italian), and a brilliant strategist and leader of men. He recaptured Algiers, which had also been taken by the forces of Charles VII, and Tripoli too once again became Muslim. In 1530 Kheir-ed-din was appointed regent of Algiers by his nominal overlord, the Sultan, and this port, like Tunis and Tripoli, became a province of the Ottoman Empire, garrisoned by Turkish janissaries. But these garrisons did not affect their high degree of independence from any central authority.

In the latter part of his life, Kheir-ed-din enjoyed a kind of glamor, even among his enemies, which was accorded to no other corsair captain, and this lingered for long after his death. Brantôme includes him in his series of great captains, and passed on the rumor that he was of French descent, saying:

> If it was true that he was French, he did honor to the name of Frenchman, and if it was not true, he was still to be praised wherever he hailed from, for he not only astounded the Christians, but also the Arabs and the Moors, having made war upon all of them, both by land and sea, and made them all tributary to him.

Kheir-ed-Din was succeeded by men as able as himself, Dragut and Ulug'Ali (otherwise Ochiali), but the Muslim impetus could not be sustained at the same level. The Turks failed to take Malta in the great siege of 1565, and their fleet was shattered at the Battle of Lepanto in 1571. This battle, combined with the Spanish failure to hold Tunis, led to the establishment of a kind of balance of power in the Mediterranean. Hostilities were conducted thenceforth in a more piecemeal and localized way; and it was only now that corsairing began to play a dominant part in the history of the area.

For both sides, the most important prizes were not cargoes but slaves and ships, and this led to great slave-markets being established not only in Constantinople and Algiers but in Malta and Leghorn. At the same time a

Barbarossa. A sixteenth-century engraving.
MUSÉE DE LA MARINE

complex system of middlemen for the redemption of captives, both Christian and Muslim, grew up. Soon, as the raids and counter-raids continued, corsairing became an industry, and the principal employment for many seamen. Corsairs were not religious fanatics but a strange mixture of merchant and pirate, exercising the profession they had adopted as prudently as possible, and usually avoiding as much as they could the necessity of fighting. Meanwhile the great European powers took a hand in the game. Though all of them suffered losses, it suited many nations, particularly the stronger ones such as England and France, to allow the corsair war to continue. Their interventions against the Barbary states were aimed not so much at completely suppressing their piratical activities as at gaining "most favored nation" status for themselves. This is why hostilities against the Algerines and others were generally confined to a show of force, with no serious attempt to follow up any initiative, once taken. The existence of the corsairs was used as a way of securing a trading advantage for the shipping and ship-owners of a particular power. Thus in the early seventeenth century it was the French who dominated Mediterranean commerce, and the bulk of trade between the various Mediterranean ports, or to and from the Levant, was carried under the French flag, since this was the one the Barbary corsairs were most likely to respect. In 1605 the French ambassador at Constantinople reckoned that a thousand ships were trading to the Levant under the French flag, and that they earned half a million crowns annually carrying goods belonging to nations at least in the technical sense hostile to France. Later in the century preference began to be given to English and Dutch vessels, and the Genoese merchants and bankers in London found the use of the English flag so beneficial that insurance rates fell by eighty percent.

It was, nevertheless, the Muslim rather than the Christian powers which depended on the corsairing industry for very existence. One reason for their dependence on plunder was economic. There was a shortage of many commodities in North Africa, particularly of the large timbers needed for shipbuilding, and of cordage and war material such as gunpowder. Some Christian nations, such as Holland and Sweden, bought immunity from the activity of the corsairs by paying a tribute in naval stores and armaments. This helped to perpetuate the system of raiding even more than the subtle interventions of French diplomacy. But even more influential was the fact that the corsairs and those who supported their efforts came to form so large a part of the population of the various North African ports. The abolition of corsairing became unthinkable because it gave employment to so many, and because those concerned with it occupied preponderant places in communities whose politics were notoriously unstable.

Though the methods employed were superficially the same upon both sides, there were many differences of detail in personnel, ships and tactics. Aboard Muslim vessels, a distinct division was maintained between the Christians who not only manned the oars but also saw to the working of the vessel, and the janissary troops who were there for no other purpose than to fight. Janissaries were Muslims, though they were often renegades or children taken from Christian families. They were never local men, but were gathered by an efficient recruiting system from all over the Levant. They were conspicuously courageous and well disciplined; and, unlike the Christian troops they opposed, they were well fed, well treated and regularly paid. Aboard ship, their chief or *agha* took precedence over the ship's commander or *raïs* in all decisions that directly concerned fighting. The Christians on Barbary ships were forbidden, on pain of being bastinadoed, from approaching either the compass or the tiller; and when the moment for combat came they were fettered four by four to great bars of iron by their hands and feet, thus obviating any risk of treachery.

Aboard both Christian and Barbary ships there was an egalitarianism which was unusual for the age. But this again took different forms. On Christian ships the captain and his officers drank and played cards with the crew; and a captain was forced to maintain respect by his personality and physical strength, as well as by his luck in taking prizes. In the Maltese courts, corsair crewmen were insistent on maintaining their agreed rights, and lawsuits against superiors were quite common. Aboard Muslim ships, the sense of equality was more profound, since it was something fundamental to the Mahommedan religion. In Barbary, legal proceedings to ensure a fair division of the spoils were seldom necessary. The Chevalier Laurent d'Arvieux, who was captured by Barbary corsairs early in the eighteenth century, and who published an account of his captivity in 1735, remarks that in his experience there was never the least difficulty about this.

Both sides made much use of the typical Mediterranean war vessel, the galley, which had been employed from about 1300. Galleys were essentially oar-propelled, and of about 800 tons at their very largest. The rowers were captives, up to six of them chained to an oar. Barbary ships were built for speed more than endurance, and their basic mode of combat was to overtake and board the enemy. For this reason they carried very large numbers of men, often as many as 100 janissaries in addition to the oarsmen and other members of the crew. Conditions aboard were

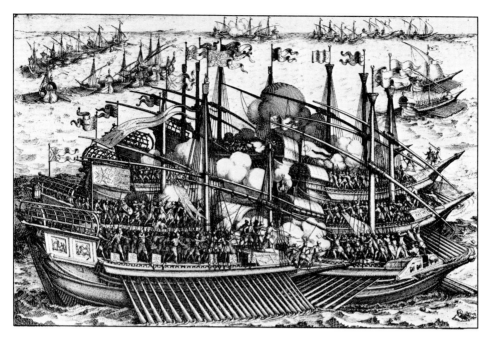

Galleys in action. Early sixteenth century.
SCIENCE MUSEUM

therefore exceedingly spartan, more so even than upon their Christian counterparts. Barbary galleys were lighter, more maneuverable and lower in the water than their opponents, and tended to have more oars in proportion to their length. They carried only one mast instead of two, and had no forecastle. Where Maltese ships carried three bow-chasers, Barbary galleys had only one, and their gunnery tended to be of poor quality, due both to bad powder and inept handling of the guns. The gunners were either renegades or inexperienced slaves, both on these and on the sailing vessels which were introduced later. Individually no match for European sailing vessels of any size, the Barbary galleys often succeeded because they cruised in company, two or three of them together, and could throw overwhelming quantities of men over the bulwarks of their prey.

Cruises, both for Barbary and Maltese galleys, were usually quite short—about forty or fifty days at most, which must have seemed long enough in such cramped conditions. The logbooks of Maltese corsairs show that the ships had to be careened at two-monthly intervals at least, in order to maintain the speed which was the secret of their success. It seems probable that the usual practice of the Barbary pirates was to leave port, snap up a prize as soon as possible, and then return home before efficiency was seriously impaired. A galley could be fully ready for sea again after

63

Eighteenth-century model of a galley of the Knights of St. John.
NATIONAL MARITIME MUSEUM

eight or ten days in harbor. The exceptions to this pattern were the Sallee corsairs, who, operating in the Atlantic, tended to stay away for much longer. They took provisions for fifty days with them, and at a pinch could be as long as sixty days at sea. But even so, it was rare for them to go much more than five or six hundred miles from the original point of departure. The Sallee vessels tended, in keeping with the rougher conditions, to be sailing ships, though still equipped with ports for oars. They were "galleys" only in a somewhat looser sense of the term—the word was often applied by English seventeenth- and eighteenth-century seamen to a type of lightly built ship which could be propelled with sweeps. It was in a ship of this type, for example, that Captain Kidd undertook his fatal voyage.

The most important of the Barbary states, and the one with the largest fleet, was Algiers. Father Dan, the Redemptionist father who visited it in the first half of the seventeenth century, and who has left some of the fullest accounts of the Barbary states, asserts that the population was then about 100,000, counting Christian slaves and Jews. He thought that the slaves formed about a quarter of this total. This compared to 7,000 Christian slaves in Tunis; 1,500 at the most in Sallee, and about 4–500 in Tripoli. Similarly, it has been estimated that Algiers always had the largest and Tripoli the smallest corsair fleet. In 1624–5, when so-called "round ships"—i.e., sailing vessels of European type—were already well

Battle between Maltese and Algerine galleys, by Reiner Zeeman.
BRITISH MUSEUM

established among the Algerines, the city had six galleys and about 100 fighting sailing ships. Of the latter, sixty were large, with twenty-four to thirty guns each, and the rest were smaller. At the same time Tunis had six galleys, plus ten or twelve brigantines (here a term for a much smaller version of the galley), and fourteen large sailing ships, but Sallee perhaps as many as sixty. The favored type, here on the Atlantic coast, was the xebec, lateen-rigged on three masts, but with some square sails, and the vessels were rarely more than 200 tons in burthen. The combined forces of the Barbary states in the early seventeenth century, when they were at the height of their power, undoubtedly put them in the same naval league as the major European maritime powers such as England and France. But there was a decline in the numbers of the Barbary corsairs from the 1620s right up to the beginning of the Revolutionary Wars, when there came a brief revival. In 1656, for example, the Salletines had only six vessels of any value, and in 1669 only nine.

Malta, of all the Christian powers, was the one most heavily involved in the corsair industry. Indeed, the degree of economic dependence may have been for a while even greater than that of Algiers or Sallee. In the 1660s perhaps one third of the adult male population was engaged in the *corso*. To these must be added the officers and crews of the regular Maltese navy, and those who were engaged in servicing the seafarers and their ships. But the

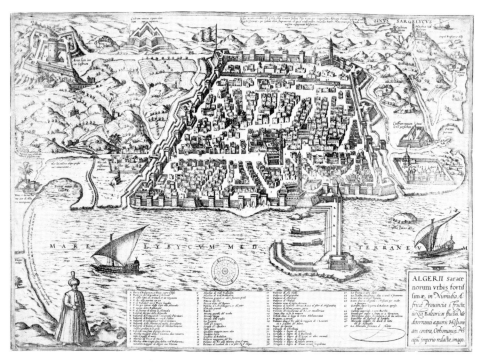

ABOVE: *a seventeenth-century view of Algiers.*
BRITISH LIBRARY

RIGHT: *Algiers (above) and Tunis (below): two views by J. de Ram.*
VICTORIA AND ALBERT MUSEUM

Maltese were far from isolated, and the cruises undertaken by their ships brought a return to big investors and to little ones, not all of them by any means connected with the Order of St. John or resident within its jurisdiction. In the seventeenth century many Maltese corsairs were financed by French capitalists—investments of this type could, after all, be thought of as a religious duty—and the captains of the ships were often French as well. The French, in addition to the financial returns which they got from the Maltese, often used their ships as a kind of unofficial training ground—a large number of the most distinguished French seventeenth-century sailors spent part of their youth in command of corsair vessels based upon the island.

By contrast, Maltese owners found an advantage in registering their ships under the Tuscan flag, both in order to avoid some of the dues to which the Order was entitled and to manipulate Tuscan legal processes to the disadvantage of the owners of Greek vessels, which were easier prey than North African or Turkish ones. If a Greek ship was taken by a corsair which was nominally Tuscan, the owner found to his cost that members of

66

ALGIERS

TUINES

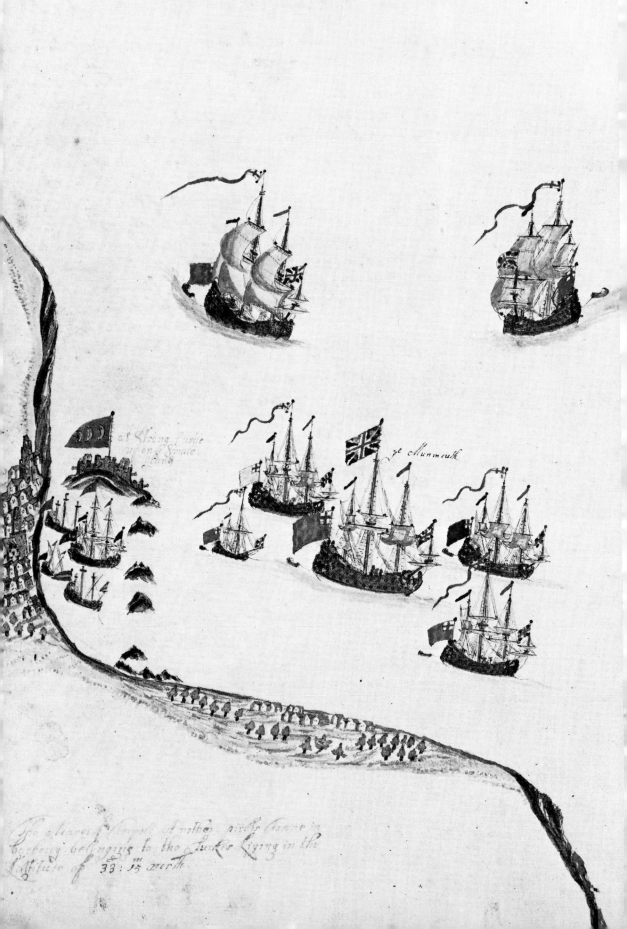

a strong castle
upon ye Smate
Iland

ye Munmouth

The abtaine[?] of shypps at nother newly come in
barbery belonging to the Tucker Lying in the
Latitude of 33:15 north

ABOVE: *a Mediterranean* xebec, *a favorite with late eighteenth-century corsairs and pirates.*
SCIENCE MUSEUM

LEFT: *a view of Tripoli, from Edward Barlow's* Journal, *late seventeenth century.*
NATIONAL MARITIME MUSEUM

the Orthodox faith were not protected in the grand ducal courts as they were in Malta. The abuse became so flagrant that it eventually had to be suppressed by the Pope. But there still remained another advantage for the cunning corsair, which was that Tuscan courts had no jurisdiction over Maltese subjects.

The Maltese *corso* shows the same steady decline in numbers and importance during the seventeenth and eighteenth centuries as can be seen across the sea in the Barbary states. The corsair fleet numbered about twenty or thirty ships between 1600 and 1675, but by the second half of the eighteenth century it had declined to under ten. There was a corresponding change in leadership. In the seventeenth century the corsair captains, equivalents of the Moorish *raïs*, were usually either knights or sergeants of the Order of St. John, with members of the three French tongues predominating.* But these were gradually replaced by Maltese and French laymen, together with some Corsicans. Since the knightly corsairs

* The eight "tongues" into which the order was divided were those of Auvergne, Provence, France, Aragon, Castile, England, Germany and Italy.

69

ABOVE: *a Greek* fousta, c. *1780, particularly vulnerable to corsairs.*
SCIENCE MUSEUM

LEFT: *Olof de Vignacourt, Grand Master of the Knights of St. John. By Michelangelo Caravaggio.*
LOUVRE

tended to be more interested in heroics than their secular successors, the *corso* became noticeably more humdrum and businesslike as it grew older. But even in its earlier days there were occasional abuses. In the seventeenth century one knight of the Order admitted that he was in fact both a Dutchman and a Lutheran—the decision to go to Malta might, in this case, just have easily been a decision to go to Algiers and turn renegade, as some of his compatriots did.

Like their Muslim rivals, the Maltese corsairs developed certain routines as the result of experience in the game. They tended to have favorite catching grounds—the sea between Palestine and Egypt, the sea around Rhodes, around Chios, around Crete and around Cyprus. In Barbary they haunted the waters between Tripoli and Tunis. One immense advantage was that the Greek islands, nominally Turkish but in fact quasi-independent, were almost invariably hospitable. Argentiera was one of their main bases in the Aegean, and they made use of Paros, Antiparos,

71

A view of Malta by Mathaus Merian, early seventeenth century.
VICTORIA AND ALBERT MUSEUM

Delos and Kimolos. Many Maltese corsairs kept wives and mistresses in the Greek islands, and led a whole domestic existence there.

We are fortunate in possessing a first-hand account of the life of a Maltese corsair at the earliest and most active period of the *corso*. Alonso de Contreras was born in Madrid in 1582, to a good but impoverished family. Having set out to make a living as a soldier of fortune, he got into trouble after a brawl in Palermo, stole a ship and fled to Naples, got into further trouble there, and was lucky enough to be rescued by a knight of St. John, who knew a likely-looking fellow when he saw one. Contreras's adventures mingle the heroic and the hilarious, and there is also a good share of the brutality which marred the warfare between the two sides. He describes, for example, how he arrived at the island of Stampalia, where he was already well known to the inhabitants, to find the whole place in an uproar because the Orthodox priest who was the most necessary member of the community had been kidnapped by Maltese Catholic raiders, and was being held to ransom for 2,000 sequins. Having rescued this worthy, he had great difficulty in getting away, for the islanders were determined that he should marry a local girl, settle among them and be their captain. Contreras sent a man to warn the crew of his ship about the fix he was in:

> My comrade went down and related what had happened, at which they all marveled. But if they loved me up yonder, how much more did my men! So that they began to arm themselves, and took a

culverin out of each of the frigates and mounted them on top of a windmill which stood before the town gates a little distance off. And they sent back word by my comrade that if I were not let out, they would force an entrance and sack the place; and that this was the best recompense I could make for all the good I had always done them. The islanders marveled at such love and said they had not been mistaken in desiring me for their lord; let me at least give them my word that I would return when I had discharged my obligations. I gave it to them, and they desired that I should give my hand to the maiden, and kiss her on the mouth; and I am sure that had I wished to enjoy her there would have been no difficulty.

Contreras is a representative figure of the milieu and the age. At one moment we find him gleefully abducting a renegade Hungarian beauty, the wife (or as it turned out, the mistress) of the Bey of Chios. At another, provoked by his Moorish opponents, he is treating a couple of prisoners with bestial cruelty:

And so, before their very eyes, I cut off the two prisoners' ears and noses and flung them to the ground . . .. Then, tying them back to back, I stood out to sea, and threw them overboard before their friends' eyes; and I sailed away, shaping my course for Alexandria.

We have no comparable account of the corsair's life written from the Muslim point of view, and indeed our knowledge of life in the corsair cities of North Africa comes from European witnesses. These can be divided into three categories: those who had at one time or another been captured and redeemed, and who afterwards wrote accounts of their experiences; the members of Christian religious orders who went to Barbary to negotiate for the release of captives; and the diplomats who were accredited to the various Barbary governments. The theme or escape or redemption from Barbary became well established in European literature, (it even appears in *Robinson Crusoe*) and was particularly popular, not surprisingly, in French and Spanish. Perhaps the most celebrated author to treat the topic is Cervantes, who himself endured a Moorish captivity. A neglected but charming instance is the brief autobiographical novel *La Provençale*, by the French eighteenth-century playwright Jean François Regnard, which tells the bittersweet story of his own love affair with a married woman, brutally interrupted when they are captured by corsairs when on a voyage from Italy to France.

Until recently, historians accepted the inbuilt bias of these European eyewitnesses without questioning it. The balance has now perhaps swung too far the other way. Not only has it now been realized that the depredations carried out by the Barbary corsairs are only one side of the coin, and that these must be weighed against those committed by Christians, but it is felt that the horrors of captivity in North Africa were grossly distorted for propaganda purposes. One newly published general history of piracy puts the case as follows:

> Slavery was seldom permanent, and its horrors were overstated by redemptionist organizations which played on racial and religious prejudices to raise funds. For merchants and corsair officers on either side, capture and ransom was a routine, almost ritual affair.

But this is to paint altogether too rosy a picture of the captive's lot.

The first-hand accounts which have been left us are, of course, the work of educated men; and they leave us in no doubt that for individuals of some consequence capture was a brutal shock. To find oneself in a twinkling not only stripped of all one's clothes and possessions but reduced to the condition of a chattel was bound to be a blow to any man's self-esteem. Nor was the business of ransom as simple as it has been made out. High prices were asked, particularly for educated men or those in possession of some useful skill—"sea-artists," such as gunners and carpenters, found it particularly difficult to obtain their release—and Moorish masters often preferred the slave's services to any ransom he might be able to offer. D'Arvieux, a French nobleman who wrote one of the best narratives of captivity in the Barbary states, remarks that at Algiers French slaves tended to be cheap because the owner's possession of them was not secure, since the French king might obtain their release by some treaty.

For most Christian slaves, the life they lived was divided into two parts—the time they spent laboring, or with their masters, or moving around within the city; and the time they spent in the *bagnios* or slave quarters, where most of them were confined at night. These have been represented as places which were not only picturesque in themselves, but which offered plenty of opportunities for advancement to prisoners who had their wits about them. The great courtyards held up to two thousand slaves, and were surrounded by stalls, taverns and cookshops, all slave-managed. There were Catholic, Orthodox and Protestant chapels, and those who could afford to pay enough money to the Turkish *concierge* or guardian could ensure themselves a certain degree of comfort. Emmanuel d'Aranda, a Spaniard who was a captive at Algiers in the 1640s, found the *bagnio* both educative and entertaining. He says that in the one in which he was confined there were 550 slaves, who spoke twenty-two different

Christian captives being tormented. By Jan Luyken, seventeenth century.
MUSÉE DE LA MARINE

languages. D'Arvieux, on the other hand, stresses the disadvantages of these crowded quarters, and describes them as: "horrible places, where the stink of cooking, which goes on in every part, the noise, the shouts, the blows and the tumult prevail everywhere."

Psychologically speaking, the greatest strain put on the captives was the necessity of adjusting to Muslim life and customs. Failure to do so could lead to extremely unpleasant consequences. Father Dan describes the brutality of Moorish punishments with gruesome relish. Essentially, the captive had to keep in mind at all times that he belonged to an inferior order of beings, and that his existence could be at risk from any fanatical passer-by. The most dangerous of these were the wandering *marabouts*, or holy men. These were often extremely aggresive towards Christians and Jews, and would fall into real or pretended frenzies and incite the crowds who followed them to attack the infidel. The result for the victim might be serious injury or even death, for these were incidents where the authorities were careful not to intervene. Another, potentially dangerous but more amusing, example of Muslim contempt for the infidel is given by Germain Mouette, another distinguished captive. He remarks that it was the custom of the women to show themselves *en déshabille* to Christian slaves, saying that, since the eyes of the soul were blind, those of the body must be so too.

The European consuls who dwelt in the various regencies were certainly

The slave market in Algiers (Jan Luyken).
MUSÉE DE LA MARINE

much better off than the captives, but they do not leave us with the impression that life in these places was either pleasant or easy for a Christian European. The chief business of the consul was to issue maritime passports, and to ensure that these were respected according to the treaty obligations in force at that time. To get over any possible language difficulties, the passports took a curious form. They consisted of sheets of paper covered with intricately engraved designs. After being signed, these were divided in half, the division being an irregular line. The top halves were given to merchant captains when they called into port, and the bottom halves to departing corsair captains. If he was stopped, the merchant captain would produce the top half of his passport, and the corsair would search among his papers to see if he possessed a matching bottom half. If he did, he would allow the merchantman to proceed unmolested. Obviously this cumbersome system belonged to an epoch when the corsairing industry was in decline, and corsair ships relatively few.

When a corsair returned to harbor after a cruise, it was the consul's duty to present himself at the ruler's ceremonial divan. Here the legitimacy of captures was established, and the consul would attempt to obtain the release of those who had some claim to be under his protection.

A resident consul faced many hazards. The most acute of these was a sudden upsurge of hostility on the part of either the local population or the ruler. In the early seventeenth century, the British consul in Algiers was torn to pieces by the mob outside the Divan of the Bey. In 1688, when French warships bombarded the city, the French consul and forty-seven of his compatriots were blown one by one from the mouths of cannon toward the attackers. In 1710 Mr. Goddard, the British consul in Tunis, was found by a naval visitor to have been kept in chains by the Bey. The ill-treatment he underwent sent him off his head. Six years later a visitor to the British consul in Algiers found that he, too, had become mentally unstable thanks to the suffering he had endured. He was "sitting up in bed with a sword and a brace of pistols by his side, calling for a clergyman to give him the sacraments . . . ."

Other dangers were those which the consul shared with the entire population, Muslim, Christian and Jewish alike. The Barbary states were frequently swept by famine, plague and revolution. In 1711 the French consul in Tripoli, Poulard, wrote a dispatch in which he described the then political situation in the city:

> The Bey, having tricked the Turks who raised him by fair words, now cheats them. Every day, he drowns, strangles or exiles them. The Moors also are torturing each other. One hears nothing in this desolate city but cries, as they rob and cut each other's throats.

In good times, Muslim justice was swift and severe, but this was preferable to the anarchy which followed any loosening of the reins. The seventeenth-century historian Paul Rycaut wrote, in his *History of the Ottoman Empire*:

> In this Government severity, violence and cruelty are natural to it, and it were as great an error to begin to loose the reins and ease the people of that oppression to which they and their first origin been accustomed, as it would be in a nation free-born . . . to change their liberty into servitude and slavery.

One of the great natural dangers to the population of the Barbary states was bubonic plague, which continued to be endemic in North Africa for many years after it had died out in northern Europe. We possess a vivid description of one outbreak in Tripoli from the pen of Miss Tully (her

Christian name is not known), who was the sister of the British consul, Richard Tully. The disease declared itself at the end of 1784. On June 14, 1785, the consul and his household were forced to begin a complete quarantine, which lasted until mid-June of the following year. During the visitation 27,000 people died in Tripoli, including nine tenths of the Christian inhabitants and all but a handful of the 500 Christian slaves then confined in the *bagnios* of the castle. When she emerged again from her seclusion, Miss Tully wrote:

> The city of Tripoli, after the plague, exhibited an appearance awfully striking. In some of the houses were found the last victims that had perished in them, who, having died alone, unpitied and unassisted, lay in a state too bad to be removed from the spot, and were obliged to be buried where they were; while others, children, were wandering about deserted without a friend belonging to them.

If the lot of the Christians, and especially the captives, in the Barbary states was unenviable enough, that of their Muslim counterparts, enslaved by Christianity, was probably still worse. In Islam, captives were specifically protected by injunctions in the *Qur'an* and the *Traditions of the Prophet* that slaves should be treated kindly. The demand for galley-slaves (and the galleys were considered the worst of all fates) was in fact much greater among the Christian powers than it was in Barbary, where it declined after the introduction of the round ship. Muslims were much valued for the work because of their outstanding powers of physical endurance. In addition, fewer of the Muslims were of high enough rank to raise a ransom from their friends and families, and there was no Muslim religious organization devoted to redeeming captives.

For many Europeans, the advantages of life in Barbary so far outweighed the disadvantages that many chose to turn Turk, even without being captured first. In 1588 when the corsair war had scarcely begun to institutionalize itself, between twenty and thirty Algerine galleys were commanded by renegades, though most of these were Greek. Father Dan goes so far as to claim that in his day all the greatest corsair captains were converts to Islam. And in 1640, when he was captured, Emmanuel d'Aranda heard Spanish, Flemish and English spoken aboard the vessel that took him, in addition to Turkish, Arabic and Lingua Franca, the common sea-language of those who plied the Mediterranean.

For southern Europeans, Spaniards and Italians, the attraction of the renegade's life was the degree of upward social mobility which it conferred. It was a way of escaping their own static social milieu of oppression and injustice, and of achieving prestige, honor and riches. In Barbary few questions were asked about one's past if one accepted the Faith. And few places held out such hopes of a prosperous and adventurous life. There were even those who saw advantages in going over to Barbary even though their only prospect was servitude. In the seventeenth century the soldiers stationed in the Spanish African fortresses, most of them transported criminals, were so starved and so miserably treated that they often gave themselves up to voluntary slavery among their enemies.

The most spectacular and most successful of the renegades, however, were northeners, mostly Englishmen and Dutchmen, who created a new era in the seafaring annals of Barbary by introducing the Moors to what were called "round ships"—sailing ships capable of enduring the storms and rough seas of the Atlantic. It was under their guidance that the Barbary corsairs burst out of the Mediterranean and started to raid elsewhere. Early in the seventeenth century some spectacular descents took place. Murad Raïs, otherwise the renegade Dutch privateer Jan Janz, raided Iceland in 1627, pillaging the town of Reykjavik, and carrying off more than 400 people captive. In 1631 he sacked the town of Baltimore in Ireland—a kind of tit-for-tat, as the town was famous throughout Elizabeth's reign as a resort of pirates. In 1641 the Irish Sea was still not safe from Barbary raiders. In that year the clergyman Devereux Spratt was captured on his way from Ireland to England, and subsequently endured a long captivity.

English privateers had already been using Algiers as a base in the late sixteenth century, and in 1600 they created an ugly incident. They brought into the harbor a Venetian prize of great value which proved to have been illegally captured. A Turkish guard was placed on the vessel, pending its return to its rightful owners. The incensed English, taking advantage of the fact that the day was Friday, when the Muslims were at prayer, set the ship on fire and came close to burning all the shipping in the harbor. Another contretemps occurred in 1609, when an English ship came into Algiers harbor and, according to custom, the English consul, accompanied by a Turkish officer, came on board to search it. The crew drowned the Turk and fled to Bougie, where they enticed aboard the captain of the castle and two of his sons, plus several other Muslims, and subsequently sold them all into slavery at Leghorn.

These uneasy relationships did not prevent bargains being made with other English seamen who now openly offered to join the Barbary service. The motivation upon both sides was very simple. The Barbary states needed the technical help that only Europeans could give them, and the

Englishmen were disgruntled with the peace policy being pursued by their new king, James I—"their passions, increasing with discontent, made them turn pirates."

An early recruit to the Barbary service, and one of the most famous of the renegades among his contemporaries, was Captain John Ward. Ward was born about 1553, and started as an east coast fisherman. He then settled in Plymouth, joined the navy, and rose through the ranks. In 1601 he had command of the *Lion's Whelp*, one of the few king's ships still in commission, and was drinking hard and inciting his crew to mutiny. A version of the speech he is supposed to have made to his men survives, and gives a good notion of the feelings of grievance among those who had known the great seafaring age of Elizabeth:

> Where are the times that we sailors esteemed chickens cheaper than your bumber Hollander doth cheese? Where are the Portugal voyages, that put portuguese into our pockets? S'blood, what would you have me say, where are the days that have been, and the seasons that we have seen, when we might sing, swear, drink, drab and kill men as freely as your cake-makers do flies? When we might do what we list, and the Law would bear us out in't, nay when we might lawfully do that, we shall be hanged for an we do now, when the whole sea was our Empire, where we robb'd at will, and the world but our garden where we walked for sport?

Having made up his mind to piracy, Ward was determined to pursue the trade as ruthlessly and profitably as possible. "I tell you," he declared, "if I should meet mine own father at sea, I would rob him, and sell him when I had done." He cast in his lot with the Barbary corsairs between 1602 and 1604, and by 1606 he was in a position to capture the largest and best-armed merchantmen that might oppose him. In June 1607 he brought back to the Goletta, the port of Tunis, what was probably his richest prize, a Venetian ship called the *Soderino* with £100,000 worth of loot aboard her. An Italian source gives a vivid description of his appearance and personality at this period:

> Very short, very little hair, and that quite white, bald in front, swarthy face and beard. Speaks little and almost always swearing. Drunk from morn till night. Sleeps a great deal, and often on board

LEFT: *A view of Leghorn, from Edward Barlow's* Journal.
NATIONAL MARITIME MUSEUM

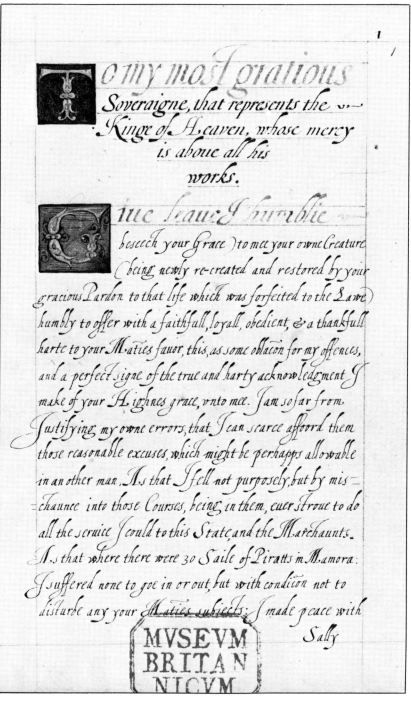

To my most gratious
Soveraigne, that represents the
Kinge of Heaven, whose mercy
is aboue all his
works.

Giue leaue, I humblie
beseech your Grace)to mee your owne Creature
(being newly re-created and restored by your
gracious Pardon to that life which was forfeited to the Lawe)
humbly to offer with a faithfull, loyall, obedient, & a thankfull
harte to your M·aties fauor, this, as some oblacōn for my offences,
and a perfect signe of the true and harty acknowledgment I
make of your Highnes grace, vnto mee. I am so far from
Iustifying my owne errors, that I can scarce afford them
those reasonable excuses, which might be perhapps allowable
in an other man, As that I fell not purposely, but by mis-
-chaunce into those Courses, being, in them, euer stroue to do
all the seruice I could to this State, and the Marchaunts.
As that where there were 30 Saile of Piratts in Mamora:
I suffered none to goe in or out, but with condicōn not to
disturbe any your M·aties subiects: I made peace with
Sally

Sir Henry Mainwaring's treatise Discourse of the Beginnings, Practice and Suppression of
Pirates, *1617.*
BRITISH LIBRARY

when in port. . . . A fool and an idiot out of his trade.

William Lithgow, that indefatigable traveler, speaks of having met Ward in Tunis, where had now built himself "a fair palace," and where he was attended by fifteen English renegades of less importance "whose lives and countenances were both alike, even as desperate as disdainful."

Ward was courted by the Grand Duke of Tuscany and the Duke of Savoy, who offered him facilities at Leghorn and Villefranche, but he resisted their seductions. He managed to live to what was then, especially for a man in his profession, a ripe old age, and died at Tunis in 1622.

Another English renegade, Peter Eston, did change back to the Christian side, though he rejected James I's offer of a pardon. "Why," he demanded, "should I obey a king's orders when I am a kind of king myself?" Eston, who started life as a Somerset farm laborer, commanded a fleet of forty vessels by 1611. In 1612 he raided the fishing-fleet on the Newfoundland banks, as West Indian-based pirates were to do after him. Here he trimmed and repaired his vessels, appropriated such provisions and munitions as he needed, and took 100 men to join his fleet. He caused havoc wherever he appeared, whether this was in the western Mediterranean or off the coast of Ireland. Eventually tiring of the renegade life, he entered the service of the Duke of Savoy, purchased a Savoyard marquisate, and married a lady of noble birth.

Henry Mainwaring, a gentleman who had seen service in the Low Countries, was sent to track Eston down—he failed to capture him in 1611. Like many pirate-hunters, he then proceeded to turn pirate himself. In 1612 he bought the fast 160-ton ship *Resistance* and obtained a privateer's licence to pursue Spanish shipping in the West Indies. Instead he sailed for Morocco and established himself at Mamurra, near Sallee. In June 1614 he arrived on the Newfoundland banks with a fleet of eight ships, and behaved just as Eston had done two years previously. Returning to Mamurra, he found it was now in the hands of the Spanish, and transferred his activities to the Christian "free port" of Villefranche. After crushing a Spanish squadron sent to suppress him in 1616 he had the choice of a free pardon and a good job from the king of Spain, and a similar pardon from his old master, James I. Accepting the latter, he was knighted in 1618, appointed Lieutenant of Dover Castle and Deputy Warden of the Cinque Ports, and got himself elected Member of Parliament for Dover. He occupied his spare time in writing a *Discourse of the Beginnings, Practices and Suppression of Pirates*. One of his chief recommendations is that no further pardons should be issued to pirates.

An anonymous portrait of Sir Francis Verney (left), and his clothes, returned to England after his death (right).

A less fortunate adventurer, like Mainwaring a man of gentle blood, was Sir Francis Verney. A turbulent youth, Verney lost a quarrel with his stepmother about his inheritance, and in the autumn of 1608 left England in disgust. He arrived in Algiers and played a part in one of the frequent wars of succession, then turned corsair. In 1609 he was reported by the English ambassador in Spain to have taken "three of four Poole ships and one of Plymouth." In December 1610 he was said by the Venetian ambassador in Tunis to have apostasized. At this period he was an associate of John Ward. But his period of success did not last long. In 1615, according to Lithgow, he was desperately sick in Messina, after being a prisoner for two years in the Sicilian galleys. He had been redeemed upon his reconversion by an English Jesuit. Though he was now free, his fortunes were broken, and he was forced to enlist as a common soldier in order to exist. Lithgow discovered him when he was on the point of death, "in the extremist calamity of extreme miseries" and having lost all desire to live.

The most famous of the Dutch renegades was Simon Danser or Dansiker, a native of Dordrecht. Father Dan states that it was Dansiker in particular who taught the Moors the use of "round ships." He came to the Mediterranean and settled in Marseilles, at which time he was already a corsair. In 1606, he accepted an invitation to transfer his base to Algiers. Here he was fabulously successful, capturing about forty ships in the space of two years, and burning and sinking others. He earned the nickname of *Dali Capitan*, or Captain Devil, amongst the Algerines, but in spite of this he would not apostasize, as his hosts were pressing him to do. By 1608 he was already secretly in touch with the court of France, and was negotiating to rejoin his wife and children, whom he had left behind in Marseilles. In January 1609 he was seen arriving in Algiers in a ship built in Lubeck "of great force", manned by Turks and about twenty Dutch and English seamen. He was then reported to be forcing English seamen from captured ships to serve with him, and to be importing Dutch sailors from the Netherlands. Later in the same year he made a magnificent prize, a Spanish galleon reputed to be worth £500,000, and this seems to have encouraged him to make the break and return to Marseilles, where he put himself under the protection of the Duke of Guise. All might have been well if Dansiker had then been content to remain where he was, but he allowed himself to be tempted to go to Tunis in order to ransom some captured French vessels. He was arrested on the orders of the Bey, and hanged in 1611.

Though Dansiker eventually proved too much for their patience, the Muslim authorities displayed remarkable tolerance towards the re-negades, who were often difficult guests. The Sieur de Bréves gave the following description of their conduct in 1606: "They carry swords at their side, they run drunk through the town . . . they sleep with the wives of the Moors . . . in brief every kind of debauchery and unchecked licence is permitted to them."

A little later, Captain John Smith felt that "any man would rather live with wild beasts than with them." But he adds reflectively, "the best was, they would seldom go to sea, so long as they could possibly live on shore." But by this time the Dutch and English renegades had already begun to outlive their usefulness, having taught the Moors all they needed to know about fighting a European ship of war.

The history of Barbary in the late seventeenth and eighteenth centuries is one of a long decline followed by a sudden recovery. The politics of the region remained as complicated as they had ever been, and it was by no means always the Maltese who were left to sustain the Christian cause. Villefranche and Leghorn have already been mentioned as "free ports" which served a purpose exactly analogous to that served by Algiers, Tunis

A battle between Barbary coast ships and a British ship, seventeenth century. The corsairs are here using "round ships," not galleys.

or Tripoli. Leghorn was the headquarters of the Knights of Santo Stefano, a military order created by Cosimo I, the first Grand Duke of Tuscany. After Lepanto, they, like the Knights of St. John, participated in the corsair war against the Barbary states, and they continued to do so until the extinction of the Medici dynasty. Even Venice in the days of her decadence found the energy to take action against the corsairs. In August 1766 a Venetian squadron appeared off Tripoli, a city which was particularly vulnerable to blockade as the land routes were bad and much food, especially grain, was imported from as far afield as Italy and Spain. In 1784 war broke out between Venice and Tunis, and peace was not finally concluded until 1792.

It was the outbreak of the Napoleonic Wars which led to a revival of corsair activity on the part of the Barbary regencies, for the European conflict removed the constraints which had been placed upon their activities, in particular by the fleets of Spain and Portugal. The renewed outrages of the corsairs sometimes had a funny side to them. One affair which amused much of Italy concerned Giovanni Luigi Moncada, Prince of Paternò, a fabulously rich and notoriously mean Sicilian nobleman. In 1797 the prince was going by sea from Palermo to Naples when he was the victim of an "arranged" meeting between his own ship and a galley from Tunis. Because, when once he got his freedom back, the prince failed to deliver the whole of the agreed ransom, the Bey of Tunis sued him in the Palermitan courts and won.

Among the victims of the renewed corsair impetus were the Americans, whose ships had been appearing in the Mediterranean from the mid-eighteenth century onward. After the War of Independence, the new nation, which possessed no navy of its own until one was authorized by Congress in 1794, approached both the British and the French to ask for their protection. Both nations refused, because they saw, as so often before, the corsair threat to ships of smaller powers as being a real protection for their own trade. "The Americans," said Lord Sheffield when the matter was debated in the House of Commons in 1783, "cannot pretend a navy, and therefore the great nations should suffer the Barbary pirates as a check on the activities of the smaller Italian states and America." By 1793 the problem had grown to serious proportions, and a dozen American ships were captured in the Atlantic. The Americans then tried the expedient of paying subsidies, and they also appointed their own consuls. But in 1801, the Bey of Tripoli, dissatisfied with the subsidy he was getting, expelled the American consul and declared war on the United States. The Americans dispatched a squadron to deal with the matter. They returned

The French frigate Clarinde *capturing an Algerine corsair, by Thomas Long*, c. *1800.*
PARKER GALLERY

to the Mediterranean in 1802 and 1803, but had little success, owing
chiefly to the incompetence of the officers placed in command. In the fall of
1803, they suffered a humiliating disaster. The fine frigate *Philadelphia*, sent
to blockade the port of Tripoli, stuck fast on a reef in the bay and was
captured by the Bey's men. The ship's crew were paraded half-naked
through the town. The situation was only partially retrieved when, in a
daring action under the leadership of a young lieutenant, Stephen
Decatur, the Americans succeeded in boarding and burning the captured
Philadelphia in the harbor. Despite several bombardments, the American
prisoners were not freed for another nineteen months, and then only at the
price of a ransom of 60,000 dollars (the Bey had originally asked for
much more, but was brought to his senses when the Americans supported
the pretensions of a rival to the throne).

The general pacification of Europe which followed the end of the
Napoleonic Wars, and which was hammered out by the leading statesmen

88

of the time at the Congress of Vienna, also spelt the beginning of the end for the Barbary regencies, which had flourished thanks to general European disorder. The nuisance they caused now began to seem intolerable, and the various maritime powers took steps to put an end to it, using the naval forces they had built up in the Napoleonic period. In 1815, the American government, now again at peace with England after the war of 1812 and able to send a fleet to the Mediterranean with impunity, dispatched Decatur to deal with the corsairs who were still troubling American shipping, and he forced Tripoli, Algiers and Tunis to pay an indemnity. The British, with even more to lose from corsair depredations, were more drastic. After a series of provocations, the British fleet bombarded Algiers in 1816, 1,600 captives were released, and the Bey was forced to make a public apology for his conduct. In 1825 the Sardinians, for similar reasons, took punitive action against Tripoli, and the Sardinian commandant Sivori succeeded in burning the Tripolitanian fleet.

The ambitions of the European powers, instead of being directed against each other, now began to be turned towards the creation of new colonial empires. Even under the French Directory, Talleyrand had advocated that France should look for an opportunity to make conquests not in Europe, but on the other side of the Mediterranean, and Napoleon's unsuccessful expedition to Egypt had been the result. The French took his policy up again and in 1830 occupied Algiers. Now a new era began in North Africa, with the French and the Spanish vying for influence and territorial gains. The still largely medieval society of Barbary was ill-equipped to resist these invasions, and entered into a period of foreign domination which lasted until our own day.

4
Pirates and Colonizers

IN THE MEDITERRANEAN THE activity of the corsairs was in one important sense the expression of a clash between two cultures. Under different sets of circumstances, the clash was to be repeated elsewhere, and was to find expression in precisely the same way. In particular, "piracy," so called, was to be an expression of resistance to colonizing powers.

During the first period of European expansion the colonizers also often behaved in a piratical way, shedding any moral inhibitions they possessed as their travels took them further from Europe and its laws. Vasco da Gama, the pioneer of the sea route to the Indies, practiced piracy or something very like it on his first voyage, and behaved with great cruelty to the Indians whom he captured. The principle upon which he and his successors acted was succinctly put, at his trial more than three centuries later, by a pirate called Darby Mullins, who sailed with Kidd and Culliford, namely, "that it was very lawful (as he said he was told), to plunder ships and goods, etc., belonging to the enemies of Christianity." While the Portuguese were still aggressors rather than possessors, they behaved in a completely lawless way, disrupting coasting traffic along the coast of India and the Persian Gulf, the Red Sea and the east coast of Africa. As late as the middle of the sixteenth century, one Captain

A Java proa, sixteenth century. Native ships of this kind were often attacked by Europeans without justification.

Mesquito was commissioned by the Viceroy of Goa to undertake a piratical cruise along the coast, at a time when the Portuguese were officially at peace with the Indian princes. He seized nearly two dozen ships, and either beheaded the crews or sewed them up in sails and threw them overboard.

Piracy had, of course, existed in Indian waters long before the arrival of the Portuguese, just as it flourished in all places where men traveled and traded by sea. The Greek geographer Ptolemy, writing in the second century A.D., refers to the west coast of India as "the Pirate Coast." Two centuries later, the pirates of Diu were forced to send hostages to the Roman emperor Constantine, one of them being a Christian bishop called Theophilus. Later still, in 1290, Marco Polo found the Indians of the west coast deeply involved in piracy. They were well enough organized to set up an offshore cordon of a hundred or so vessels, so that no trader could escape the net. Marco Polo adds the picturesque detail that it was their custom to administer a strong purge to the merchants they captured, in case they had managed to swallow their precious stones and pearls.

With the coming of the Portuguese, piracy increased rather than diminished, first because the European intruders made an always fluid political situation less stable than ever, and secondly because piratical acts could be thought of as part of a war of revenge, provoked by the robberies and cruelties of the European intruders. The Kunjali family, originally admirals of the Zamorin of Calicut and later rebels against his authority, were the chief protagonists on the Indian side. The techniques used were those common to pirates with a secure land-base all over the world—a swarm of light craft, usually called *paroes*, each rowed by thirty or forty armed men, would be stationed in creeks and river mouths, ready to surround and overcome by superior manpower and maneuvrability any unescorted merchantman that came into sight. Naturally, the pirates

Departure of an English Indiaman for the east, by A. Willaerts.
NATIONAL MARITIME MUSEUM

spared their own compatriots no more than they did the Portuguese. By 1565 the sea route from Goa to the Red Sea was so infested with robbers that only very large and strong vessels or those under Portuguese convoy were even moderately safe from attack. Sometimes very rich prizes fell into Indian hands. In 1592, for example, Mohammed Kunjali Marakkar captured a rich treasure-ship from China almost within sight of Goa, and it was not until 1599 that the Portuguese were able to lay siege to his base at Kotta, and capture and execute him. Even so, the dynasty did not cease to give them trouble. A cousin of the fallen leader, who had been taken prisoner and subsequently Christianized as Don Pedro Rodriguez, escaped from Goa and promptly turned pirate. In 1618 he was ranging the coast with five fully armed war paroes.

When the English established themselves at Bombay, they inherited the problem of native piracy. Their chief scourge was the Angrians, named after their chief, Kanhoji or Conagee Angria, who succeeded to the

A view of Bombay, from Edward Barlow's Journal.
NATIONAL MARITIME MUSEUM

93

command of the Mahratta navy in 1698, and then became, like Mohammed Kunjali Marakkar before him, an independent ruler. His base was a strip of territory about forty miles wide and 240 miles in length, extending along the line of the coast from Bombay southward. He first made himself a serious nuisance to the East India Company around 1706 or 1707—in the latter year his ships attacked the frigate maintained by the Bombay factory for anti-pirate duties, and blew it up after a brief engagement, and in 1712 they took the Governor of Bombay's armed yacht. The Angrians were formidable opponents because they were so tenacious. In October 1707, for instance, two English frigates reported that they, together with an East India Company ship and two galleots, had fought a whole day's fight with the Malabar pirates, and had lost the two galleots as a result. The powerful Indiamen which maintained the Bombay factory's link with Europe were sometimes attacked, but not usually successfully. An exception was the capture of the *Derby* in 1750. On this

Bombay in 1732, a view by Lambert and Scott.
INDIA OFFICE LIBRARY

94

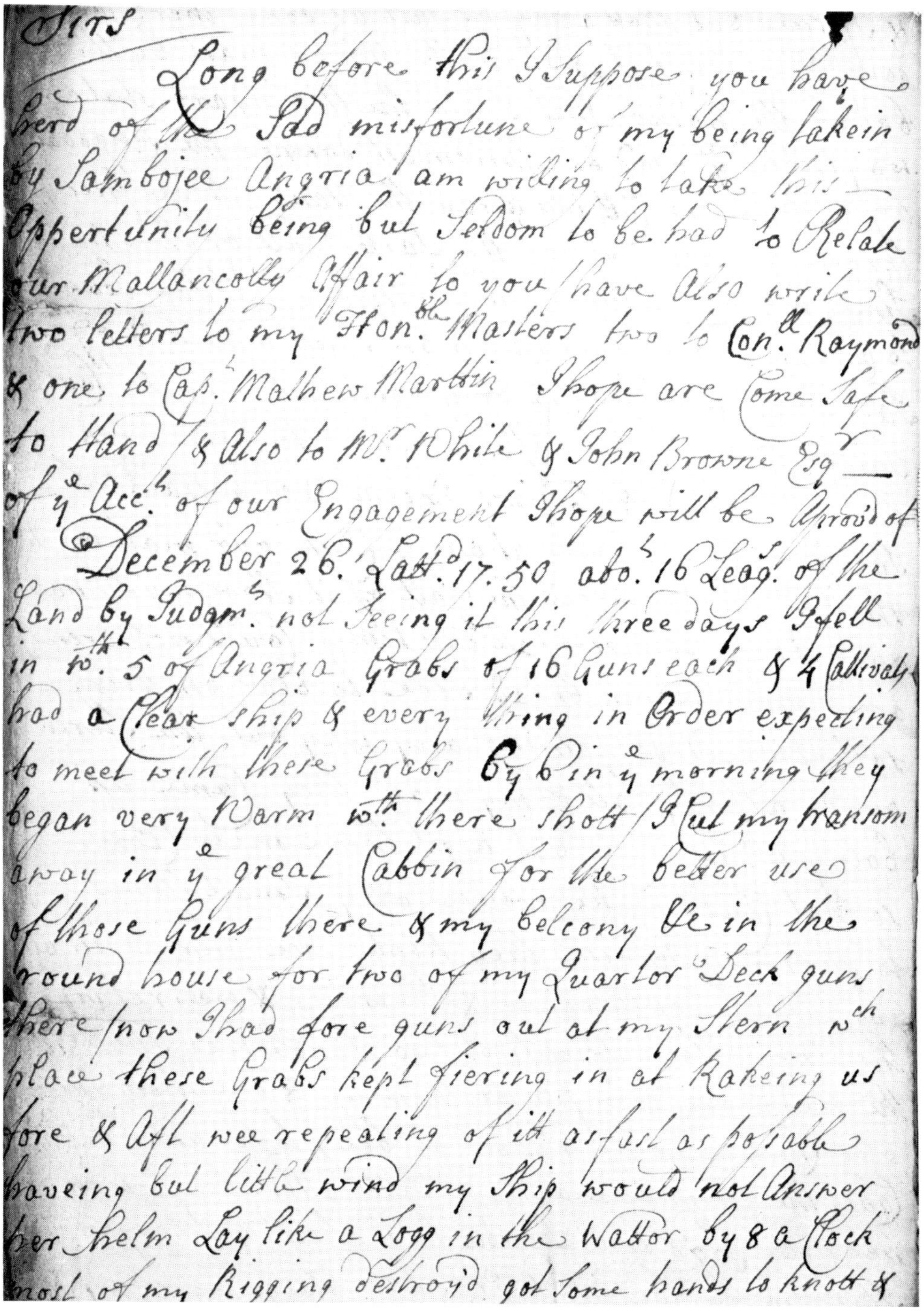

Sirs

Long before this I suppose you have herd of ye Sad misfortune of my being takein by Sambojee Angria am willing to take this Oppertunity being but Seldom to be had to Relate our Mallancolly Affair to you have also writ two letters to my Honble Masters two to Conll Raymond & one to Capt Mathew Marttin I hope are come Safe to Hand / & also to Mr White & John Browne Esqr of ye Accts of our Engagement I hope will be Aprov'd of

December 26 Latd 17.50 abots 16 Leags of the Land by Judgmt not Seeing it this three days I fell in wth 5 of Angria Grabs of 16 Guns each & 4 Gallivats had a Clear ship & every thing in Order expecting to meet with these Grabs by 6 in ye morning they began very Warm wth there shott / I Cut my transom away in ye great Cabbin for the better use of those Guns there & my belcony Bl in the round house for two of my Quartor Deck guns there / now I had fore guns out at my Stern wch place these Grabs kept fiering in at Rakeing us fore & Aft wee repealing of it as fast as posable haveing but little wind my Ship would not Answer her Helm Lay like a Logg in the Wattor by 8 a Clock most of my Rigging destroy'd got some hands to knott &

The captain of the Indiaman Derby *describes the ship's capture by Angrian pirates in 1750.*
INDIA OFFICE LIBRARY

95

Angrian territory. The plan shows an Angrian encampment at top left.

occasion the crew fought with little spirit because their captain did not offer them the usual reward—it was customary on such occasions to place two treasure-chests on deck for subsequent distribution if the attackers were beaten off. The captain, who was called Anselme, offered no leadership, and insisted on surrender when many of those who surrounded him were willing to continue the fight. He and 114 others spent eleven months in captivity.

Many of Angria's best vessels were commanded by Europeans, usually Dutchmen, and for the most part adventurers in search of a new occupation after the Peace of Utrecht in 1713. It was perhaps under their guidance that extremely effective maritime tactics were evolved. The vessels chiefly used by the Angrians were called "grabs"—a corruption of *ghorab*, the Arabic word for "raven." They were generally two-masted ships of 150 to 300 tons burden, built to draw very little water, and excellent sailors, especially in light airs. Attacks on large European vessels were often made at night, in the period of calm that prevailed between the land and sea breezes. The grabs came on toward their intended victim in line abreast, coming up astern of her and keeping the masts of the enemy just sufficiently out of line to afford a good target to the powerful guns—either nine- or twelve-pounders—which they carried projecting over the bow. Two or three grabs would then run alongside the shattered

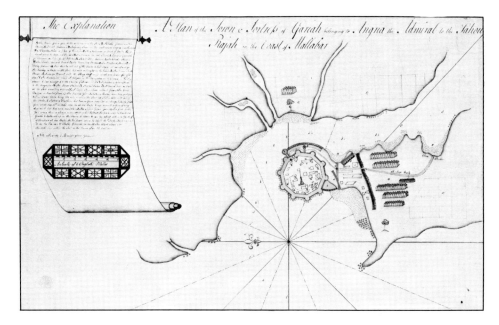

The Angrian headquarters at Geriah, besieged by Clive, 1756.
BRITISH LIBRARY

sternquarters of the enemy ship, and the crews would board her, sword in hand, along the beaked prow of their own boats.

The East India Company made any number of efforts to suppress the Angrians, and to capture their headquarters at Geriah. The first attempt to take this fortress was made in 1717, but success was not finally achieved until 1756, when the place fell to an expedition led by the great Clive. But piracy on the Malabar coast was not completely suppressed even at the very end of the eighteenth century. The East India Company was still having trouble in 1798, and the grab continued in employment. In Gujerat, the Sanganian pirates, whose peculiarity was their insistence on being ruled by a queen rather than a king, were finally brought to order in 1818.

The Kunjalis, Angrians and their successors are one instance of a pattern of piracy which is at least partly seen in the activities of the Barbary corsairs, and repeats itself from the Adriatic eastward to the coast of Manchuria. It long preceded, just as it has far outlasted, the activities described by Defoe in his *General History*. What seems to happen is that a hardy maritime people, perhaps still only in the tribal stage of social development, and positioned upon the flank of some important trade route, compensates for the lack of natural resources in its own territory by preying upon the trade that passes by. Often the guerrilla warfare waged

97

H.M.S. armed patimar Powna, Bombay. *Ships like this continued to be used off the coast of India into the early nineteenth century to protect commerce against pirates.*
INDIA OFFICE LIBRARY

by the pirates upon their victims is fueled not merely by a mixture of greed, bravado and economic necessity, but by religious differences and by the resentment felt by the colonized towards the colonizer. Thus the Dalmatian Uskoks of the Adriatic, who have already been described, turn out to have much in common with the Arab pirates of the Red Sea, using the same tactics, and (despite the religious difference), professing the same attitudes towards their opponents and following much the same code of conduct.

Piracy in the Arabian Gulf has a recorded history that goes back to as early as 1600 B.C. According to the ancient historians Strabo and Arrian the Persians were forced to block the mouth of the Tigris in order to prevent pirate raids, and it was not until the time of Alexander the Great's conquest of the Persian Empire that these obstructions were removed. Pliny describes how, in Roman times, archers were kept aboard ships sailing in the Gulf in order to defend them from pirate attack. The East India Company first began to have trouble with native pirates in these waters in the late seventeenth century. In 1683 the Company ship *President* was attacked, but managed to beat off her attackers. In 1696 there was a striking outrage—a Company vessel carrying horses to Surat was taken by Arab pirates. Captain Sawbridge, who was in command, expostulated with his attackers, and when he refused to hold his tongue they sewed his lips together with a sail-needle and twine. He was kept for several hours with his hands tied behind him, then taken on board the pirate dhow while his

An Arab pirate dhow.
SCIENCE MUSEUM

ship, with the horses still in it, was set on fire. Sawbridge and his crew were eventually put on shore, where soon afterwards he died.

Piracy in the Gulf increased in the mid-eighteenth century. In this period the Joasmi people (properly Qawasim), who were converts to the fanatical Wahabi sect, began to molest trade. The principal Joasmi town was Ras-al-Khaima, north of Muscat, and they controled the narrow straits at the entrance to the Gulf. Their activities soon spread as far as the west coast of India, and put the East India Company authorities in a dilemma. The council of the Presidency of Bombay knew that it was essential to maintain the important Gulf trade-route, but were reluctant to engage in open combat with the Wahabis, who were known to be the most warlike element in Arabia. At first they tried the feeble compromise of

Arab coasting prows. These ships too were often used by pirates.
INDIA OFFICE LIBRARY

instructing their own ships not to fire until fired upon. The consequence of this was that a British vessel, by the time she had allowed herself to be surrounded by pirate dhows, had little chance of making a defence.

At this time the Joasmi pirate fleet was estimated to consist of over sixty large ships, and several hundred smaller vessels, manned by about 20,000 men. Many of the ships were armed with guns taken from captured vessels, but these were seldom efficiently used. The technique of the pirates, here as elsewhere, was fast sailing to run the quarry down, an approach from the stern to avoid a broadside and instant boarding in overwhelming force. The Joasmi usually respected "the persons and virtues of females," and treated European captives better than Indian or Arab ones. The traveler J. B. Fraser remarks that:

> The horrid coolness and even solemnity with which they were wont, after a capture, to take the survivors to the fore part of the ship, and cut their throats upon the gunwale with their crooked knives, uttering a prayer the while; and the formal purification of the vessel afterwards, evinced a seriousness of purpose that rather bore the character of some dreadful religious rite; and had there not been strong reasons to the contrary, would have led to the conclusion that the practice had originated in religious zeal.

100

In fact, it did originate in just such zeal, as the Joasmi believed it was much less of a sin to kill a man who did not share their beliefs than it was to rob him.

An English punitive expedition was at last sent against Ras-al-Khaima in 1809, and the town was destroyed. But in 1816 the menace was as bad as ever, and had spread to the Red Sea. A second punitive expedition was needed in 1819, which combined the forces of the Royal Navy, the East India Company and the Sultan of Muscat. This destroyed the pirate strongholds on the Arabian coast as far as Bahrein.

Other strongholds of piracy were the Malay Archipelago, the Philippines and the South China Sea. For many years after the Portuguese established themselves in India, the Straits of Malacca were thought to mark a kind of boundary where the rule of maritime law came to an end, and it was every man for himself. One of the first Europeans to return with a narration of his experiences in this unknown and dangerous area was the Portuguese Fernão Mendes Pinto who claimed, when he returned to his native land in 1558, to have been five times shipwrecked and seventeen times sold as a slave in his twenty-one years of adventure. Mendes Pinto's book, the vast and immensely entertaining *Grand Peregrination*, has earned him a reputation as a liar in the same league as Baron von Munchausen, but recent research tends to demonstrate that it contains more than a basis of truth.

An early section of the book concerns the pursuit of the Gujerati pirate Koja Achem by the Portuguese Antonio de Faria, who is accompanied on his adventures by the narrator. Koja Achem's father and two brothers have been killed near Jeddah in the Red Sea in a fight with a Portuguese captain. Now, off the coast of Siam, he indemnifies himself by taking another Portuguese vessel. Those who have been robbed set forth in pursuit, and eventually get their revenge. But Antonio de Faria wants to go further—he likes the pirate life to which he has been introduced by becoming a victim of piracy, and he decides to continue his career in these lawless regions as the "King of the Sea." Hubris leads him to attempt to plunder some royal tombs on an island near Hainan; he is then solemnly cursed by the guardian priests, meets a great storm and his ship goes down with all hands. Though the edifying conclusion of the tale is fairly obviously fictional, Mendes Pinto gives a lively and convincing picture of a world in which there can be no distinction between trader and pirate because the concept of law does not exist, just as it had been non-existent upon all the seas known to Europeans in the early part of the Middle Ages.

One of the most eminent of Elizabethan navigators, John Davys, met his end in the same quarter of the globe in 1605, in circumstances very like those described by Mendes Pinto. He was acting as pilot to an expedition led by Sir Edward Michelbourne. They were anchored off Patani, on the eastern side of the Malay Peninsula, when they encountered a junk manned by Japanese pirates who had lost their own ship. Seeking to improve their fortunes, the Japanese tried to take Michelbourne's vessel the *Tiger* by means of a treacherous surprise attack. Though they were driven off, Davys was killed in the mêlée. But Michelbourne's expedition also illustrates the fact that, in these unknown waters, an encounter with strangers could be a curious mixture of war and trade. A member of the expedition describes how they met two Chinese ships: "We fought a little with them, and boarded them and brought them to an anchor." Nevertheless, good relations were soon restored: "After we had taken some of their silks we let them depart the fifteenth of January, and gave them twice as much as we had taken from them."

At a later epoch, the archipelago was famous for the piracies of seaborne tribesmen, such as those who terrorized the Straits of Macassar until their

The return of Sir Edward Michelbourne from the East Indies, by A. Willaerts, 1606.
NATIONAL MARITIME MUSEUM

stronghold was destroyed in the early nineteenth century by a punitive expedition of American marines, conveyed to the spot by the frigate *Potomac*. In the 1840s James Brooke, the White Rajah of Sarawak, conducted a campaign against the piratical head-hunting Dyaks. His success, and the large bounties claimed by some of the European participants, caused an outcry in Parliament. Brooke was reproved for "unseemly behaviour" by a Royal Commission because he had made use of native allies whom those in England considered no better than the savage tribesmen he had set out to repress. The affair is an early instance of European anti-imperialism.

Chinese piracy was stimulated in the early 1800s by the decline of the Manchu regime, and the inability of the central government to impose order. The initial impetus was provided by the end of the war with Annam, which left a number of bold seafarers at a loose end, but piracy soon, like other occupations in China, became an inherited profession. The most celebrated of the first generation of pirates on a grand scale was Mrs. Ching—Ching Yih Saou, the widow of Ching Yih. She took command

Sir James Brooke, by G. R. Ward after F. Grant.
BRITISH MUSEUM

when her husband perished in a gale in 1807. She inherited a fleet of 600 junks, and expanded it until it contained 800 large vessels and a thousand smaller ones. Her methods were businesslike—she kept strict records and refused to have dealings with anyone who did not first submit a request in writing. But she evidently decided after a brief while that piracy was too demanding a profession, and looked around for another way of making a living. In 1812 she negotiated a pardon with the Chinese government, bringing with her 212 vessels, 791 guns and nearly 7,000 small arms. She then set up as the director of a large smuggling combine.

Richard Glasspoole, fourth officer on the Indiaman *Marquis of Ely*, was captured by Chinese pirates who were probably part of Mrs. Ching's force in 1809, when he took the ship's cutter to Macao from the anchorage at Whampoa and failed to regain his ship due to adverse weather conditions. He describes in a memoir the way in which the pirates systematically levied

South China trading junk. These were frequently converted for use by pirates.
SCIENCE MUSEUM

English operations against Amoy, 1841, provoked by Chinese piracy.
INDIA OFFICE LIBRARY

tribute from the coastal towns and villages, and says that they were divided into five squadrons, distinguished by flags of different colors. The largest ships they possessed were quite formidable—they were of five or six hundred tons, and mounted up to thirty guns.

In the 1840s there was a change in the character of Chinese piracy thanks to the growth of the opium trade, which was forbidden by the Emperor but supported by the British government because of the revenue it brought to India. The pirates started to raid the opium clippers, chiefly because their cargoes were very valuable, but also because robbery of this kind could be represented as patriotic. The British China Squadron entered the fray, and found little difficulty in destroying large numbers of pirate junks. Yet piracy itself was far from finished. In 1854 a Frenchwoman called Fanny Loviot, traveling alone and unprotected (one is left wondering darkly precisely why she made the long journey to China) was one of those taken prisoner aboard the Chilean bark *Caldera* as it left Hong Kong for California. Her experiences, related in lively style, were much the same as Richard Glasspoole's. But adventurers from outside had also begun to enter the game. In 1857 a handsome young American called Eli Boggs was put on trial in Hong Kong for crimes committed in association with Chinese seafarers. Wingrove Cooke, the correspondent of

The destruction of shap-'ng-Tsai's piratical fleet by the British in the Gulf of Tonkin, 1850.

The Times, attended his trial and gives a colorful description of the defendant:

> In form and feature he was like the hero of a sentimental novel; as he stood in the dock, bravely battling for his life, it seemed impossible that that handsome boy could be the brute whose name had been for three years connected with the boldest and bloodiest acts of piracy. It was a face of feminine beauty. Not a particle of down upon the upper lip; large lustrous eyes; a mouth the smile of which might woo coy maiden; affluent black hair, not carelessly parted; hands so small and delicately white they would create a sensation in Belgravia, such was the Hong Kong pirate Eli Boggs.

Boggs was acquitted of murder, though only because nobody had actually seen him kill anyone; but he was found guilty of piracy and sentenced to be transported for life.

Piracy outlived the collapse of the Manchu dynasty and was still flourishing in Chinese waters in the earlier part of the present century. In the 1920s an average of three ships a year bearing British or foreign flags were attacked by the pirates who based themselves on Bias Bay near Hong Kong. The method resembled that of the present-day skyjackers—the pirates would board the ship as passengers, and take the crew by surprise in the course of the voyage. One of the most notorious cases of piracy at this time was the capture of the S.S. *Sunning* on November 15, 1926. The existence of real-life pirates, still at work in the modern world, naturally attracted the attention of enterprising journalists. The most successful in his quest was the Finn A. E. Lilius, who managed to get in touch with a female pirate chief who sounds, from his description, like the reincarnation of Mrs. Ching. He spent some time on one of her junks, and wrote an account of his adventures, complete with photographs to authenticate the narrative, which appeared in English in 1930. This must be one of the very few occasions on which the everyday existence of professional pirates has been recorded by the camera. When the Japanese moved into Manchuria, Chinese piracy again took on a nationalistic and even patriotic tinge. The piracy of the steamer *Nanchang* off the Manchurian coast in 1933, and the kidnapping of her officers, who were British, created a situation in which the consular officials responsible for trying to obtain the release of their compatriots found themselves the shuttlecock in a diplomatic game

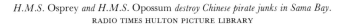

H.M.S. Osprey *and H.M.S.* Opossum *destroy Chinese pirate junks in Sama Bay.*
RADIO TIMES HULTON PICTURE LIBRARY

The cruiser H.M.S. Frobisher *(above) and the aircraft carrier H.M.S.* Hermes *(below) were both used to hunt Chinese pirates in the 1920s.*

between the Chinese themselves and the occupying power. The officers were at last freed after a long-cherished principle had been abrogated and a ransom paid. The money seems to have been exacted as much to prove a point to the European powers as it was for its own sake. Many incidents in the story have an atmosphere which is once again strongly reminiscent, not only of the world of Richard Glasspoole and Fanny Loviot, but of that of Fernão Mendes Pinto. The East had not changed all that much since his day, and might prove to be much the same even now if more information was available to us. Certainly there has in recent years been occasional news from the Philippines of piratical forays made by left-wing nationalists basing themselves on the remoter islands.

5

The Indies, East and West

Vasco da Gama's voyages to India in the service of the Portuguese crown, followed by Columbus's discovery of the Americas on behalf of the Spanish rulers Ferdinand and Isabella, led to the creation of a monopolistic system of trade and colonization which eventually put a girdle round about the earth. The Portuguese and the Spanish were at first rivals. Ferdinand of Aragon exerted his influence with the Spanish-born pope, Alexander VI Borgia, to obtain a grant of sovereignty over all lands lying to the west and south of an imaginary line drawn north to south a hundred leagues west of the Cape Verde Islands and the Azores. Later, the papal grant was expanded to include "all islands and mainlands whatsoever . . . in sailing or traveling towards the west and south, whether they be in regions occidental or meridianal and oriental and of India." Alarmed by the mention of India, which he regarded as his own preserve, King Manuel of Portugal managed to get Ferdinand to sign the Treaty of Tordesillas, which guarded Portuguese rights in the Far East. Spanish jealousy of the wealth which their neighbors derived from the spice trade later prompted Ferdinand's son Charles V to finance Magellan's voyage, the first circumnavigation. Yet gradually the two nations came to realize that their commercial interests had much in common; and they tended, too, to organize their commerce in a similar way. For a crucial forty years, after Philip II invaded Portugal in 1580, the two powers were united under one authority.

When Columbus made his voyages of discovery, he was disappointed not to find gold, which was a prime object of the venture. It was only after the conquest of Mexico and Peru, and the discovery of rich silver mines at Potosi, that precious metals began to flow eastward across the Atlantic. The supply of wealth, though apparently endless, was in fact not so abundant as the Spaniards believed. Nor was it healthy for Spain herself. The Spanish crown was encouraged to take an exaggerated view of its own power and international responsibilities, and its commitments cost it dearly in both blood and money. The flood of bullion ruined the balance of the national economy, and impoverished the nation. By the seventeenth century Spain was visibly in decline—her population was only half that of France and three quarters that of Italy, thanks to constant wars and epidemics. From the mid-sixteenth century onward she had ceased to be self-sufficient in grain, and there is evidence that the population was chronically undernourished. It was hunger which prevented the Spanish people from making the rapid recovery from major outbreaks of disease which was customary in other European countries. The Americas themselves were a direct drain. Probably at least 100,000 people left Spain for the Americas in the sixteenth century, and the migration was still going on in the seventeenth. This did not represent a particularly high proportion of the total population, but it meant the constant loss of men of vigor and initiative.

Meanwhile, the Spanish government counted on the wealth of the Americas to pay its garrisons in Italy and in the Low Countries, the fleets it maintained in the Atlantic and in the Mediterranean, and the armies that campaigned in Germany. In order to do all this, it was forced to borrow, and the chief security offered was naturally the revenues from overseas. But what came in was never quite enough to service these immense borrowings and to make adequate repayments, so the government fell deeper and deeper into debt. Any interruption or delay in the silver shipments meant an immediate financial crisis, and damage to Spanish credit which was hard to repair. For this reason alone, the government was particularly rigid in its attitudes towards trade with its new dominions.

The Americas, or, as the Spaniards called them, "the Indies," had been shaped as a social organism by the desires, the needs and the prejudices of the Europeans who followed in Columbus's track. The Spaniards were convinced of their own natural superiority to the indigenous population; they were convinced of the right of the first discoverer to do what he liked,

Old colonial architecture in Havana, probably the most magnificent city in the Antilles. From Isla de Cuba Pintoresca.

particularly when this right had been confirmed by papal decree. They easily persuaded themselves of their right to rule over the native Indian population, noting:

> The naturally servile nature of the barbarians, and their consequent need for a civilized master; their habitual crimes against natural law; the plight of the subjects of barbarian rulers, who were the victims of oppression, unjust war, slavery and human sacrifice; and their duty of making possible the peaceful preaching of the gospel.

Despite the inherent idealism of some of their attitudes, many of the conquistadors behaved with horrible and reckless cruelty. The natives were soon decimated. In many parts of New Spain the Indian population was, by the beginning of the seventeenth century, reduced to a tenth of what it had been a hundred years before. This was due not only to Spanish oppression, but to diseases introduced by the invaders against which the

Indians had no immunity. This declining population was expected to support, by its tribute and its labor, not only its own nobility, insofar as this survived, but also an increasing number of Spaniards.

The lack of precious metals in the West Indian islands which Columbus had first discovered and the presence of abundant supplies on the mainland of South America led to a neglect of those areas which were most easily reached by sea. The chief inland cities—Lima, the capital of the Viceroyalty of Peru, and Mexico, the capital of Neuva España or New Spain—soon became very magnificent. They approximated, in their open and regular street-plans, to the ideas put forward in Renaissance textbooks on architecture. The English Jesuit Thomas Gage, who traveled extensively in the Spanish Americas, saw the city of Mexico at the beginning of the seventeenth century, and reported that it was completely stone-built, and that there were then some 30 or 40,000 inhabitants. These lived very luxuriously indeed: "a hatband and rose made of diamonds in a gentleman's hat is common, and a hatband made of pearls is ordinary in a tradesman." He estimated that there were no less than 15,000 coaches in the city.

The condition of the outlying islands, and of the ports through which the treasure passed on its way to Spain was very different. In 1582, the acting warden of the chief fortress on the island of Santo Domingo wrote to Philip II:

> In all this island, which is indeed large and uninhabited, there are some six or seven thatched villages and only this city of 500 houses of which most (anyway, many) have fallen in and are unoccupied. Masters and servants—in villages and on estates, whites, Indian half-breeds and mulattoes—in all, there are scarcely 2,000 men, many without weapons, living in an abandonment which cannot be exaggerated.

In addition to 2,000 free men there were also some 25,000 Negro slaves, brought in to replace the now-exterminated native Indians. The need to procure these Negroes was to produce some of the sharpest disagreements between the Spanish colonists and the government at home.

Santo Domingo was a staging-post for the fleets going to and from the mainland—the West Indies had not yet acquired their later wealth and importance from sugar, though some was grown. The ports of the Spanish Main by no means lived up to the image which romantic storytellers have subsequently formed of them. Here is an English description of Nombre de Dios in 1587:

113

Nombre de Dios is builded upon a sandy bay hard by the seaside; it is a city of some thirty households or inhabitants: their houses are builded of timber, and most of the people which are there be foreigners; they are there today and gone tomorrow.

Vera Cruz when Thomas Gage saw it was larger but scarcely more impressive. The buildings, he says, "are all, both houses, churches and cloisters, built with boards and timber." He estimated that there may have been as many as 3,000 inhabitants.

The ports only came to life when the annual fleets arrived. The Porto Bello Fair was a famous event, when the notoriously unhealthy collection of wooden hovels which called itself a city was suddenly filled with feverish bustle. Gage says that in the year he was there one merchant was forced to give no less than 1,000 crowns for a shop "of reasonable bigness" in which to transact his business. Gage says he saw great mounds of silver ingots and even, he claims, mounds of jewels, lying in the filthy streets.

The brevity and intensity of the fair reflected the way in which trade was organized by Spanish government regulation. Between 1504 and about 1660 the commerce between Spain and the Americas was the biggest, the most varied in terms of merchandise, and the farthest ranging of its time. The rules which governed it were extremely complicated, often altered, and only codified and regularized as late as 1680. But the basic principles were clear. The colonists were forbidden to trade with foreigners, just as no individual could go to the Indies without permission. The foreign ship which made its appearance in an American port was automatically considered to be a pirate, and all intercourse with it was outlawed. But Spanish maladministration led to frequent hiatuses in regular and authorized commerce, and to a steady growth of contraband trading. Spanish industry, which the regulations were supposed in part to protect, was unable to supply the needs of the colonies and trade fell more and more, even when authorized, into the hands of foreigners sailing under the Spanish flag.

The Spanish were always very nervous about piratical attack, and by 1561 an elaborate convoy system had been evolved. Seville was the only permitted starting point, and one fleet or *flota* set out every year for Vera Cruz in New Spain, and another for the *Tierra Firma* (Colombia, Venezuela, Panama), where it collected the bullion sent from the Viceroyalty of Peru. The *Tierra Firma* squadron consisted almost entirely of galleons, and was therefore known familiarly as "the Galleons." Both

Spanish carrack and galleons, 1561.
SCIENCE MUSEUM

squadrons together were known as the *Carrera de Indias*. The departure of
the Galleons was set, after many changes, for the end of March; and the
fleet for New Spain left soon afterwards, at the beginning of April. In the
course of the seventeenth century the custom grew up that both fleets
would sail together, and would separate only when they got as far as
Dominica in the West Indies.

The types of ship used in the *Carrera de Indias* were the galleon, the
caravel, the urca, the carrack, the não, the galleoncete and the patache.
These words were sometimes used to mark a distinction of function rather
than form. A galleon was a ship used for fighting and convoy duties. It was
usually forbidden to carry cargo except for "official" or registry treasure. A
não was the same type of vessel, but used as a transport and equipped with

115

A late seventeenth-century view of Havana by J. de Ram.
VICTORIA AND ALBERT MUSEUM

fewer guns. The galleon prototype was developed around 1450, before Columbus's first voyage, and was fully in service by 1510. In the period 1550 to 1600 such ships were typically of 300 to 600 tons, but were sometimes as large as 1,000 tons. A 400-ton ship of about 1590 would have been some hundred feet long, with a thirty-foot beam and a draft of twenty feet or less. The reason for designing for a shallow draft was the existence of a bar blocking the entrance of the Guadalquivir River. This had to be passed before the ship could reach Seville to load or unload. Shallow draft and a high freeboard made the galleon type unwieldy, and they needed high winds to make them move. As the years went on, there was an increasing tendency for size to outrun design. In the seventeenth century the largest nãos exceeded 1,200 tons, while the galleons called *Capitanas* and *Almirantes*, which carried the commanding admirals and vice-admirals respectively might be as large as 2,000 tons, and rose as much as forty-five feet above the water, carrying ninety bronze cannon in three tiers. The largest ships, unhandy, heavily armed and often overloaded, were far more dangerous than those of more moderate size, especially in the crowded open anchorages which the Indies fleets had to use when they reached the end of the outward voyage. But it was not until the eighteenth century that galleons gradually ceased to be employed. In 1748 they were at last officially abolished, and replaced by "register" ships which maintained communications between Spain and Peru by going round Cape Horn. The last *flota* arrived in Vera Cruz as late as 1778.

Two other ship types which call for comment are the carrack and the caravel, which lay at opposite ends of the scale of size. The carrack was a kind of warehouse-fortress, with a cargo capacity of up to 1,500 tons, and often carrying as many as 1,000 passengers and crew. It was a notoriously poor sailor, but was nevertheless much used by the Portuguese on the voyage to India. The annual Manila galleon also conformed to this type. The caravel was small—between thirty-five and ninety tons, though later Portuguese caravels might be up to twice this size. The crew was usually one man per ton. This type, which was the one used by Columbus on his pioneering voyages, was nearly obsolete by 1575.

A certain variation was introduced into the ship types used for the *Carrera de Indias* because fewer and fewer were Spanish-built. Not only did the custom arise of building ships in the Indies (where superb hardwoods could be obtained) but vessels were hired or purchased from foreign owners. By 1650 about a third of the ships in the *flotas* were small merchantmen of Dutch origin.

The convoy system survived so long not merely because of Spanish conservatism, but due to the fact that it was basically a success. It might make rapid turn-arounds impossible and prevent the economical use of shipping, but, with a few brief intermissions, it kept Spain's lifeline to the Indies intact. In fact, the main threat to the *flota* was always natural disaster rather than the activity of corsairs or even of hostile fleets. The proportion of all losses was often surprisingly low. On outward voyages from Seville in the period 1504 to 1550, they averaged only 0.54 percent. On return voyages during the same period, they were 2.13 percent. From 1551 to 1600, losses on outward voyages averaged 3.43 percent, and on return voyages 7.08 percent. From 1601 to 1650, the loss on outward voyages averaged 2.41 percent, and on return voyages 4.19 percent. There were some bad years in the second half of the sixteenth century—in 1554 and 1591, for instance, the losses on the return voyage (when the bullion was carried) were nearly 35 percent. Losses to corsairs formed a relatively small part of the total, though there is evidence that the pressure of their attacks began to step up around 1537–8. In 1542 five vessels were lost on the return voyage from this cause, in 1588 (the year of the Armada) there were six, totalling 1,850 tons, and in 1624 there were twelve. But the average was between one and three ships a year. The long voyage across the Atlantic could be an ordeal, but it could also be very pleasant. Gage, who supplies so many vivid details, describes a play which was acted aboard the ship which first took him to the West Indies:

> For the afternoon's sport they had prepared a comedy out of famous Lope de Vega, to be acted by some soldiers, passengers and some of the younger sort of friars, which I confess was as stately acted and set forth both in shows and good apparel, in that narrow compass of our ship, as might have been upon the best stage in the Court of Madrid.

If the Spanish consistently overestimated the size of the revenue they got from the Americas (and thus persuaded others to overestimate it also) the English and other corsairs who tried to intercept it always underrated the difficulty of the task.

Portuguese commerce to India was never as well organized as the Spanish trade to the Americas. It was mostly carried in immense carracks with three of four flush decks and high castles stem and stern, which sometimes sailed in company but often alone. Even when they left together from port they would seldom remain in sight of one another for long, as there was intense rivalry to reap the profit of being first at Lisbon or at Goa. Not that the carracks were in any sense racehorses. Their sailing qualities, bad enough at the best of times, were further spoilt by overloading—it was said of them that: "There is not the smallest corner that is not given as a favor or sold, and the same on deck." In 1602 the Dutch pirates who took the Portuguese ship *Santiago* were astonished by the degree to which she had been overburdened, even though much cargo had already been jettisoned by the time they boarded her:

> Tell us, you Portuguese, has there ever been such a barbarous and greedy nation in the world, who would try to round the Cape of Good Hope, buried to the bottom of the sea with cargo, putting your lives in such probable danger of losing them, and only because of your greed? It is not to be marveled at that you lose so many ships, and so many lives.

Losses could indeed be high. There were usually five or six sailings a year, of one of two ships each. But between 1605 and 1612 no less than twenty-four carracks were lost along the East Indies route. Though there was also a great deal of corruption, poor maintenance and provisioning, and gross overloading for private profit aboard the ships of the Spanish

Havana harbor, showing the fortifications.
VICTORIA AND ALBERT MUSEUM

flotas, the situation never seems to have been as bad as it became aboard the great Portuguese hulks.

The danger was increased by the poor quality of the crews. Even when Portuguese maritime power was at its height, the professional seaman was universally despised in Portugal. Their fellow-countrymen thought of the sailors who manned the carracks as clownish, undisciplined, selfish and brutal. Perhaps for this reason local Portuguese shipping in the East was largely operated by Asian seamen, and even the carracks that visited Japan might carry only a few white men besides the captain, pilot and master-gunner. In the Indian ocean, the captain was often the only white man aboard, and even the pilots were Gujeratis. On the great carracks of the *Carreira da India* the captain was often a landsman chosen for his rank, and by prudent royal regulation it was not he but the pilot who had sole charge of the ship's navigation.

The third great trade route controled and regulated by the nations of the Iberian peninsula was the one which linked the port of Acapulco in Mexico with Manila in the Philippines. The Spanish had established themselves here in 1564, and had discovered that the place was the perfect entrepôt for trade with the mainland of China. The Spanish government did not at first regard the idea of direct trade with Mexico with much favor, as they feared the loss of bullion which would result. But the pressure of Mexican demand for luxuries, particularly silk, was too great to be successfully resisted. In 1593 the number of ships that might make the voyage yearly was fixed at two only by royal decree, each ship to be limited to 300 tons. A third vessel was to be maintained at Acapulco to act as a reserve. But often just one huge vessel was sent. By 1614 1,000-ton ships were being regularly employed. They were built of teak by native craftsmen at Cavite in Manila Bay, and were considered "the strongest and best ships in the world," just as the voyage from the Philippines to Mexico was thought of, thanks to the adverse currents and winds, as being "the longest, most tedious and most dangerous voyage in the world." In some years the Manila galleon took so long to cross the Pacific that provisions were exhausted and there was heavy mortality among the crew and passengers.

Even after the warnings given by Drake's capture of the Lima–Panama ship *Cacafuego* in 1579, and Cavendish's taking of the Manila galleon *Santa Ana* in 1587, the great argosies from the east were usually lightly armed for their vast size. Those in charge preferred extra loading space to additional protection against pirates. And on the whole history proved them right. The Manila galleons continued to make their voyages until 1815, but in all this time only four were lost to the English, who were the most aggressive of their foes—one in 1587, one in 1709, one in 1743 (to Anson), and one in 1762. Losses from causes other than war or piracy were considerable. In the period 1600 to 1609, for instance, six galleons were lost. Many of these disasters, like losses to the *flotas* in the Atlantic, could be attributed to Spanish inefficiency. For example, while the galleons were supposed to leave Acapulco for Manila in January or February, because to depart any later meant contrary winds and arrival in the Philippines at the height of the typhoon season, sailing was in fact nearly always delayed. Of 148 recorded sailings in the period 1566 to 1784, eighty-seven were in March and forty-two in April.

It was natural that other European nations should be immediately envious of the new dominions the Spanish and Portuguese had carved out for themselves. It was equally natural that their seamen, still close to the piratical free-for-all which had prevailed throughout the Middle Ages, should try to divert some of this new-found wealth into their own pockets. It was the French who took the lead. They appeared sporadically in the East Indies: in 1506 a French corsair, Pierre de Mondragon, took a

Portuguese ship in the Mozambique Channel; and in 1530 the Rochellois pirate Captain Boudart was hanged by the Portuguese at Mozambique for having pillaged their caravels. But the political rivalry between France and Spain made the French even more interested in what the Spanish were up to. The Dieppe corsairs were organized by a ship-owner called Jean Ango, and it was one of his captains, Jean Fleury, in charge of a squadron of eight vessels, who in 1522 intercepted three unarmed Spanish ships at the Azores. These turned out to have been dispatched by Fernando Cortez to the King of Spain, and to be loaded with the spoil of Montezuma. The loot included "an emerald as large as the palm of a hand," and the incident revealed to the rest of Europe the full extent of the wealth the Spaniards had found. It was this disaster which led the Spanish government to decree that ships of less than 100 tons must not in future make the Indies voyage, and that all ships must carry at least four guns and sixteen gunners, plus twenty-six soldiers.

After this initial coup, Ango's luck was never as good. In 1523 another of his captains captured a galleon with three chests of gold ingots aboard, and five quintals of pure gold. But he himself was promptly attacked and taken by six Portuguese ships. A private war soon broke out between Ango's men and the Portuguese, to the displeasure of the French government. In 1527 Jean Fleury was captured and hanged; and in 1531 Ango was warned that his men would be treated as pirates if they persisted in attacking the Portuguese. He died in 1551, a more or less ruined man.

By this time the French had begun to raid in the Caribbean itself. In 1537 there was a successful Gascon freebooting expedition to the West Indies. It consisted of 150 men and two small ships, and was repulsed when it attacked Santiago de Cuba. But it nevertheless returned to France with much booty. Such enterprises received a fresh impetus after war broke out between France and Spain in 1542. Francois Le Clerc, called Pié de Palo, or Wooden Leg, by the Spaniards, received privateering letters of marque from Henri II of France, and was sent to scour the Spanish Main. In 1553 he ravaged Santo Domingo, Puerto Rico and Cuba. In the same year Vincent Bocquet of Dieppe, in command of two ships, took eight of fourteen vessels in a Spanish convoy returning from the Indies. In 1555 Pié de Palo's lieutenant, Jacques de Sores, stormed Havana with 200 men. He gave a truce so that a ransom could be collected, but when the Spaniards broke it he burned and pillaged the town, holding it for eighteen days in all. A Protestant who was later to organize the Channel blockade for the Huguenots during the Wars of Religion, Sores made a special point of destroying the churches. Dressed in church vestments, his men paraded

Sixteenth-century French privateers attack a Spanish settlement in the New World.
BRITISH LIBRARY

through the ruins of Havana, bearing aloft the religious images, insulting them and stabbing them with their poniards. It was the first sign of the part that the bitter opposition between the two faiths, the Catholic and the Reformed, was to play in the history of the area.

As they made more frequent forays into the Caribbean, the French began to realize how much they were hampered by lack of detailed knowledge of its geography. A clandestine traffic in renegade pilots grew up. A family of Lucchese Italians, called the Abagni, who settled in La Rochelle, were specialists. But perhaps the most famous of these renegades was a one-eyed Portuguese called Francisco Dias Mimoso, who in the 1560s became expert in capturing Spanish ships along the West Indian trade routes, near Havana and en route to Florida. The king of Spain, when he again had an ambassador at the French court, made strenuous efforts to have Dias Mimoso executed for piracy. Having been twice condemned and twice reprieved, the man was at last hanged in 1569, as part of some dubious diplomatic bargain. But the same day Charles IX of

The sixteenth-century sack of Cartagena.
BRITISH LIBRARY

France appointed another Portuguese pirate called Sordeval chevalier of the Order of St. Michael, and reappointed him governor of Belle-Isle, a function previously taken from him at the Spanish ambassador's insistence.

Of course, legitimate privateering and even colonizing expeditions at this period easily turned into what can only be described as outright piracy. In 1565 some French colonists who had gone to Florida found that the reports of wealth which had brought them to the place were greatly exaggerated. A number of them rebelled against their leader, stole a ship, and cruised southward. They terrorized Jamaica, and held prisoner the Spanish governor of the island. On their return to base they were promptly condemned and executed, but even this act of justice did not save the fledgling colony, which was wiped out by the Spaniards the next year.

In the first half of the sixteenth century the English were less active in the West Indies than the French, though, from the evidence of a Spanish document, they were the first foreigners to invade the New World. An

123

English ship appeared in West Indian waters in 1527. In 1541 an English corsair was cruising in Caribbean waters under the guidance of a French pilot. But at the time of the earlier Tudors English seamen were already going to the Newfoundland Banks to fish, and clearly they had the capacity, if not yet the will, for West Indian voyages. Pirates abounded in home waters, and were to continue to do so well into Elizabeth's reign. Various attempts were made to put a stop to the nuisance, but they were almost as fruitless as they had always been. After the peace between England and France in 1514 a joint effort was made by the two nations to suppress pirates, and in 1517 it was arranged that a commission of three or four suitable persons should sit at Calais to hear French complaints, and that a similar court should hear English grievances at Dieppe. In 1536 a new and revolutionary statute was passed against piracy, which brought it at last within Common Law jurisdiction and deprived pirates of benefit of clergy, the customary immunity extended to those who could read and write. A new court was set up, and more pirates were hanged in the first two years of its existence than in the previous three centuries. But by

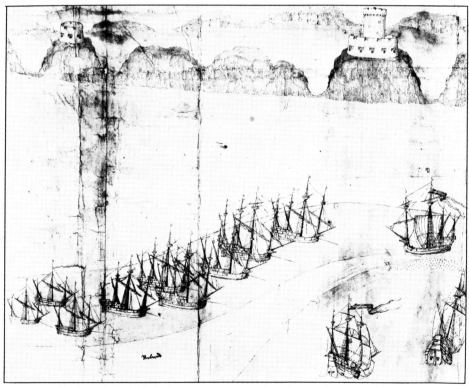

Merchant ships in Calais Roads, 1545—a time at which merchant vessels were extremely vulnerable to piracy in home waters.
SCIENCE MUSEUM

1544–6 piracy assumed gigantic proportions thanks to the renewed war with France, and Lord Admiral Seymour was accused of abetting it. The accusation occurs in the Act of Attainder by which he was condemned to death—his real crimes, of course, were an ambition to seize the throne and a bold attempt to seduce the young Princess Elizabeth.

1545 saw one of the most spectacular captures yet made by an Englishman. One Robert Reneger of Southampton, who felt himself aggrieved by the way he had been treated in the Spanish prize courts, lay in wait ten leagues off Cape St. Vincent and took the Spanish galleon *San Salvador*, on the return voyage from Hispaniola. In her he found, besides sugar and hides, gold worth more than seven million *maravedis*. The Spanish captain begged him to keep quiet about the gold, as it was being shipped illegally. When he got home Reneger had a good reception at court—"he swaggers about everywhere," the Spanish ambassador reported bitterly. The gold, held in the Tower of London for eight years, was at length returned to Spain, or about a third of it was.

At the beginning of Elizabeth's reign the machinery for dealing with pirates remained totally ineffective. No ship was safe from attack, and local officials charged with the task of repressing piracy were usually hand-in-glove with the pirates themselves. Between 1558 and 1578, no more than 106 English freebooters were hanged, a ridiculously small proportion in view of the number of capital crimes committed. Pirate goods were disposed of by means of an elaborate network of middlemen. Ten days after a Dutch vessel was attacked off Land's End, much of her cargo of linen was in the hands of London's Cheapside drapers. Things got so bad that in 1563 there were over 400 known pirates sailing the four seas that washed the coasts of England.

Three areas were particularly favored as pirate bases—eastern Dorset, the area round Falmouth, and South Wales. In Dorset the pirates used Lulworth Cove, and also the Isle of Purbeck, the peninsula stretching eastwards from Lulworth towards Poole Harbour. Sir Christopher Hatton, titular Lord of the Admiralty there, was said to be mixed up in their doings; and his deputy, Francis Hawley, used to send his men out to the pirate vessels anchored in Studland Bay "to see what they would give him."

In the Falmouth area, piracy was the profession of the Killigrew family, hereditary captains of Pendennis Castle at the entrance to Falmouth. In 1555 the English ambassador at Paris wrote in alarm to the English court: "The Killigrews are at sea, with four or five barks, and have taken good prizes, trusting to take yet more, and in case the worst fall, the gains thereof

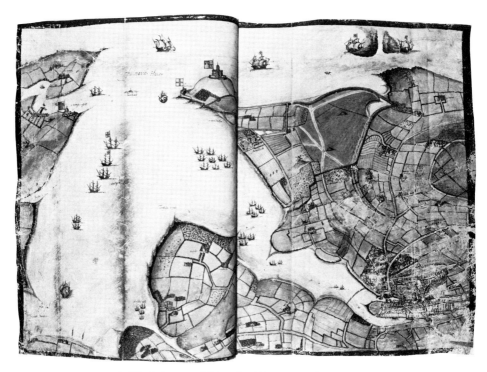

An Elizabethan map of Falmouth, which was a notorious pirate haven.
BRITISH LIBRARY

will be able to find them all this next winter in some island." Yet in 1577 Sir John Killigrew, the then head of the clan, was actually appointed the head of the Commission for Piracy. He was an extravagant man, and by 1592 had got himself deeply into debt. He tried to repair his fortunes by openly plundering a Spanish ship, the *Marie* of San Sebastian, which had been driven into Falmouth by adverse weather. The ship itself was carried to Baltimore in Ireland, and there disposed of. Sir John's mother, old Lady Killigrew, played a leading part in the affair, and we are told that, when she discovered what the ship was carrying "she was very discontented that it was of no more value."

In South Wales, Sir John Perrot, who was probably the natural son of Henry VIII by Mary Berkeley, acted as almost absolute ruler of Pembrokeshire. Dismissed as Vice-Admiral of South Wales in 1565, he never forgot the slight, and got his revenge by positively flaunting his patronage of pirates. His headquarters was at the castle of Laugharne, granted to him for services in Ireland.

Though the high tide of English coastal piracy had passed by the early 1580s, the same trade continued to flourish in the remoter corners of Ireland. Berehaven (Bantry Bay) and Baltimore were famous as pirate havens. Berehaven belonged to the O'Sullivans and Baltimore to the O'Driscolls. Clew Bay, thirty miles south of Broadhaven, was the base of the female pirate Grace O'Malley, who had her headquarters on Clare Island in the mouth of the bay. She married first an O'Flaherty, and then Richard MacWilliam Bourke, "Richard of the Iron," who was knighted in 1576 by Sir Henry Sidney, Viceroy of Ireland. Nevertheless she was on one occasion arrested for piracy, and spent some time in Dublin Gaol, though in the end she was not charged and was allowed to return home. She seems to have renounced her profession around 1586, and seven years later, now aged over sixty, she crossed to England to petition Elizabeth I for pardon and financial help. But even after this the Irish pirates continued to give trouble. It was not until 1602 that Berehaven was taken by the English, and Dunboy Castle demolished.

In the circumstances, it may seem surprising that English aims in the New World were at first directed towards trade rather than spoilation. The directing spirits seem to have been the Hawkins family of Plymouth. What was innovative about them was not merely their boldness as seamen, but the fact that the ships they took to sea were their own. This led to bolder and more flexible decisions on the spot, when they were a long way from home and anyone who might help them. The founder of the dynasty was the first William Hawkins, who pioneered the trade in ivory with Upper Guinea (now Liberia), and also ventured to the Portuguese colony in Brazil. He made three voyages in the years 1530–2, on the second of them bringing back a local chief from Bahia who caused a great deal of wonderment at Henry VIII's court, especially because of the jewel he had set in his lower lip and the bones thrust through his cheeks.

William Hawkins never made another voyage himself, though there is evidence that his ships continued to do so. He died in 1554, and his sons William junior and John Hawkins succeeded him. William junior was the biggest ship-owner in Plymouth and served three times as mayor, but it was John who was to be the bolder voyager. In the early 1560s he decided, on the basis of the considerable information he had gathered on trading voyages to the Canaries, to set up a triangular trade between West Africa, the West Indies and England. The venture was designed to exploit the difference in interests between the Spanish colonials and Spaniards in Spain, and the chief merchandise carried on the middle leg was to be slaves. His first voyage was in 1562, with three ships. In West Africa, partly through capture and partly through forced trading with the Portuguese factors who manned the forts at the mouths of the rivers, he acquired about 500 slaves. In Santo Domingo he was already expected, and after a token

Anonymous portrait of Sir John Hawkins.
NATIONAL MARITIME MUSEUM

show of force on the part of the planters, designed to keep them out of trouble with the bureaucrats back home, he traded profitably, taking much of his payment in bills of exchange on finance houses in Seville, and returned home with a cargo of hides.

A second venture left for Africa in October 1564, and once again returned safely, though Hawkins lost some men helping the Portuguese attack a neighboring town. As well as helping them, however, he also attacked them, taking seventeen Portuguese ships. In the Americas the Spanish were a little more resistant than before to Hawkins's approaches, but he got rid of all his slaves and even took orders for more. Philip II of Spain, however, was now determined to put an end to these breaches of the Spanish trade monopoly. The Spanish ambassador in London was told to get in touch with Hawkins and attempt to discover what he was up to, and advised his master to try to get the newly returned Englishman away from the scene "so that he may not teach others, for they have good ships and are greedy folk with more liberty than is good for them." There was even a suggestion that Hawkins might serve Philip against the Turks in the Mediterranean. But in 1566–7 there was yet a third Hawkins-organized voyage, now under the command of John Lovell, who was accompanied by the young Francis Drake.

Meanwhile an even more ambitious expedition was being fitted out, to which the Queen herself had agreed to lend two of her ships. These were large, but old-fashioned and in poor condition, which was to prove a decisive factor in the fate of the project. One was the *Jesus of Lubeck*, of 700 tons. Henry VIII had bought her in 1544 from the Hanseatic League, and she was rotten from prolonged neglect under Edward VI and Mary. At the beginning of Elizabeth's reign she had actually been condemned as beyond repair, though she had later been reprieved and patched up. Hawkins had used her on his 1564 expedition, and must have known her deficiencies. The other royal ship was the *Minion*, built *c.* 1536 for Henry VIII, and almost as rotten as her companion. The *Jesus* gave trouble from the very beginning of the voyage, and nearly foundered in a gale off Brest. When at last they all got to Sierra Leone, they acquired slaves as merchandise for the second leg (though not as many as they wanted) by the classic expedient of allying themselves with one native ruler who was making war against another.

In the Indies, conditions were difficult. At Rio de la Hacha, Hawkins had to take the town and burn part of it before the Spaniards would agree to trade, and the *Jesus* nearly sank in another storm—"the living fish did swim upon the ballast as in the sea." Hawkins decided to risk a visit to San

Juan de Ulua, the port of Vera Cruz, which was also a regular port of call for the ships of the *flota*, come to carry away the silver from the Mexico mines. He took the Spanish governor by surprise, got possession of the shingle-bank studded with gun emplacements which guarded the anchorage, and obtained facilities for repairing his ships. It was bad luck that the plate fleet appeared the morning after his arrival, having made a record crossing. Hawkins could not refuse them entry to their own port, for England was still at peace with Spain, and the result would have been a major diplomatic incident. So he allowed them in, on the understanding that the English would not be molested. The precarious truce was shattered by a Spanish surprise attack on the island and the English ships. After a confused six-hour battle in the harbor, Hawkins was lucky to get away with most of his men, though he succeeded in extricating only the *Minion* and another ship, the *Judith*, commanded by Drake. The *Minion* and the *Judith* became separated immediately after they had worked their way out of the port and out of range of the Spanish guns. Both reached home safely, but in Hawkins's ship there were only fourteen survivors. He had been forced to land a hundred others on the Mexican coast, for want of food and water and at their own request. Some died, and the others fell into the hands of the Inquisition.

After San Juan de Ulua, the dream of trade with the Spanish Indies was no longer practical. If the English wanted a share of Spanish wealth, they would have to get it by force. The decision was made easier for them by the religious conflict which was engulfing Europe. Even before Drake and Hawkins arrived back in England at the beginning of 1569, the Huguenot privateers were swelling in numbers, and at the end of 1568 there were fifty of them working under Condé's flag. At least thirty of these were alleged to be in fact English by the Valois ambassador at the English court, who protested to Elizabeth about them. The Dutch "Sea-Beggars," operating under commissions from the Protestant leader, the Prince of Orange, operated out of Flushing and Brill, but also based themselves on Dover. In the autumn of 1569, they numbered eighteen sail, but by the spring of next year over a hundred. In this fleet, too, English ships were to be found. In fact, English, French and Dutch privateers together formed a formidable Protestant navy. One of those who lent his aid after San Juan de Ulua was William Hawkins junior. His ship, the *Paul*, inherited from his father, who had used it for his original trading voyages to Guinea, was at one time actually commanded by the famous Jacques de Sores. William Hawkins himself was in effect commander-in-chief of the whole flotilla based on Plymouth.

LA VERRA CRVS

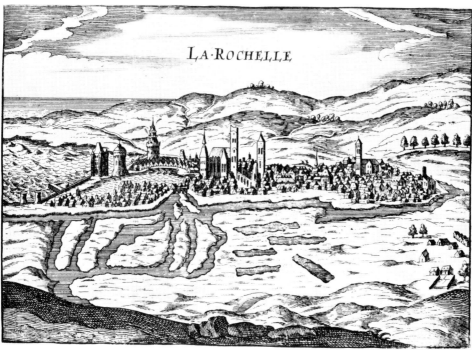

LA·ROCHELLE

Privateering havens: Vera Cruz (above), still called San Juan de Ulua when Hawkins's fleet anchored;
La Rochelle (below), base of the Huguenot privateers in the sixteenth century.
BRITISH MUSEUM

In 1571 Drake made his first independent voyage to the Spanish Main with a single ship, the *Swan*. He knew that bullion from Peru was sent first by sea to Panama, on the Pacific side of the isthmus, and that it was then brought by mule to the Caribbean port of Nombre de Dios. His aim, eventually, was to ambush the treasure, which he thought easier than taking it from the *flota*. He counted for help on the Negro slaves who had escaped from the Spaniards, and now formed communities of their own.

The next year he returned with two ships, confident that he would have a free hand because, while England and Spain were not yet at war, the Spanish ambassador had just been expelled, and relations were at a low ebb. He took Nombre de Dios, but was disappointed of the treasure he had hoped to find there—new regulations laid down that treasure was now to be sent from Panama only when the vessels of the *flota* had actually anchored in the port. Despite this, Drake decided to stay in the area, rather than return home. He explored the whole isthmus and had his first sight of the Pacific in February 1573. Allying himself with a Huguenot privateer from Le Havre called Le Testu, who had newly arrived in the area, and who brought him news of the Massacre of St. Bartholomew, he surprised three mule-trains loaded with silver, and finally made a rich haul of gold. He took a Spanish frigate to replace his one remaining ship, which was now too dilapidated to make the crossing, and returned home in April with £30,000 in booty to inflame the imaginations of his fellow-countrymen.

The next Englishman to appear in the vicinity of Panama was John Oxenham, and he was less fortunate. He crossed the isthmus safely, built a pinnace and crossed to the Pearl Islands. Here he ambushed two very rich treasure-ships from Peru. But when he landed on the mainland again, his luck ran out. The natives of the Pearl Islands revealed his presence to the Spaniards, who first of all recovered the loot that Oxenham had hidden, and took the ship he had left at Nombre de Dios, and finally surrounded and captured the man himself. He was sent to Lima for questioning about his faith as well as about his deeds, and died at the hands of the Inquisition.

In November 1577 Drake sailed from Plymouth on the voyage that was to take him round the world. Five ships accompanied him, but only the *Pelican*, later renamed the *Golden Hind*, completed the voyage. As they passed southward they took prizes, one of them a Portuguese caravel called the *Mary*. Drake pressed her pilot, Nuño da Silva, into his service, and kept him for the next fifteen months. Once they reached the Pacific, Drake and his men began to make havoc with virtually undefended Spanish towns and shipping. They attacked Valparaiso and caused a panic in the harbor at Callāo, the port for Lima. Between Lima and Panama they took the

*Sir Francis Drake: the portrait by Nicholas Hilliard (above left); Drake's drum (above right); a modern
model of his ship the* Golden Hind *(below).*

NATIONAL PORTRAIT GALLERY/PLYMOUTH CITY ART GALLERY

treasure-ship *Cacafuego*, and spent no less than six days in transferring her cargo to the *Golden Hind*. It consisted of "fruits, conserves, sugars and a great quantity of jewels and precious stones, 13 chests of royals of plate, 80 pounds of gold, 26 tons of uncoined silver." On September 26, 1580, after many further adventures, Drake returned to Plymouth. Later, at Deptford, he was knighted on the deck of his own ship—when the Queen called him her "pirate," she meant it as a compliment. The investors in the voyage received a return of 4,700 percent.

The 1580s and 1590s were the great age of English privateering. As Sir Walter Raleigh remarked: "No man is a pirate for millions." The profession of corsair was patriotic, recognized and respectable. The successes, when they came, were impressive—Cavendish's capture of the Manila galleon *Santa Ana* in 1587, which has already been mentioned; and the richest prize of all, the Portuguese carrack *Madre de Dios*, taken off the Azores in 1592 by a privateer fleet which had the financial backing of the Earl of Cumberland, a great nobleman turned sea-adventurer. Cumberland never forgave himself for not being present in person. He lost his glory and he lost money too. The *Madre de Dios* was a ship of 1,600 tons, so large indeed that no one could think of any use for her when once she had been brought to England and emptied out. Sea-architects wonderingly took her measurements and then she was left to rot at her moorings. Those who captured her "broke bulk" as it was called, and plundered her pretty thoroughly, but there was nevertheless £150,000 worth of loot left when an inventory was taken. Meanwhile, every packhorse on the road from Exeter to London smelled of cloves. The Queen, who was a principal shareholder, appointed commissioners to try to recover what had been taken, and Robert Cecil, who was one of them, reported: "Everyone I met within seven miles of Exeter that either had anything in a cloak, bag or malle which did but smell of the prizes at Plymouth (for I could well smell them also, such had been the spoils of ambergris and musk among them) I did retain him with me to the town."

But increasingly there were failures to balance the successes. The enemy was capable of putting up a stubborn resistance, even in adverse circumstances. In 1594 Cumberland's privateers intercepted a Portuguese carrack called the *Chagas* (more properly *Cinque Chagas*, or *Five Wounds of Christ*) between Pico and Fayal in the Azores. She was a new ship and a very big one—even bigger than the *Madre de Dios*—but she had few fit men on board after a difficult voyage from Goa: only seventy, out of more than 500 people. She was exceedingly richly laden. Francesco Vendramin, the Venetian ambassador to Spain, was afterwards to write that she was the

Elizabethan privateers commanded by Sir Walter Raleigh attack a Spanish settlement.

richest ship ever to leave an East Indian port and that her cargo was worth more than three million ducats.

Despite her lack of hands, the *Chagas* put up a stout defence. Of the three English ships who attacked her only one succeeded in boarding her. The Portuguese used the cargo which was heaped on deck to make barricades and twice drove the English off. At a third attempt the English flag was hoisted but immediately pulled down, and the attackers were once more forced to sheer off. There are two different accounts of what happened next. According to the English, burning cordage from one of their ships, the *Mayflower*, set the galleon on fire at the stern. According to the Portuguese account, she was bombarded with red-hot shot. At any rate, the ship became an inferno, and the passengers and crew started to leap overboard in large numbers. The commander of the English flotilla sent out a boat, and told the man in charge of it to "use his own discretion" in saving them. As a result only those who had the forethought to hold out jewels and gold pieces were rescued. Two noble Portuguese ladies, who had endured an earlier shipwreck on the same voyage, deliberately drowned themselves rather than fall into English hands, and only thirteen

George, 3rd Earl of Cumberland. One of Elizabeth's gloves is pinned to his hat, and Nicholas Hilliard's painting reflects the self-conscious chivalry of her court.
NATIONAL MARITIME MUSEUM

136

people survived altogether. The English had approximately ninety men killed and 150 wounded, and got nothing for all their efforts, apart from ransoms, for the *Chagas*, once abandoned, burned furiously for the best part of two days and finally blew apart. The episode illustrates not only the growing Spanish and Portuguese willingness to fight, but the extreme bitterness with which the two sides now regarded one another.

The Spanish even began to show signs of fight along their formerly unprotected Pacific coastline. Richard Hawkins, son of Sir John, met with disaster when he tried to repeat the feats of Drake and Cavendish in the same year that the *Chagas* was sunk. His success was spoilt by the undisciplined greed of his crew. The expedition, like many undertaken at this time, was being conducted on a profit-sharing basis. As a result Hawkins was forced to delay to make prizes when he should have been showing the Spanish a clean pair of heels. At Callão the Viceroy was able to equip six vessels, with about 2,000 men on board. Though these were largely inexperienced, Hawkins eventually succumbed to the over-

Callão, the port for Lima, by J. de Ram.
VICTORIA AND ALBERT MUSEUM

137

whelming numbers of his assailants. The Spanish also had the advantage that their ships were locally built to suit conditions on the west coast of South America, where tempests were unknown and stoutness of build could therefore be sacrificed to speed and handiness. Hawkins was chagrined to find that his opponents comfortably outsailed his own vessel, the *Dainty*. The Spaniards took him prisoner, but treated him much better then they had Oxenham. He was honorably entertained, cured of his wounds, and at length sent home. When he reached England, it was to find that the Elizabethan privateering epoch was over.

Yet, for a while at least, Spanish losses were so serious as to bring the colonists close to despair. As late as October 1595, Diego de Ybarra, the treasurer of Santo Domingo, was complaining that:

> For the last four years . . . corsairs are as numerous and as assiduous as ever, as though these were ports of their own countries. They lie in wait on all the sailing routes to the Indies, particularly the courses converging on this city of Santo Domingo. Coming or going, we always have a corsair in sight. Not a ship coming up from the outside escapes them, nor does any which leaves the harbor get past them. If this continues, either this island will be depopulated or they will compel us to do business with them rather than with Spain.

He did not know that the situation was about to change. At the time when this letter was written, a joint expedition mounted by Drake and John Hawkins was in the West Indies, but Hawkins, old and worn out, would die within a few weeks; and Drake too would die and be buried at sea before the ships returned to England to report a disastrous loss for the investors. It was a sad contrast to the venture of ten years before, when Drake had sacked both Santo Domingo and Cartagena. The Earl of Cumberland's last and most ambitious cruise, in 1597-8, was also a failure. He took Puerto Rico at a second assault, but got little plunder and could not hold it because of the ravages of yellow fever.

As long as Elizabeth lived, however, privateering continued to be smiled upon. There was an abrupt change when James I ascended the throne. The new king thought that hostilities with Spain had gone on long enough, and he was determined to have peace if he could get it. In 1603 a proclamation was issued recalling all letters of marque. And to close the last loophole, this was followed in 1605 by another which forbade English seamen to seek service in foreign ships.

ABOVE: *Drake's attack on Santo Domingo.*
BRITISH LIBRARY

BELOW: *Puerto Rico in the seventeenth century, a view by J. de Ram.*
VICTORIA AND ALBERT MUSEUM

6

The Buccaneers

JAMES I'S BAN ON privateering did nothing to discourage piracy in
home waters. On the contrary, it probably made the situation worse,
as adventurous seamen found themselves thrown out of employment.
Some of the attacks made at this time were extremely audacious—in
1603 the Venetian ambassador was assailed on his way to London, and in
1614 it was the turn of James's brother-in-law, the King of Denmark, who
was attacked by pirates on a voyage to Yarmouth.

One reaction of seasoned privateers to James's peace policy was to go off
and join the Barbary corsairs. But it was only for a brief period that the
rulers of the Barbary states were able to tolerate allies who were unwilling
to turn renegade, or at least unwilling to do so permanently and sincerely.
The conduct of men such as Eston, Mainwaring and Dansiker, all of whom
deserted their new masters as soon as they saw the possibility of returning
successfully to Christendom, shows that they were right.

Another solution was to look for adventure and profit not in the West,
but in the East Indies, where the political situation was less precisely
defined. The courtiers of James I and Charles I occasionally tried for a
quick return by supporting ventures of this sort. In 1616, for instance, Sir
Robert Rich, the heir to the earldom of Warwick and later Lord Admiral,
went into partnership with Philip Bernardi, a Genoese merchant resident

An English privateer off La Rochelle, by Cornelius Claes Wieringen, mid seventeenth century.
NATIONAL MARITIME MUSEUM

in London, to mount a privateering voyage to the East Indies. Two ships, the *Francis* and the *Lion*, took part in the venture, equipped with commissions not from the King of England but from the Duke of Savoy. In 1635 there was another venture, backed by Endymion Porter, Gentleman of the King's Bedchamber, in partnership with two London merchants. Once again two ships were dispatched, the *Samaritan* and the *Roebuck*. Both ventures caused trouble to the fledgling East India Company. The *Francis* and the *Lion* almost succeeded in taking a large Gujerat ship of 1,400 tons, with thirty-five tons of silver and other goods worth not less than £100,000 aboard, plus the mother-in-law of the Great Mogul, returning from a pilgrimage to Mecca. But at the last moment they were cheated of their prize by the intervention of the Company ship, *Royal James*, which by coincidence happened to be nearby. The *Roebuck*, though she lost her consort in a wreck at the Comoro Islands, took two rich Mogul ships at the mouth of the Red Sea. The East India Company's servants at Surat were forced to pay compensation for what had been looted. Porter was sufficiently satisfied by the returns of the cruise to back another, which made more captures in the same waters. This was the beginning of a system of interlopers and permission ships which competed with the Company's vessels and infringed its monopoly. These often plundered native vessels to fill their holds, and sometimes the crews mutinied and quite openly turned pirate. At all times they represented a threat to trade and to the good relations which the Company itself was trying to build up with Indian rulers, and their existence is striking proof of the influence exercised by corrupt favorites at the Stuart court, to the detriment of the national interest.

In the early seventeenth century, however, it was not the English but the Dutch who caused the greatest damage to Spanish and Portuguese commerce, though it was sometimes the English who were in bad odor for their misdeeds. In July 1617, for instance, President George Ball of the English factory at Bantam wrote despairingly: "The Hollanders have covered the ocean with their ships from the Arabian Gulf to the coast of China, spoiling and robbing all nations in the name and under the colours of the English."

The Dutch corsairs, called *pechelingues* by the Spaniards—a word supposedly derived from the name of their native port, Vlissingen or

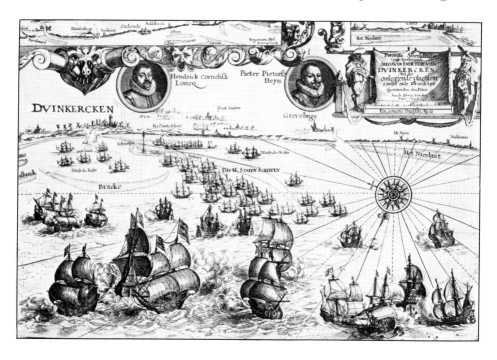

The Dutch fleet off Dunkirk. Piet Heyn is portrayed in the medallion to the right. 1629.
RIJKSMUSEUM

142

Flushing—raided in the West Indies and along both the west and east coasts of South and Central America. In 1602 Santiago de Cuba was taken by Dutch privateers. In 1605 a Spanish fleet was successfully attacked off the coast of Mexico by Dutchmen in league with Spanish colonists, who were finding the yoke of Madrid and Seville increasingly heavy. In 1615 the Dutch admiral Joris van Speilbergen fought a twenty-four-hour engagement with a superior Spanish fleet off Cañete in Peru, and was victorious; and in 1623 another Dutch admiral, Hugo Schapenham, had the bad luck to let a Spanish fleet containing two years' accumulation of Spanish silver escape him off Callão. The failure was redeemed by Piet Heyn who, five years afterwards, when in command of thirty-one ships of the Dutch West India Company, succeeded in capturing almost the entire *flota* as it set off laden with bullion for Spain. The disaster wrecked Spanish credit in Europe and gave the West India Company's shareholders a dividend of fifty percent.

Dutch incursions at this period were so serious that they upset the whole equilibrium of Spanish rule in the West Indies. No sea journey in the area was safe from corsairs. Thomas Gage, who sailed in the galleons from Portobello to Cartagena in 1637, describes how four privateers hovered near them, and succeeded in carrying away two merchant ships under cover of darkness. Later, as the fleet was leaving Havana, two strange ships singled out a Spanish vessel that had strayed from the rest, suddenly gave her a broadside, and forced her to yield. The Spanish admiral and two other galleons gave chase, but with no success. The entire business was so skilfully conducted that the action lasted for only half an hour. Meanwhile, the Dutch were almost as active elsewhere, and were not always too scrupulous as to whether their activities could be classified as privateering or piracy. In 1622 the great Portuguese carrack *São João Baptista*, on her way home from Goa, encountered two Dutch corsairs and fought a vicious running battle with them that lasted for nineteen days. In the end she escaped from their clutches, but was so badly crippled that she was afterwards wrecked on the coast of Africa. In 1625 a Dutch pirate called Claes Campane was hovering off Youghal in Ireland, with seven ships under his command. As a Danish writer naively reported: "He was a man of much experience, surpassing all others, both at sea and in drinking-bouts, and much practiced in navigation." In the 1640s the prosperity of the just-planted English colonies in New England was being affected by the activities of Dutch and Flemish privateers and of flushing and Ostend pirates off the English coast.

The *pechelingue* era officially ended with the Peace of Westphalia in 1649, and Dutch energy then turned toward legitimate trade. More and more long-haul cargoes were carried in Dutch hulls, whether or not the owner of the goods was himself a Dutchman. In the second half of the seventeenth century, for example, the Dutch were sending about a hundred ships per annum to the French Caribbee islands alone, and were returning with immensely valuable cargoes of tobacco, ginger and sugar. Having won their struggle for independence from the Spanish crown, the Dutch were so prosperous as to be inclined to leave the more dubious adventures to others. However, they were engaged in a bitter commercial rivalry with England, which intermittently flared up into open warfare. When it did so, Dutch privateers immediately became the danger to English shipping that they had once been to the Spaniards. In the First Dutch War of 1652–4 six Indiamen were lost to the Dutch on voyages from Persia to Surat. In the Second Dutch War of 1665–7 there was a panic in Surat when it was learned that the Dutch corsair Lambert Hugo was loose in the Red Sea. There were serious English losses nearer home as well. We learn of Dutch privateers taking prizes in the traditional hunting grounds off the Lizard and off the Scillies.

The partial breakdown in the Spanish colonial system caused by Dutch privateering in the first half of the seventeenth century opened the door to a period of colonization by nations other than Spain. The Dutch themselves seem to have had a foothold in Guiana by as early as 1580, but they were inclined, on the whole, to let others produce what they afterwards carried across the oceans, and did not press their colonizing efforts as briskly as they might have done, except in Brazil. The first English settlement to achieve permanence, Jamestown in Virginia, was founded in 1609. In 1624 the first English settlers arrived in the West Indies, and settled on St. Christopher. In 1625 the island was formally divided between the English and the French, and became the nucleus from which other colonies were seeded. The English spread to Nevis and Barbuda, then to Antigua and Monserrat. Barbados, which was to become the most important of the English colonies in the early years, was settled separately in 1627. The French colonized Guadeloupe, Martinique and the Windwards. After 1631 the flow of European colonists started to increase very rapidly. Most of these were the product of a recruiting drive for indentured servants, who bound themselves for a term of years in return for being transported across the Atlantic to a place of fresh opportunity. They were illiterate, rootless, vigorous and young, and of course there were very few women among them—of the colonists who departed from London in 1635 for Barbados and St. Christopher, only one percent were female.

ABOVE: *trading in the Dutch East Indies, by Hendrik Cornelius Vroom, early seventeenth century.*
RIJKSMUSEUM
BELOW: *the visit of a Dutch embassy to the Sultan of Visiapur, near Goa—an example of Dutch ambition to replace the Portuguese as a commercial power in the East. By J. B. Weenix.*
NATIONAL MARITIME MUSEUM

145

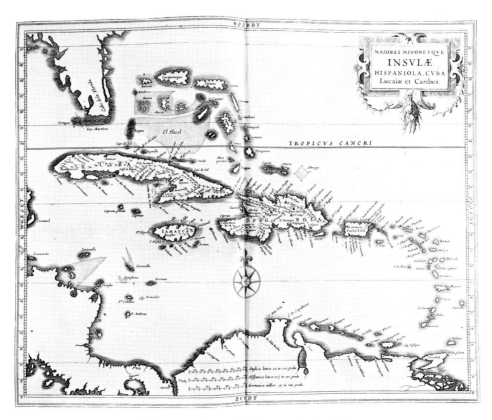

A late seventeenth-century Dutch map of the West Indies.
LONDON LIBRARY

The average age was twenty-four and a half years, and twenty-eight percent of the males ranged from eleven to nineteen years of age.

Of all these settlements, one was particularly significant for the theme of this book. The island of Tortuga lying just off the north side of Santo Domingo (otherwise Hispaniola), near the entrance to the Windward Passage, was first colonized in 1630. The settlers were English, and came from Nevis. The settlement had only a brief life. In 1635 it was destroyed by the Spaniards, who had a colony, dating from the earliest years of their penetration of the Americas, on the southern side of Santo Domingo itself.

The Spanish had found the Tortuga colony particularly provocative because those who belonged to it had soon established relations with the buccaneers. The buccaneers were outlaws of many nationalities, the flotsam of the whole new area of settlement, who had drifted together in the semi-deserted north-western part of the main island. The majority of them were at first probably French, and originated in Normandy, but their numbers were soon swelled by English indentured servants from Barbados

A buccaneer, from a French edition of Exquemelin.

and elsewhere who, when their term of service expired, found themselves free but landless. They were at first not primarily seamen, but hunted the wild cattle of Santo Domingo, trading the hides and also the meat which they turned into *boucan*, preserving it by a process of smoking on wooden racks which they had learned from the native Indians. The dried meat took on a bright red color and acquired an attractive flavor from the process, and it was valued as a convenient form of ship's provisions.

The buccaneers had evolved for themselves a characteristic costume—a shirt and pantaloons of coarse linen, with boots of hogskin, a strap of rawhide for a girdle, and a round cap on their heads. They were well-armed. Each man usually had a short sabre, several knives, and a long firelock. They lived in small groups of six or eight at the most, and acknowledged no authority except the agreements they made among themselves. Their most curious custom was that of living in *matelotage*, a kind of homosexual marriage. Two matelots agreed to hold everything in common and, in later years, when women were available, a matelot would

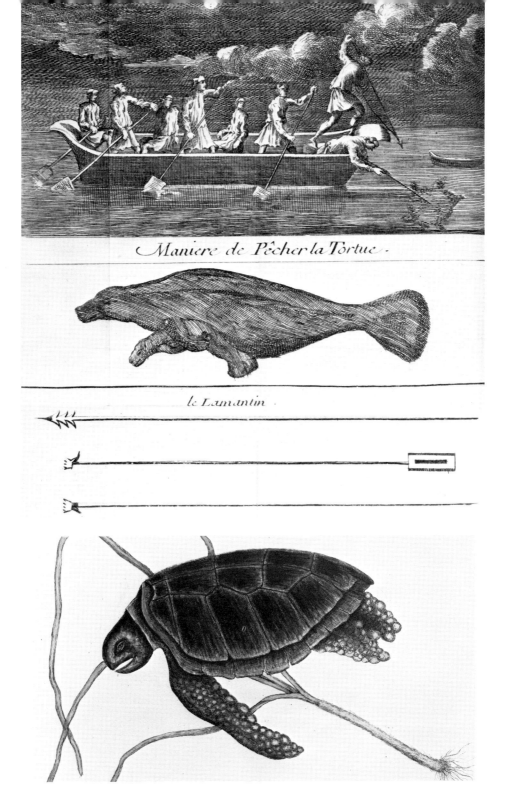

Maniere de Pêcher la Tortue.

le Lamantin.

ABOVE: *Buccaneers fishing for turtle—their favorite dish. From Exquemelin.*
LONDON LIBRARY
BELOW: *the green turtle, from Mark Catesby's* Natural History of Carolina.
BRITISH LIBRARY

even have the right to sleep with his partner's wife. The Spaniards found their anarchic, devil-may-care existence an affront, and since 1620 had been making constant attempts to exterminate them, just as they tried to exterminate the communities of runaway slaves in the isthmus of Panama. The sack of Tortuga in 1635 was therefore merely an incident in a struggle which already had a considerable history behind it. One effect of Spanish hostility had been to make the buccaneers take increasingly to the sea, where they had even greater mobility than they possessed on land. The boats they used were at this stage little better than canoes, but they soon graduated to handy, one-masted fast-sailing sloops which could carry up to fifty men at a time, and which used oars as well as sails. Their tactics were, when attacking a large sea-going vessel, to try and pick off the helmsman and any men who might be working aloft. They then lowered the mast of their sloop and rowed under the counter of the vessel they were attacking to jam its rudder and render it helpless.

Tortuga was too convenient a base to remain deserted for long. By 1639 the colony had revived, and there were about 300 men living on the island, most of whom, as had been the case before, were English. In 1642, however, the French had succeeded in taking over. The instigator of this move was Philippe de Loinvilliers de Poincy, a knight of the Order of St. John who was governor of the French portion of St. Christopher. His emissary was a Huguenot called Le Vasseur—whom he was anxious to get rid of, together with as many of his co-religionists as possible. Le Vasseur accepted the bait and was soon master of the island, where he built a virtually impregnable fort and organized a market where the buccaneers could sell their products and also their plunder. In 1643 a renewed Spanish attack was beaten off. But success went to Le Vasseur's head. He rebelled against his superior de Poincy, and at the same time antagonized the Catholics on the island, by trying to make Tortuga into a semi-independent Huguenot state. De Poincy was helpless to do anything about it in the practical sense, but theoretically at least he acquired a freer hand when, in 1647, the French Compagnie de Saint-Christophe went bankrupt, and he acquired, on behalf of the Knights of St. John, the French parts of St. Christopher, St. Croix, St. Bartholomew, half of St. Martin (the rest belonged to the Dutch), and last of all Tortuga. By 1652 he was at last ready to move in on the rebel, and at that moment Le Vasseur was assassinated by two of his lieutenants. De Poincy's nominee, the Chevalier de Fontenay, who had been poised to make an attack from the mainland, was able to seize control. It was he who initiated a more active policy of freebooting than Le Vasseur had pursued, though the colony was again assaulted and retaken by the Spaniards in 1654. The next year, when the buccaneers once more returned to Tortuga, their appetite for freebooting was fully established, and there were other developments, too, to send them out into the seaways of the West Indies, and even on to the mainland of Central America in search of booty.

While Tortuga was still only a relatively minor thorn in the Spanish flesh, the West Indies and indeed the whole western hemisphere continued to be plagued by pirates and privateers. There were those who were intruders from outside and those who were, so to speak, home-grown. Both sides in the English Civil War sent expeditions to try their luck on the other side of the Atlantic. In 1642–3, Captain William Jackson, provided with letters of marque from the Earl of Warwick (formerly the Sir Robert Rich who had had a hand in the East Indian venture of the *Francis* and the *Lion* in 1616, and now Admiral of the Fleet for the Long Parliament), plundered the Central American towns of Maracaibo and Truxillo. On

Prince Rupert. Portrait by Gerard van Honthorst.
WILTON HOUSE

March 25, 1643, he dropped anchor in what is now Kingston harbor in Jamaica, landed about 500 men, and marched inland to the Spanish capital of Santiago de la Vega, which he ransomed back to its inhabitants for 200 head of cattle, 10,000 pounds of cassava bread and 7,000 Spanish dollars. Later it was the turn of Prince Rupert, the commander of the royalist fleet in the second Civil War. After trying his luck as a privateer in the Mediterranean, he made a difficult passage across the Atlantic to the West Indies, where he had very little success. Rupert's much-loved brother Prince Maurice was drowned when his ship was lost with all hands in a West Indian hurricane, and in 1653 the remaining royalists returned to Europe with their tails between their legs.

In the first half of the seventeenth century, home-grown aggressors included privateers based on Bermuda. In the 1640s they were already making good prizes. On one occasion the Bermuda ship *Anne* captured a Spanish vessel which was freighted, among other things, with "a fair new

Truxillo (by J. de Ram): a town sacked several times by the buccaneers.
VICTORIA AND ALBERT MUSEUM

sedan, worth forty or fifty pounds" which one of the Spanish viceroys was sending to his sister. North America produced its first known pirate in the unimpressive person of Dixey Bull, a fur-trader on the Maine coast who in 1632 lost his shallop and stock of trade goods to a roving company of Frenchmen. He set out to plunder the French in revenge, and finished up by robbing his fellow colonial traders, causing an excitement out of all proportion to the damage he did.

There seems to be a number of interlocking reasons why buccaneering became far more important after 1655 than it had ever been previously. Some are political, others economic. The English capture of Jamaica, accomplished almost accidentally by a Commonwealth force under Penn and Venables in 1655, provided the buccaneers with another base in addition to Tortuga. When the latter fell into French hands, as it did in 1660, and still more so when the able Bertrand d'Ogeron became governor on behalf of the French West India Company in 1665, there was a rivalry between the two centers which led to a great increase in activity. At the same time, the buccaneers were able to preserve their cherished independence by playing the English authorities off against the French ones. The Jamaican authorities in particular feared that, if they tried to impose too many restraints, the English privateers who now based themselves on Port Royal, and brought the struggling colony much of its prosperity, would sail away and join their brethren in Tortuga. In addition to this, there were political tensions within Jamaica itself. After the Restoration in 1660 many members of the old republican (Commonwealth) faction, who were well entrenched in the island because they had been responsible for capturing it, turned pirate as a way of relieving their feeling of frustration at being robbed of power by the new regime.

But the most important reasons for the rise of buccaneering are, first of all, the population explosion which had taken place in the French and English colonies, secondly the increasing decadence of the Spaniards— Governor Modyford of Jamaica described them as being "in all places very weak and very wealthy"—and thirdly the general state of anarchy to which the whole region had been reduced by the political rivalries which were being played out in Europe. The first and last of these points perhaps need to be a little further expanded, if their significance is to be grasped. By 1650 St. Christopher and Barbados were the two most densely populated communities, not only in the West Indies, but in the whole of the known world. Those who lacked land—the majority—were forced to think of migrating, as free white labor was now meeting with formidable competition from the black slaves who had begun to be imported in ever-

The Towne of Puerto del Principe taken & sackt
Part 2: Chap: 5.

Port au Prince, sacked by the buccaneers.

153

Two depictions of buccaneers in action, from Exquemelin.

increasing numbers. A small proportion of rich planters controlled all the wealth, and there seemed no hope of achieving a more equitable distribution of it. What could be more natural, in these circumstances, than to seek one's fortune by freebooting? This is why it was henceforth always easy for a well-known and successful leader to raise a large force of reckless fighters at short notice. They had much to gain and little to lose.

Throughout the second half of the seventeenth century the West Indies were shaken by political shock waves from Europe. The great powers were usually at open war with one another. Even at those times when they were not, a bitter trade war continued among English, Dutch and French merchants overseas, often involving the use of force. Because the region was remote, and because many parts of it remained wild and undeveloped, the rule of law in any case tended to be weak. The buccaneers were as much frontiersmen as the pioneers of the American West.

Like the cowboy, the buccaneer soon developed his own mythology, and it is this which is enshrined in Exquemelin's book; and also in the recently discovered (and apparently heavily edited) memoirs of a French buccaneer called Louis Le Golif, otherwise known as Borgne-Fesse, or Half-Arse, because one buttock had been carried away by a cannon-ball.

Francis Lolonnois, from Exquemelin.
LONDON LIBRARY

It is Borgne-Fesse who describes his own appearance when he was on the way to raid Caracas in Venezuela: "I marched in front, as was right, with my pistols in my belt, my fine deep boots and plumed hat, and a sword at my side." Exquemelin, Le Golif, and other sources tell us of the many extraordinary characters to be found among the buccaneer captains. Some, like the Comte de Grammont and the Sieur de La Mothe, were gentlemen-born, others were men of low origin. Their personalities were as different as their backgrounds. Grammont, for example, was a Gascon naval officer who arrived in the West Indies and won enough money gambling to buy and equip a fifty-gun ship, whereupon he handed in his commission. His fellow buccaneers were shocked by his "libertine" views—that is, not by his bad morals but by his atheism. Two other Frenchmen were remembered not for their atheism but for their cruelties. One was Montbars, surnamed the Exterminator because of the vigor with which he pursued the Spaniards. Le Golif says of him: "He had this peculiarity, that his eyebrows were larger than his moustaches, which gave him such a terrible air that his aspect alone assured him of victory before a fight was joined." The other was Jean-David Nau, called Lolonnois from his birthplace at Sables d'Olonne. On one occasion, after capturing a

"The cruelty of Lolonnois," from Exquemelin.

Roche Braziliano, another picturesque buccaneer who figures in Exquemelin's pages.

frigate, he personally executed the whole of the crew, licking the blood from his sabre as he decapitated each one. He met his end by being torn to pieces and then burnt to ashes by the Darien Indians "to the intent no trace or memory might remain of such an infamous, inhuman creature."

Equally formidable, to his foes and sometimes to his friends, was the Dutchman from Groningen who bore the nickname Roche-Braziliano by reason of his long residence in Brazil:

> In his domestic and private affairs he had no good behavior or government over himself; for in these he would oftentimes show himself either brutish or foolish. Many times being in drink, he would run up and down the streets, beating or wounding whom he met, no person daring to oppose him or make any resistance. To the Spaniards he always showed himself very barbarous and cruel, only out of an inveterate hatred he had against that nation. Of these he commanded several to be roasted alive upon wooden spits, for no other crime that they would not show him the places or hog-yards where he might steal swine.

To Exquemelin's description, here quoted, Le Golif adds another picturesque detail: "Contrary to what one sees in other human beings, his visage was broader than it was high."

Père Labat, a French missionary who arrived in the West Indies at the very end of the buccaneer era, also gives some lively descriptions of the customs and manners of the "Brethren of the Coast." He tells us, for instance, how a certain Captain Daniel, running short of provisions, landed at the nearest island and kidnapped the local curé. When the buccaneers had collected what they needed, they asked the priest to say mass aboard their ship before they released him:

> They sent for the church ornaments, put up an altar on the poop under an awning, and then chanted Mass lustily. A salvo of eight cannons marked the commencement of the service, they fired a second salvo at the Sanctus, a third at the Elevation, a fourth at the Benediction, and lastly a fifth after the Exaudiat, while the prayer for the King was marked by a most hearty *"Vive le Roi."* Only one incident slightly marred this ceremony. One of the pirates adopted an offensive attitude during the Elevation, and on being rebuked by the captain, he replied insolently with a horrible oath. Daniel promptly drew his pistol and shot him through the head and swore by God that he would do the same to anyone else who showed disrespect to the *"Sainte Sacrifice."*

Labat comments drily that it was an effective method of preventing the poor fellow from repeating his offence.

In their early, heroic period, the buccaneers behaved with reckless bravery. It seemed there was no risk they would not dare, no hardship they could not withstand: "Their patience was inexhaustible: they endured hunger, thirst and the most excessive fatigue with unalterable serenity, and without permitting the slightest complaint to escape from their lips." This is the verdict of Archenholz, one of the best of the early buccaneer historians. But he also says, with equal justice: "Everything was done from motives of cupidity, and nothing from a principle of valor." The booty was often enough to settle any man's greed. When Maracaibo was sacked by Morgan in 1667, the loot was 260,000 pieces of eight in cash alone.

In the short term, buccaneering had a tremendous impact on the life of the West Indies. This was particularly true of Jamaica, where the colony was at first dependent on the privateers not only for most of its trade but for its defence—a fact which was recognized by the Council, and officially recorded in their minutes for February 22, 1666. The harbor town of Port

ABOVE: *Bartolomew Portugues, from Exquemelin.*
LONDON LIBRARY
BELOW: *Maracaibo Bay, 1686.*
LONDON LIBRARY

A view of Port Royal, Jamaica, as it was before the earthquake. From Edward Barlow's Journal.

Royal experienced a period of mushroom growth. Immediately before the earthquake that destroyed it in June 1692, it was nearly twice as large as New York at the same period. Visitors were struck by how crowded it was—more than 200 buildings, many made of specially imported English bricks, were jammed together in a solid mass on the sandspit that encircled the harbor. The edges of the town reached out into the harbor itself, where some dwellings were built on pilings driven into the soft sand. In 1682, the lawyer Francis Hanson described it as being "always like a continual mart or fair, where all sorts of choice merchandizes are daily imported." And he added: "Almost every house hath a rich cupboard of plate, which they carelessly expose, scarce shutting their doors at night, being in no

160

Artefacts lost in the earthquake at Port Royal: a silver pocket watch made in London (left); a Spanish coin (above right); bottles, pestle and mortar (below right).
INSTITUTE OF JAMAICA

apprehension of thieves, for want of receivers as aforesaid."

Other observers noted less salubrious aspects:

> There is not now resident in this place ten men to every house that selleth strong liquors ... besides sugar and rum-works that sell without licence. All the tavern doors stand open as they do in London on Sundays in the afternoon.

In the novel *Captain Falconer*, there is heartfelt and clearly non-fictional reference to the settlement's boom-town prices:

> Provision is prodigious dear here; two or three of us went on shore to dinner one day at Port Royal, where we had only a roasted turkey, wretchedly lean, and nothing nigh so well-tasted as our English turkeys, and our eating came to thirty shillings; but then, to make amends, money is plenty enough.

In 1698, when Port Royal had already been laid low by catastrophe, the

161

Two portraits of Sir Henry Morgan: from Exquemelin (left), and an eighteenth-century impression (right).

satirist Ned Ward hyperbolically described the whole colony of Jamaica as being:

> The dunghill of the universe, the refuse of the whole creation, the clippings of the element, a shapeless pile of rubbish confusedly piled into an emblem of chaos, neglected by Omnipotence when he formed the world into its admirable order.

This social rather than physical chaos, combined with great wealth, was the product of the confusion brought with them by the race of freebooters.

Is it, however, fair to see the buccaneer fleets led by men like Henry Morgan, Grammont and Laurent de Graff as being the "floating republic" which they have been labeled by many historians, the model of a rough-and-ready egalitarian society in which a kind of thieves' honor prevailed? "As soon as they had given their word they were invariably bound by it," asserts Archenholz, "and they not infrequently gave it on the bare proposal to become a party concerned in some enterprise." On the whole, the evidence suggests the contrary. Buccaneer honor, like buccaneer democracy, was a necessary legend to those who took up this way of life. The facts tended to be rather different.

The most successful of all the buccaneer leaders, and the one who, because of the daring of his exploits, has attracted most attention is the Welshman Henry Morgan. Morgan was born in 1635, the eldest son of

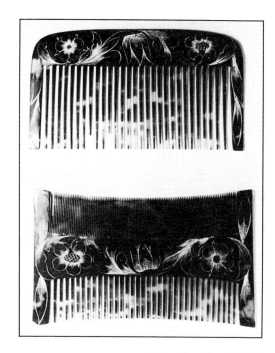

Henry Morgan's tortoiseshell combs and comb cases.
INSTITUTE OF JAMAICA

Robert Morgan of Llanrhymney, a small squire with an estate in Glamorganshire near Tredegar Castle. He was thus definitely a gentleman. Nevertheless, he seems to have arrived in Barbados as an indentured servant, and may have succeeded in winning his freedom by enlisting in the expedition led by Penn and Venables which, failing in its assault on Santo Domingo, took Jamaica as a kind of consolation prize. He may then have participated in Admiral Christopher Myngs's assaults on Santiago de Cuba and Campeche in 1662–3. He first came to prominence, however, in alliance with Mansvelt, a veteran Dutch privateer captain, who in 1665 recaptured the island of Santa Catalina, otherwise Old Providence, which had been one of the earliest British colonies in the West Indies. The garrison they installed did not succeed in holding the place for long, but it was the beginning of Morgan's hugely prestigious career. Like Drake before him, he showed an uncanny knack of routing superior Spanish forces both by land and sea. In 1668, he took and sacked, with a force of between four and five hundred men, the town of Porto Bello, then reckoned the third strongest in the Spanish Indies. The attack was made in canoes, from a point more than a hundred miles away. This was followed by a second sack of Maracaibo in 1669 (following the capture of the place by French buccaneers two years previously), and then by Morgan's best-

163

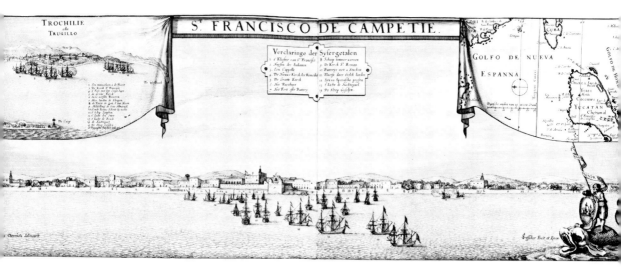

known exploit, the taking of Panama after a forced march across the isthmus, at the beginning of 1671. The town was set on fire by its inhabitants, and was afterwards rebuilt on a new site. At the time when Morgan took it, it had a population of about 30,000 and was reckoned to be the wealthiest settlement in the New World.

Morgan does not emerge well from Exquemelin's pages—the book is indeed so hostile that Morgan was forced to bring a libel action against the printer when it was published in English. In particular, Exquemelin asserts that captive priests and nuns were forced to raise the scaling ladders against the walls of Porto Bello, and that Morgan often had prisoners tortured to make them disclose where they had hidden their wealth. But these were not the deeds of a man who cared little what society thought of him, as the libel action proved. Morgan had every intention of taking his place in the Jamaican plantocracy when opportunity offered, and in due course he did so. His way was eased by the fact that he was the nephew of a one-time deputy governor, Sir Edward Morgan. He married his uncle's daughter soon after Sir Edward died, and in due course attained both a knighthood and the deputy governorship himself, a good example of poacher turned gamekeeper. In 1680, when he was acting governor, we even find him saying unctuously:

Morgan's attack on Panama, with the city burning. From Exquemelin.

Morgan's men torturing the citizens of Panama, from Exquemelin.
BRITISH LIBRARY

Nothing can be more fatal to this colony than the temptingly alluring boldness of the privateers which draws off white servants and all men of unfortunate or desperate condition.

Few men can have known this better than Henry Morgan himself.

The Panama episode virtually put an end to large-scale buccaneering based on Jamaica, both because it created so much trouble for the English government back home, and because the colony now had a strong and varied enough economy to do without what the filibusters brought in. By 1685 Port Royal had virtually ceased to be a buccaneer haven. It now prospered on contraband trade with the Spanish colonies and on the slave trade until wiped out by the great earthquake, to which there succeeded within a few years other natural disasters such as fire and hurricane. Some of the buccaneers went back to their original occupation of logwood cutting, others traded with the Central American Indians, others fled to the French to avoid the press-gang, and some few undertook the daring expeditions to the South Seas which were the true beginning of piracy as Defoe understood it.

French buccaneering continued for rather longer, thanks largely to the encouragement offered by the French government. The attitude of Louis XIV and his ministers towards these troublesome subjects was not, however, entirely consistent. On the one hand they wanted the governor of Tortuga to turn them into peaceful colonists, and on the other they saw them as a useful offensive weapon. France had a long tradition of using privateers as auxiliaries to the king's own ships, and after the Treaty of Nymwegen in 1678 Louis was willing to allow Governor de Pouçay of Tortuga to issue privateering commissions even when he himself would no longer issue them at home. Under the leadership of Grammont and the handsome Laurent de Graff a series of spectacular raids were made upon the Spanish possessions in the Indies. The sack of Vera Cruz in 1683 was actually instrumental in bringing about a brief renewal of war between France and Spain.

Most historians assert that the last great buccaneering expedition was the siege of Cartagena in 1697. This involved an alliance between a squadron of French filibusters on the one hand, and ships of the French navy commanded by Baron de Pointis on the other. De Pointis was a naval officer with considerable influence at court, and he had long cherished the idea of such a raid. When part of the French fleet was laid up in 1696, he succeeded in getting the use of some of the ships for a joint-stock venture almost on the Elizabethan pattern. He expected to get additional help once he arrived in the West Indies from Jean Ducasse, the ex-buccaneer who was now the *de facto* French governor of Santo Domingo, which was soon to be formally ceded to France by the Peace of Ryswyck.

From the very start there was trouble between the two halves of the expedition. Ducasse was outstandingly able, but he had poor material to work with. He spoke of the filibusters as men "composed of the refuse of all the kingdom, without honor and without virtue," and said acidly that "they bear arms here as if they were at a carnival, without the least principle of discipline." They were not particularly eager for the fray, and de Pointis only succeeded in recruiting the number he wanted by threatening to burn their ships. When the joint force arrived in front of Cartagena, the disagreements continued. De Pointis thought his allies were no better than cowards, and did not hesitate to let them know it. But at length the city was taken, and a rich booty was found. De Pointis then proceeded to interpret the written agreement he had made with the buccaneers very much in his own favor. Powerless to do anything about it, the force from Santo Domingo proceeded to reimburse themselves by sacking Cartagena for a second time. De Pointis returned to France with a

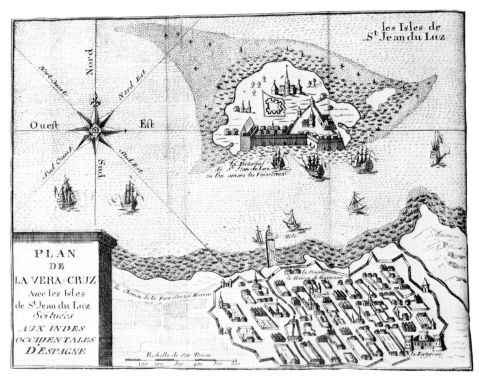

ABOVE: *a bird's-eye view of Vera Cruz.*
BRITISH LIBRARY

BELOW: *Cartagena, at the time of De Pointis's expedition. From Charlevoix's* Histoire de l'Isle
Espagnole.
LONDON LIBRARY

total of 7,646,948 francs in gold and silver bullion, and a collection of emeralds that weighed 1,947 marcs (1,051 pounds avoirdupois). There were in addition other trifles such as a statue of the madonna in a silver robe studded wth jewels, and a chest full of ecclesiastical silverware. During the second sack, the buccaneers possessed themselves of about a million crowns' worth of plunder in four days. The only person to emerge from the affair with his honor intact was Ducasse, who came to France to fight for the rights of the men he had commanded, and not only won the case (though without much financial reward) but was made a knight of the Order of St. Louis and promoted to admiral. It was at this time that Saint-Simon met him, and afterwards described him in his *Memoirs*:

> He was a tall, thin man who, with his corsair's manner and much fire and vivacity, was gentle, polite, respected and who was never false to himself. He was very obliging and had a good deal of wit, with a certain natural eloquence; and, even in matters outside his calling, pleasure and profit were to be had in hearing him expound.

Ducasse was to be another poacher turned gamekeeper, for in 1712, after he had safely brought home a vital plate-fleet, Philip V, the new Bourbon King of Spain, rewarded him with the Golden Fleece, an order

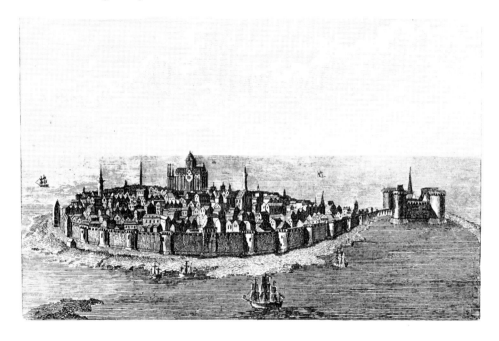

A view of the corsair port of St. Malo, showing the fortifications.
BRITISH MUSEUM

170

usually only given to royalty and members of the highest aristocracy. Saint-Simon, predictably, was shocked, and speaks of the "prodigious scandal" which the gesture caused.

The last, French-dominated, period of buccaneer activity in the West Indies overlaps with a time when French corsairs were extremely active in home waters. The royal policy of refusing letters of marque was soon reversed, and by the end of the century the privateers formed a most effective irregular arm of the French navy, causing tremendous losses to their nation's enemies. In 1689, for example, no less than 4,200 English and Dutch craft were captured by the French corsairs. The allies, in turn, tried frantically to rid themselves of the nuisance, but without success. St. Malo, a principal corsair base, was repeatedly attacked—by the English and Dutch together in 1692, by the English alone the next year, by the English and Dutch again in 1695. By the time of the War of the Spanish Succession (1701–13) the partnership between the St. Malo privateers and the French navy had become so close that the two elements often operated as part of the same squadron.

France was fortunate, at this time, in possessing some very able privateer captains. The ablest were René Duguay-Trouin of St. Malo, Jean Bart of Dunkirk, and Jacques Cassard of Nantes. All three were of bourgeois stock,

The capture of a French privateer. Anonymous, 1703.
SCIENCE MUSEUM

171

Two French privateer captains: Duguay-Trouin (left) and Jean Bart (right).
BRITISH MUSEUM/BIBLIOTHEQUE NATIONALE

though Cassard had the humblest origin—the Trouins were merchants and ship-owners, Bart came of a long line of privateers, and Cassard's father was the captain of a small ship trading between Naples and the Levant. Duguay-Trouin and Jean Bart were both in the course ennobled by Louis XIV. Cassard was less fortunate. He ended up as a kind of skeleton at the feast at the Court of Versailles, and was finally imprisoned for being too importunate in his search for redress for the wrongs which had been done to him. All were highly successful in making prizes. Bart took some 250 ships in the course of his privateering career; and in addition destroyed 500 fishing boats. Duguay-Trouin took sixteen ships of the line and over 300 merchantmen, having risen to the command of a forty-gun ship when he was still in his early twenties. Both Duguay-Trouin and Cassard commanded successful overseas expeditions—Duguay-Trouin took Rio de Janeiro in a brilliantly planned operation in 1711, finding a vast quantity of treasure and receiving in addition a ransom of 610,000 Portuguese crusadoes, 500 cases of sugar, and all the Portuguese and English ships in the harbor. In 1712 Cassard, in alliance with the remaining filibusters from Santo Domingo, took the rich Dutch colony of

172

An eighteenth-century view of Nantes, home port of Jacques Cassard.
MUSÉE DE LA MARINE

Curaçao. The venture showed a profit of ten million livres. But its success aroused so much jealousy that Cassard was relieved of his command before he had even left the West Indies, and his career never recovered. The expeditions undertaken by these two corsairs clearly have a great deal in common with de Pointis's earlier assault on Cartagena.

While it may be argued that the delightful personality revealed in Duguay-Trouin's *Memoirs*, which show a strange combination of quick-witted practicality and mystical faith in the promptings of his *daemon*, has nothing in common with the brutishness of a Lolonnois, it is often very hard, especially in a French context, to draw the line between privateering and buccaneering, and even between privateering and piracy. Though privateers were supposed to have letters of marque, the way in which they were issued and employed was often very irregular. In the West Indies of the 1670s, for instance, it was possible for a ship's captain to carry at one and the same time an English commission against Holland and a French commission against Spain, the latter issued by the always-obliging French governor of Tortuga. Many of Ducasse's force, in theory French privateersmen, were in fact English seamen who had fled to Santo Domingo to avoid being impressed. In 1695 the number of seamen in Jamaica, once estimated at 1,200, had fallen to 300. Nearer home, while matters were apt to be less confused and commissions were less easily given, privateer vessels broke the rules once they were at sea, and often came close to outright piracy. In particular, the rule about showing the national flag when once a vessel had been ordered to heave to was frequently infringed.

A striking feature of this and the succeeding age—the apparently vast preponderance of English pirates over French and Spanish ones—may perhaps be best explained by looking at respective national attitudes towards letters of marque. The Spanish were, from the beginning, reluctant to issue them at all, as they feared that such commissions might lead directly to an infringement of their commercial monopoly. Only in 1674 was privateering at last permitted, and a special type of boat, the pirogue or periagua, was developed for the work. Pirogues were small, fast, flat-bottomed galleys, often with a draft of only a foot and a half, though they mounted quite heavy armament. Like the Mediterranean galley, two or three of them could outmaneuver a larger ship and destroy or capture it. But the Spanish attitude remained basically defensive rather than aggressive, and it was not until late in the succeeding century that Spanish pirates, using much the same type of craft, were to become a menace in the

A Spanish pirogue, *used in anti-buccaneer operations in the West Indies. From Exquemelin.*

174

West Indies. In the buccaneer period, those who chiefly suffered from Spanish attentions were the unfortunate logwood cutters in the Gulf of Campeche.

The French never seem to have made any clear distinction in their own minds between a privateer and a pirate, provided that both were, in some sense, working in the national interest. An early buccaneer, the Sieur de La Mothe, who probably did not have a commission of any kind, habitually subscribed himself "a well-intentioned subject of the king." The close connection between the regular French navy and the privateer ships fitted out by private individuals who were specialists in this kind of venture (a St. Malo or Dieppe family might concern itself with privateering over several generations) tended to give the privateer an accepted place in the community; and even though privateers at some periods were only allowed to carry a certain proportion of trained French sailors, for fear of depriving the regular navy of their services, no man who served in one need think himself an outcast. There was always a home port to return to.

The English, though of course they made use of letters of marque ships whenever there was an outbreak of hostilities, had no continuity of privateering tradition, except in the American colonies. The regular navy thought of privateering vessels as places where seamen learned bad habits of freedom, and of privateering enterprise in general as something that competed with itself. In the 1740s Admiral Vernon wrote:

> It is surprising that anyone can submit to such a wretched situation as to be a captain of a privateer, lorded over by the company's quartermaster, supported by the crew, who have chosen him for their champion; and till the constitution is altered I fear they will generally prove a nursery of pirates.

This puts the point plainly enough. In English terms privateering was an undesirable compromise, which inclined towards illegality rather than legality because of the close similarity between pirate and privateer discipline. One can even go so far as to say that the English became pirates in Defoe's sense because of the English desire to enforce a separation between regular and irregular forms of nautical conduct—a separation upon which other nations were loth to insist.

175

7

The Classic Age of Piracy

THE CONVENTIONAL PICTURE of the way in which buccaneering became piracy is provided by James Burney, once the companion of Captain Cook, in his classic *History of the Buccaneers of America*. The theory he puts forward is quite simple, and on the face of it persuasive:

> After the suppression of the buccaneers, and partly from their relics, arose a race of pirates of a more desperate cast, so rendered by the increasing danger of their occupation, who for a number of years preyed upon the commerce of all nations, till they were hunted down and, it may be said, exterminated.

It is only when one starts to examine the evidence a little more closely that this neat design falls to pieces.

The West Indies cannot be treated as an isolated geographical unit, especially in a book devoted to the doings of seafarers. The ocean might divide one island from another, and it might also divide the Caribbean not only from England, but from other areas of English colonial settlement, such as the east coast of North America. But it was a highroad as well as a barrier. The phenomenon of piracy, as it appeared in the late seventeenth and early eighteenth centuries, can only be understood if we think about it in global rather than regional terms. The men who sometimes based themselves upon the West Indies also had friends in the American colonies. They were often in Madagascar; they haunted the coast of Sierra Leone; they made prizes in the Red Sea. Mauritius, the Comoro Islands and the Galapagos were also familiar to many of them. Any place which could be reached by water was accessible. Though their ships had to touch land for repairs, food and fresh water, the source of power that took them from one haven to the next was everywhere and always available, since it was only the wind.

Another consideration is the way in which plundered goods were disposed of. The popular image of pirate loot is that it was always either ready cash, or, failing that, plate and jewels. Obviously this was not the case. Pirates needed markets; and they also needed places where they could spend their gains in security, even if they only spent them on drinking and drabbing. In the buccaneer heyday Port Royal had provided these necessary facilities. Now, as the rule of law became more firmly established in the West Indies, and as the colonists there began to feel that freebooting did them injury rather than being to their advantage, unscrupulous seamen had to look elsewhere.

The rise of Elizabethan privateering, and after it of buccaneering, was closely connected with the restrictions placed by Spain upon trade with her colonies. Spain was not the only nation to impose such restraints. From the middle of the seventeenth century, all European nations grew increasingly protectionist in their economic thinking. England, as she gradually replaced Holland as the leading commercial power, was perhaps the most protectionist of all. The first English Navigation Act was passed in 1647, and the provisions it contained were constantly enlarged and elaborated. There were new acts in 1651, in 1660, in 1663; and later yet other restrictions were brought in. The "mercantile system," as the economist Adam Smith was afterwards to christen it, aimed at encouraging English trade in two ways—by duties and prohibitions, and by bounties and favorable treatment. There were import and export restrictions. For example, since England was still a major wool-producing country it was forbidden to export raw wool, and forbidden to import foreign manufactured goods made of wool. The colonies were considered an important factor in maintaining national prosperity. All goods to and from colonial destinations had to be shipped in ships which were built and owned by Englishmen, and which were manned by English crews—those who were resident in the colonies were, however, technically English, and thus were permitted to share the monopoly. Where exports from the colonies were concerned, certain "enumerated commodities" could be sent only to England. They included the most valuable colonial products: sugar, tobacco, raw cotton, indigo, ginger and dye-woods. Colonial imports—goods produced or manufactured in Europe—with rare exceptions had to be laden in England. And by the end of the seventeenth century the home government had even begun to regulate what the colonists themselves might manufacture: in 1699 their woollen manufactures were restrained.

These restrictions bore less heavily upon the West Indies than they did on the settlers in North America. The West Indian colonies had settled down to the production of valuable staple crops, and England was the natural market for them. But in America the English attempt to monopolize colonial markets met with increasing resistance, because the economy of the North American colonies, though still underdeveloped, was more various than anything to be found in the Caribbean. There was a great deal of smuggling, and American ports were a willing market for goods which had been irregularly acquired by those who were now offering them for sale—still more so because they were offered at below-market prices.

Both pirate and privateer cargoes had one thing in common: they had been got without the necessity of paying for them. The result was that they tended to be sold not only more cheaply than normal, but without much regard for the current state of the market. Privateering in particular, being more lightly embarked upon, tended to withdraw shipping from normal trade, which in turn restricted the flow of goods coming in by legitimate channels and made the impact of prize-goods all the greater.

Many Americans began to think of this as the usual, rather than an exceptional, way of acquiring certain kinds of merchandise, particularly commodities such as fine cottons and muslins which came from the East. At the same time they more and more tended to blur the distinction in their own minds between legitimate privateering and piracy. "We have a parcel of pirates called the Red Sea men in these parts," reported a New Yorker in 1695, "who get a great booty of Arabian gold. The governor encourages them, since they make due acknowledgment." New York was at that time simply a poorly governed, raw colonial port with about a thousand houses in the Dutch style, and four or five thousand inhabitants. Its resident merchants were most of them little better than fences, or distributors of smuggled and pirated goods, and they liked their trade so well that it was even proposed by one of them that a subsidiary colony be established in the notorious pirate haven of Madagascar. At the same period, other colonists were just as easy in their consciences about their relationship with pirates

New York in the late seventeenth century, by J. de Ram.
VICTORIA AND ALBERT MUSEUM

and piracy. In 1684 the French pirate vessel *La Trompeuse* was openly making use of Boston harbor, and the inhabitants of the city traded with her captain, Michel Bréha, without any attempt at concealment. In 1700 William Penn, one of the few to have a conscience about such things, estimated that the colonies neighboring his own Pennsylvania had earned a million pounds in the ten years which had just passed, supplying flour to pirates.

The two colonies which had perhaps the worst reputation for favoring pirates were Carolina and Rhode Island. Once, when a prisoner was actually foolish enough to plead guilty to piracy, a Rhode Island jury assumed that they must of course have misheard him, and acquitted nonetheless. Carolina was equally lax in its attitudes. In 1692 there was even an attempt made to pass a bill in the State Assembly, granting complete indemnity to all pirates and their accomplices. Carolina piracy is

Captain Teach, the notorious Blackbeard, from the General History.

Alexander Spotswood, governor of Virginia, was largely responsible for bringing Blackbeard to bay.

summed up in the figure of Edward Teach or Thatch, alias Blackbeard, just as the attitudes which prevailed in Rhode Island and to some extent in New York are illuminated by the career of Thomas Tew.

Blackbeard, who based himself for part of his career on the town of Bath in North Carolina, accepted a pardon in 1718, after a career which had begun in Bristol and taken him from there to the Bahamas, where he formed part of the pirate community on New Providence. After only a few months in retirement he returned to his old ways and was the subject of a pursuit instigated not by the North Carolina authorities but by Governor Spotswood of neighboring Virginia. The former were so much put out by this turn of events that they actually applied to England for a second dispensation in Blackbeard's favor, and this was on its way across the Atlantic when Spotswood's men brought him to bay and killed him.

Tew was more fortunate. Having held a privateering commission from Rhode Island (obtained at a cost of £500, at a time when his reputation was already none too salubrious), he went to Madagascar and openly turned pirate. Returning home with his wealth, he was allowed to settle in

Newport quite unmolested. Later, though he was still on the East India Company black-list, he got himself another privateering commission from Governor Ben Fletcher of New York. At this time he appeared publicly in the governor's coach, and exchanged presents such as gold watches with him. Fletcher, by way of excuse for his own conduct, said sheepishly that Tew "was also what is called a very pleasant man, so that sometimes after the day's labor was done, it was divertisement as well as information to hear him talk." It was with this sentiment on his lips that he allowed Tew to set off on his final voyage in 1695, which was just as piratical as any of the others.

In order to understand the new situation one must, however, look further than the social attitudes and economic needs of the North American colonies. It was quite true that the buccaneers were becoming increasingly unpopular in the English West Indies, chiefly because they had begun to interfere too seriously with the steady flow across the Atlantic of the valuable crops which the islands were now organized to produce. Out of self-interest, the planters soon turned against the buccaneers whom they had once cosseted, and severe measures were taken. "I abhor bloodshed," wrote Morgan to the government at home, "and I am greatly dissatisfied that in my short government I have so often been compelled to punish criminals with death." It was some of his old comrades that he was referring to, and they in turn felt bitterly that he had cheated and deserted them.

As the pickings grew slimmer, some of the West Indian buccaneers began to go further afield. In particular, like the Elizabethan privateers before them, they tried their luck in the Pacific. The first of these expeditions, unfortunately ill-documented, seems to have taken place as early as 1673, only two years after the sack of Panama. It was led by one Thomas Peche, and it is supposed that after going round the Horn he got as far as the Aleutians. By 1675 it was being reported that English pirates were appearing off the coast of Chile, and it is likely that these were of West Indian origin. But the earliest Pacific expedition of which we have any detailed knowledge is the one associated with the name of Bartholomew Sharp. In 1680 Sharp and his companions crossed the Isthmus of Darien to try to repeat Morgan's success of nine years earlier. Their motivation, as one of the participants frankly tells us, was "the sacred hunger of gold." When they arrived on the Pacific shore, they found themselves opposed by a squadron of eight Spanish ships, and after a desperate fight managed to take five of them.

The party now divided, and part of it decided to cruise the

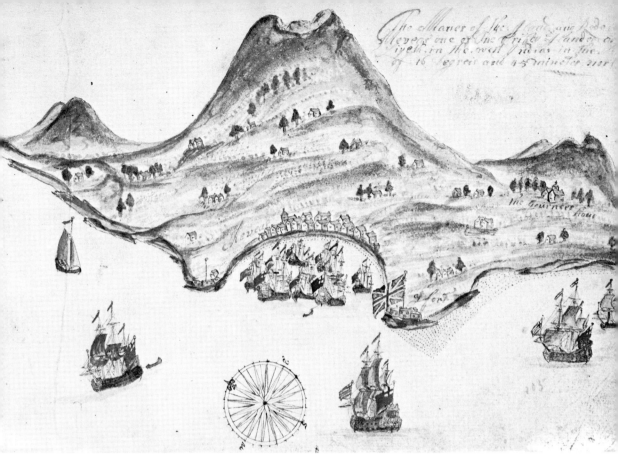

A view of Nevis by Edward Barlow. Several famous pirate cruises ended here.
NATIONAL MARITIME MUSEUM

Lima–Panama trade route, while the others made their way back across the isthmus to their own ships. After various changes of fortune Sharp had been elected captain of a vessel which was by the summer of 1680 cruising off the north coast of Peru. But by January 1681 his men had become disillusioned with him, and they deposed him in favor of another captain. Sharp recovered his position within a few weeks, when his successor was killed in an assault on Arica. But many of his men remained discontented with him, and by April the buccaneer crew had divided again, leaving Sharp with only seventy-three of the nearly 300 men who had set out to cross the isthmus. With these, after a further cruise northward, and then again southward, he finally rounded Cape Horn, having failed to find his way through the Straits of Magellan because of bad weather. He arrived off Barbados in January 1682, rightly unsure of his welcome, and at last landed at Nevis. He then returned to England as a passenger, and was promptly put on trial for piracy. He pleaded self-defense, and managed to get his acquittal with the help of an important volume of Spanish charts which he had prudently managed to bring with him. He returned to the West Indies, where, after further adventures, he was twice more acquitted

William Dampier. A portrait by T. Murray, c. 1697.
NATIONAL PORTRAIT GALLERY

on charges of piracy. He is last heard of in 1688, as "commander" of the tiny island of Anguilla, whose population was at that time described as being "without government or religion."

With one exception—the privateering cruise led by Woodes Rogers in 1708 which succeeded in taking one of the Manila galleons and rescued Alexander Selkirk, the original Robinson Crusoe—the freebooting voyages in the Pacific which followed Sharp's were just as confused as his, if not more so, and the men were just as insubordinate and prone to change their leaders at the slightest excuse. By behaving in this way about the leadership, they were in fact following an established buccaneer pattern. But the situation differed from a psychological point of view because of the isolation which the buccaneers felt once they were cut off from their West Indian bases by the great land-masses of Central and South America. For the first time we get a glimpse of the way in which the pirates of the new generation were to live, that is as outcasts, with no secure roots anywhere in the world, and no preference for one place over another. The shrinkage of the freebooting republic to the cockleshell size of a ship, the need to explore unknown territory and cope with unfamiliar conditions, brought out both the best and worst in those who participated in these voyages. One strange feature of them was that they made a considerable contribution to the stock of scientific knowledge, through the participation of men such as William Dampier and Lionel Wafer.

Dampier had tried his hand at a number of things before he joined the buccaneers. He had sailed to the East Indies as a foremast hand in 1671, and had set out for Jamaica in 1674 (then aged twenty-two) in order to manage a plantation. By 1675 he had gone to Campeche to do the backbreaking work of a logwood-cutter, and this in turn introduced him to buccaneering, since the two occupations were by tradition closely allied. Dampier was not a good leader of men—when he was later given the command of a naval ship, the *Roebuck*, on a voyage of exploration, he finished by being courtmartialed and declared "not a fit person to be employed as a commander of any of Her Majesty's ships"—but he was inexhaustibly curious, a keen observer, and less interested in money than he was in knowledge. The books which he published describing his voyages were immediately recognized by his contemporaries as being something quite remarkable. Wafer, who had been trained as a surgeon, was an almost equally good observer, and wrote a book which gives a vivid description of the Darien Indians, among whom he lived for some time.

The eager public appetite for books about voyages, which benefited Dampier, and which Defoe too was to try to exploit, was a symptom of the

185

Captain John Avery, from the General History.

intellectual change which was taking place in England. The late seventeenth century had witnessed a rapid growth in scientific inquiry, spearheaded by Isaac Newton and others who belonged to the Royal Society, of which Charles II had become patron in 1662. By the time Dampier turned buccaneer there was a new spirit abroad even among men who were not intellectuals. It brought with it a pragmatism which, if not always moral, was certainly revolutionary in its clearsightedness. Morgan and the buccaneers who accompanied him to Panama had been bold enough in a physical sense, and had overcome the most prodigious odds. Their way of looking at the world, however, was traditional—the Spaniards remained the enemy, just as they had been in Drake's day, and the way of getting wealth was to plunder them in the Indies, using a long-established hostility as cover for the deed. But now was to occur an act of outright piracy with no such pseudo-historical justification which would rivet public attention and arouse the cupidity of all those who, a little earlier, might have been content to follow in Morgan's footsteps. It is always difficult to be sure why a particular action at a particular time has the power to excite men's imaginations. This one certainly did. The man responsible for it, called John Avery, or Henry Every, or Henry Bridgman, or Long Ben, was born in Plymouth around 1665, the eldest son of a sea-captain whose brothers and sister owned ships employed in the Jamaica trade. He served first as a junior naval officer and then transferred as mate to a family-owned ship and made a series of voyages to Port Royal in the years 1691–3. At this period he may also have had some experience as a slaver on the coast of West Africa.

In 1693, Avery had a serious disappointment: he was refused the command of one of the family ships, something he had confidently expected to be given. Forced to take alternative employment, he signed on as first mate of the *Charles II*, a ship leased by Sir James Houblon, chairman of the Spanish Company of Merchants, to the Spanish for *guarda costa* service off the coast of Peru. The ship reached Corunna, where she was delayed by a dispute about pay. Dissatisfied with conditions aboard, Avery managed to seize her, and put her drunken and incompetent captain ashore. The vessel, fast and well-armed, with forty-six guns and a crew of 150, was renamed the *Fancy*, and Avery headed first for the coast of Africa and then for Madagascar, where he revictualled at St. Mary's. He next proceeded to station himself at the mouth of the Red Sea.

He was not the first to appear in these waters with the notion of turning pirate. The nuisance had existed ever since the arrival of the Europeans, and was increasing rapidly now that the buccaneers were under pressure in the West Indies—a perfect example of the way in which events in one sea or ocean might produce important reactions in another area which was perhaps very distant. In 1705 the Great Mogul wrote a letter of bitter complaint to Louis XIV about the piracies being committed by Frenchmen against his subjects. In this he dated the beginning of the plague to about twenty years previously—that is, to around the year 1685. The so-called Pirate Round, which linked the ports of the American colonies to Madagascar, does indeed seem to have been established about this epoch, and Avery had precedents for choosing the hunting ground he did.

When he arrived, he found a competitor at work: the Rhode Islander Thomas Tew, who has already been mentioned. Tew had already made an important capture between Jeddah and Surat in July or August 1693. On sighting each other, the Englishman and the American decided to join forces. Tew's ship, the *Amity*, became the *Fancy*'s consort, and Avery found other allies as well. One was the *Dolphin*, a renamed Spanish prize commanded by Captain Want, who had formerly been Tew's mate, and there were, in addition, three other pirate ships from Rhode Island. It amounted to a formidable squadron.

The first prize Avery made was important enough. It was a ship called the *Futteh Mahmood*, the property of the richest merchant in Surat, and it yielded some £30,000 to £40,000 in gold and silver. It seems likely that Tew was killed in the engagement. But the next prize was richer still, perhaps the richest ever made by any pirate. She was the *Gunj Suwai* (*Exceeding Treasure*), an eighty-gun ship belonging to the Emperor Aurungzebe, the Great Mogul himself. Aboard were a considerable contingent of soldiers, armed with 400 matchlocks, and a number of Muslim ladies of high rank who had been making the pilgrimage to Mecca. She also carried a huge amount of treasure—estimates vary between £525,000 and £325,000 in the English money of the day. There was a subsequent share-out of £1,000 per man when the pirates reached the isle of Bourbon, which they often used as a rendezvous, though Avery was afterwards said to have swindled his associates. Some of the ladies were so seriously mistreated by their captors that they leapt overboard.

The impact of the news was everywhere tremendous. At Surat President Annesley and sixty-seven others were arrested, and were kept in irons for eleven months. Avery returned tranquilly to the pirate haven of New Providence (now Nassau) in the Bahamas, where he landed in 1696, presenting the governor Nicholas Trot with his ship and other rich gifts, and being allowed in consequence to bring his booty ashore. From here he

This nineteenth-century view of Madagascar shows conditions almost identical to those encountered by the pirates of the seventeenth and eighteenth centuries.

took passage to England and disappeared. Some accounts have it that he was subsequently cheated out of all his gains by Bristol merchants, and died a pauper. He is reported to have been buried in Bideford Church, Devon, in 1727 or 1728, under the name of Bridgman. By this time he had long been legendary. One popular belief, reflected in the play *The Successful Pirate*, was that he had married a beautiful Indian princess he found aboard the *Gunj Suwai*, and had settled down to rule a kingdom in Madagascar. At any rate it was he rather than anyone else who gave the professional pirate a new glamor. Hearing of his good fortune, many discontented seamen were inspired to try to emulate him.

One consequence of the outbreak of piracy in the Red Sea during the 1690s was the last voyage of Captain Kidd, perhaps the most controversial figure in the history of piracy, and certainly the best-remembered. Kidd was a citizen of New York, prosperous and successful. In 1692 he had been the commander of a privateering expedition against the French, and after an initial success he suffered the humiliation of having some of his men run off with his ship, the *Blessed William*, in order to turn pirate in the Red Sea as everyone else seemed to be doing. This incident did not affect his credit, and when in 1695 he found himself in London at a moment when piracy

189

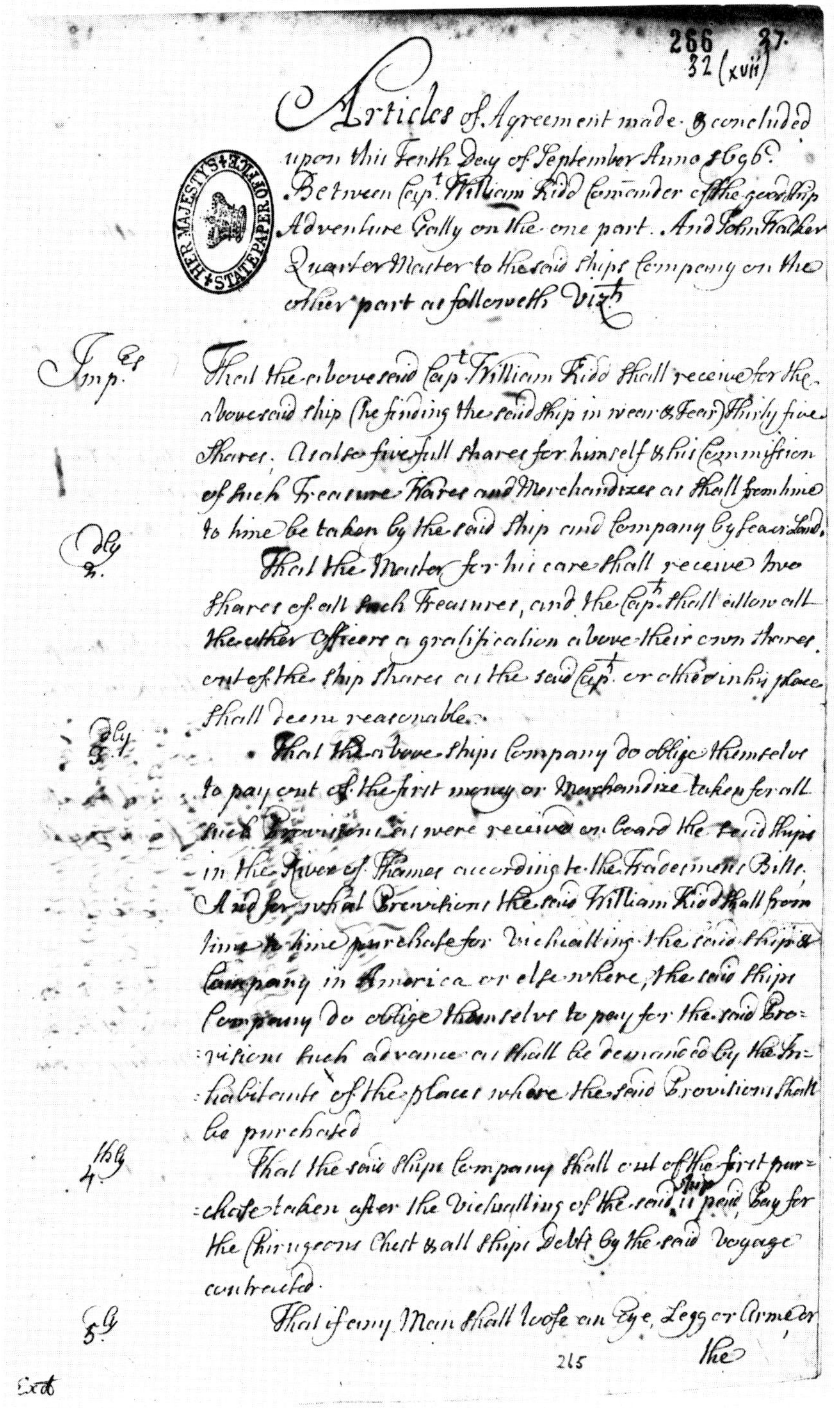

Articles of Agreement made & concluded
upon this Tenth day of September Anno 1696.
Between Cap.ᵗ William Kidd Comander of the good Ship
Adventure Gally on the one part. And John Walker
Quarter Master to the said Ships Company on the
other part as followeth viz.ᵗ

Imp.ˢ

That the abovesaid Cap.ᵗ William Kidd shall receive for the
abovesaid Ship (he finding the said Ship in wear & Tear) Thirty five
Shares. As also five full Shares for himself & his Commission
of such Treasure Wares and Merchandizes as shall from time
to time be taken by the said Ship and Company by Sea or Land.

2ly.

That the Master for his care shall receive two
Shares of all such Treasures, and the Cap.ᵗ shall allow all
the other Officers a gratification above their own Shares
out of the Ship Shares as the said Cap.ᵗ or other in his place
shall deem reasonable.

3ly.

That the above Ships Company do oblige themselves
to pay out of the first money or Merchandize taken for all
such Provisions as were received on board the said Ships
in the River of Thames according to the Tradesmens Bills.
And for such Provisions the said William Kidd shall from
time to time purchase for Victualling the said Ship &
Company in America or else where, the said Ships
Company do oblige themselves to pay for the said Provisions such advance as shall be demanded by the Inhabitants of the places where the said Provisions shall
be purchased

4ly.

That the said Ships Company shall out of the first purchase taken after the Victualling of the said Ship is paid, pay for
the Chirurgeons Chest & all Ships Debts by the said Voyage
contracted.

5ly.

That if any Man shall loose an Eye, Legg or Arm or
the

215

The first page of Captain Kidd's articles.
PUBLIC RECORD OFFICE

Richard Coote, Earl of Bellamont. Engraving by Charles B. Hall.

was much in the news, it was suggested that he be sent to the East to hunt the marauders down. The voyage was, as usual, to be a joint-stock venture, and William III actually had a tenth share reserved for him of any profits from the intended voyage. Those who actually put up most of the money (the total required was £6,000, of which Kidd himself provided £600) were leading figures in the Whig ministry which was then in power—Somers, who was Lord Chancellor; the Earl of Oxford, First Lord of the Admiralty; and the two Secretaries of State, the Earl of Romney and the Duke of Shrewsbury. However, their names were not publicly used, though the Earl of Bellamont, Kidd's patron and newly appointed governor of New England, was mentioned in the grant.

From the very start, the adventure went wrong. Kidd had a new ship, the *Adventure Galley*, and a handpicked crew, but most of them were pressed as he was leaving the Nore. He had to pick up a fresh crew in America, and many of these seem to have had piratical connections. After a long period of unsuccessful cruising, during which his crew grew more and more discontented, Kidd killed his gunner, a man called William Moore, who

The Charles *galley, by William van der Velde. William Kidd's* Adventure Galley *would have been a less elaborate ship of this type.*
NATIONAL MARITIME MUSEUM

spoke insolently to him, with a blow on the head from an iron-bound bucket. But after further misadventures, he eventually took the Surat ship the *Quedagh Merchant*, which he afterwards claimed was fair prize since it was carrying a French pass. In her he found considerable plunder. He then went to Madagascar and proceeded to fraternize with the pirates he was supposedly pursuing, perhaps because his crew were too untrustworthy to make any other course possible. After abandoning the *Adventure Galley*, which was now in unseaworthy condition, he took the prize to the West Indies, arriving at Anguilla in 1699. He then made his way to New York, despite the fact that he knew he had been proclaimed pirate, expecting Bellamont to help him. Bellamont did no such thing, but instead confiscated as much of Kidd's property as he could lay hands on, and sent the man himself to England to stand trial. The affair aroused intense public interest, and was used by the Tories to try to discredit the members of the Whig ministry who had been Kidd's backers. There was already an assumption in England that Kidd was in fact guilty of piracy, thanks to reports which had come back from the East about his activities there, and

192

Edward Barlow's ship Septer, *in which he encountered Captain Kidd in the Red Sea.*
NATIONAL MARITIME MUSEUM

from the beginning he stood very little chance of acquittal. Some ex-members of his crew, who had deserted him at Madagascar, were found to turn King's Evidence, and Kidd was given little opportunity to prepare his own defense. He was condemned first for the murder of Moore and secondly for the unlawful seizure of the *Quedagh Merchant*.

Kidd's innocence has been passionately upheld by a number of twentieth-century authors, but the public opinion of his own time undoubtedly believed he was guilty and turned him into an arch-pirate even more legendary than Avery. Certainly there are some pieces of evidence that still seem to go against him. For example, the seaman Edward Barlow (not a witness at Kidd's trial) describes in his *Journal* how a fleet he was with encountered the *Adventure Galley* in the Red Sea. Barlow

193

describes it as "a pretty, frigate-built ship" which "fired four or five times at one of the Moor's ships," but, being unable to cut out a prize, eventually gave up the attempt and sailed away. When Kidd returned to the port of New York in the sloop *San Antonio* he had with him a very considerable quantity of loot—sixty pounds of gold, 100 pounds of silver, and East Indian goods—silks, muslins and brocades—valued at £10,000. Most, if not all, of these must have come from the *Quedagh Merchant*'s cargo, and it is by no means clear that the latter was really a legitimate prize. Despite the "French pass" upon which Kidd founded his action, her master, one Wright, was an Englishman, and her two mates were Dutch. In fact, she probably, like so many native-owned vessels, carried both English and French passes to be used as occasion offered.

The English authorities by no means succeeded in checking the pirate menace by making a spectacular example of Kidd. As the years passed, the pirates grew increasingly unscrupulous about their methods, and also increasingly brutalized. Jakob Bucquoy, who was a prisoner aboard a pirate vessel around 1722, calls his captors "wretches, capable of any crime, who had stripped themselves of all humanity when they abandoned their own countries, of which they are the execration." Where Avery and many of his contemporaries who embarked on the Pirate Round seem to have confined themselves strictly to plundering Muslim ships, later pirates would attack anyone. The number of captures they made was often considerable. Of those who make their appearance in Defoe's *General History*, Lowther is said to have made thirty-three prizes in seventeen months; Low 140 in twenty months; Spriggs forty in twelve months; and Bartholomew Roberts no less than 400 in three years. All of these were active at the end of the second and the beginning of the third decade of the eighteenth century, and this seems to have been the time when the terror reached its height. In 1718 Governor Lawes of Jamaica wrote to the authorities at home: "There is hardly any ship or vessel coming in or going out of this island that is not plundered."

One reason for the huge increase in piracy at this period seems to have been a change in the rules that governed privateering in 1708, followed five years later by the Peace of Utrecht which brought about a general settlement between the various European powers. The new English Prize Act of 1708 transferred the entire interest in a prize to those who took it, instead of, as previously, reserving a percentage for the crown, and even offered a bounty in addition. The Woodes Rogers voyage to the South Seas was one of the ventures mounted in response to the liberality of the new provisions. When peace came, privateering as an industry had grown to an

Captain George Lowther, from the General History.

Captain Edward Low, from the General History *: "capable of disgusting cruelty . . . worthy of Lolonnois, and with even less reason."*

enormous extent and many seamen were thrown out of work. The situation was exactly parallel with that of little more than a century earlier, when James I had decided to make peace with Spain, and had abruptly ended the privateering of Elizabeth's reign. And on each occasion the results were the same.

Pirates were mostly men of little education. Major Stede Bonnet, a Barbados planter who "went on the account," as the phrase had it, in order to get away from a nagging wife, was very much an exception to the rule. Some, exaggerating their own natural roughness, enjoyed playing up to their roles as the devils of popular mythology. One of the most picturesque of these ruffians was Blackbeard, who seems to have combined a self-conscious pleasure in his own performance with a streak of genuine neurosis. He gained his sobriquet because of his extraordinary hirsuteness:

> This beard was black, which he suffered to grow of an extravagant length; as to breadth it came up to his eyes. He was accustomed to twist it with ribbons, in small tails, after the manner of our Ramillies wigs, and turn them about his ears. In time of action he wore a sling over his shoulders, with three brace of pistols, hanging in holsters, like bandoliers; and stuck lighted matches under his hat, which, appearing on each side of his face, his eyes naturally looking fierce and wild, made him altogether such a figure that imagination cannot form an idea of a Fury from Hell to look more frightful.

Blackbeard was full of strange freaks. It was he who, for instance, with the words "Come, let us make a hell of our own, and try how long we can bear it," betook himself in the company of two or three others to the hold of his ship, and closing the hatches "filled several pots full of brimstone and other combustible matter, and set it on fire, and so continued until they were almost suffocated, when some of the men cried out for air." Blackbeard at last opened the hatches again, well pleased that it was he who had held out the longest.

Another story about him might be of interest to a psychoanalyst. When he married a girl of sixteen (who was said to be his fourteenth wife) it was his custom, after he had lain with her himself, to ask five or six of his crew to come and have intercourse with her, one after another, while he watched their proceedings.

Yet if Blackbeard was brutal and perverted, he could also be genial. Defoe prints a delightful fragment of his journal which, if genuine, makes one long to read more:

The execution of Major Stede Bonnet at Charleston, from the General History.

> Such a day, rum all out:—Our company somewhat sober:—A damn'd confusion among us!—Rogues a-plotting:—Great talk of separation—so I looked sharp for a prize:—Such a day took one, with a great deal of liquor on board, so kept the company hot, damned hot; then all things went well again.

His own favorite tipple, which he succeeded in popularizing in the pirate community despite what must have been its extreme nastiness, was a drink called "rumfustian"—a mixture of beer, gin, sherry, rum and gunpowder.

Edward Low and his crew seem to have represented a more ordinary type of pirate. Low himself was perhaps capable of disgusting cruelty, acting in a way worthy of Lolonnois, and with even less reason. It is Defoe, once again, who supplies the details. When the captain of one of his prizes displeased him by throwing overboard a large sum of money, Low ordered his "lips to be cut off, which he broiled before his face, and afterwards murdered him and all the crew, being thirty-two persons." Another captain he tortured by putting lighted matches between his fingers; and, after taking two whale boats near Rhode Island, he disemboweled the master of one, and forced the other to eat his own ears, garnished with pepper and salt.

Philip Ashton, for a while a most unwilling member of Low's crew, paints a rather different picture, one of an environment which is violent, squalid and disorganized, rather than imbued with deliberate sadism. A good New England puritan, Ashton abhorred his companions' manner of conducting themselves:

> Prodigious drinking, monstrous cursing, hideous blasphemies and open defiance of Heaven and contempt of Hell itself was the constant employment, unless when sleep sometimes abated the noise and revelings.

Low he seems to have found more maudlin than truly dangerous. The pirate captain constantly referred to the orphan child he had left behind him in Boston "which (upon every lucid interval from reveling and drink) he would express a great tenderness for, insomuch as I have seen him sit down and weep plentifully upon the mentioning of it." Similarly, the rest of the crew, when caught in a storm, showed a tendency to panic, and constantly cried out: "Oh, I wish I were at home!" It is not quite the picture of the enemies of humankind which Defoe is careful to build up in the *General History*.

The two most improbable members of Defoe's gallery of pirates are women, Mary Read and Anne Bonny. Mary Read went in disguise to serve as a soldier in Flanders, and successfully kept up the deception for some years, only dropping it when she fell in love with a comrade. Later, she reverted to masculine costume, and became successively a seaman, a privateer and a pirate. Anne Bonny, the illegitimate daughter of a Cork lawyer who had settled with his mistress at Charlestown, South Carolina, got into the game by eloping to New Providence and there falling in with a successful pirate captain called Calico Jack Rackham, so called from the elegant costumes in colored calico which were his trademark. When justice caught up with them all off the coast of Jamaica, it was the two women who fought boldly, and the male members of the crew, including Rackham, who fled and took refuge in the hold. At the subsequent trial the two women managed to escape hanging by "pleading their bellies," that is, by announcing that they were both with child. Rackham, when the day of execution came, was brought to take his farewell of Anne. She turned from him, saying coldly: "That she was sorry to see him there, but if he had fought like a man, he need not have been hanged like a dog." This extraordinary history of female piracy is confirmed in outline by documents which are still preserved in the Jamaican archives, and must serve as a warning against assuming that all pirates are in essence the same.

The general pattern of early eighteenth-century piracy is nevertheless clear. The pirates often wintered in the Bahamas or in the West Indies, perhaps in the latter case at an island belonging to one of the minor powers. The Danish island of St. Thomas was a favorite choice in the late seventeenth century because the governor, Nicolas Esmit, was notoriously corrupt. When the good weather came, they might go north to recruit their crews. The Newfoundland fishing stations were a good source of men, because the fish-splitters who worked there were wretchedly paid, and often so deeply in debt to those who employed them that they had no other hope of getting away. Other men were "forced" from prizes as they were taken—sea-artists, such as skilled coopers and carpenters, were especially sought after, and once taken were unlikely to be released easily. From Newfoundland the pirates would go to the Azores, the Cape Verde islands, and then to Sierra Leone and the Guinea coast.

Life aboard a pirate vessel was governed by the articles which each member of the crew was asked to sign, and these were based, with certain modifications, on the articles which regulated life aboard a privateer. Defoe reproduces several typical sets of regulations in the *General History*. Here is the list he gives in his chapter on Bartholomew Roberts, with his own comments interpolated in brackets:

Mary Read, from a Dutch edition of the General History.

Anne Bonny, another Dutch portrayal.
BRITISH LIBRARY

Anne Bonny and Mary Read, the most famous women pirates.

I. Every man has a vote in affairs of moment; has equal title to the fresh provisions or strong liquors at any time seized, and may use them at pleasure unless a scarcity (no uncommon thing among them) make it necessary for the good of all to vote a retrenchment.

II. Every man to be called fairly in turn, by list, on board of prizes, because over and above their proper share they were on these occasions allowed a shift of clothes. But if they defrauded the Company to the value of a dollar, in plate, jewels or money, Marooning was the punishment. (This was a barbarous custom of putting the offender on shore on some desolate or uninhabited cape or island, with a gun, a few shot, a bottle of water and a bottle of powder, to subsist with or starve.) If the robbery was only between one another they contented themselves with slitting the ears and nose of him that was guilty, and set him on shore, not in an uninhabited place, but somewhere where he was sure to encounter hardships.

III. No person to game at cards or dice for money.

IV. The lights and candles to be put out at eight o'clock at night. If any of the crew at that hour remained inclined to drinking, they were to do it on the open deck (which Roberts believed would give a check to their debauchs, for he was a sober man himself; but he found that all of his endeavours to put an end to this debauch proved ineffectual).

V. To keep their piece, pistols and cutlass clean and fit for service. (In this they were extravagantly nice, endeavouring to outdo one another

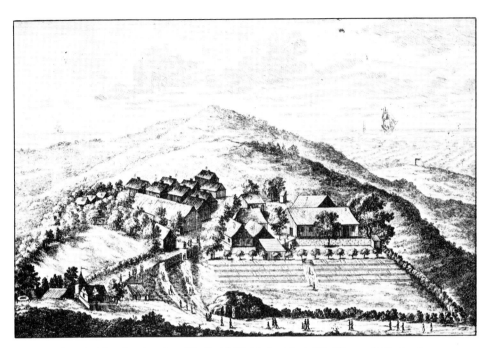

An early eighteenth-century view of the Danish West Indian island of St. Thomas. At this time it was a favorite pirate haunt.
BRITISH MUSEUM

in the beauty and richness of their arms, giving sometimes at an auction at the mast, £30 or £40 for a pair of pistols. These were slung in time of service with different coloured ribbons over their shoulders in a way peculiar to these fellows, in which they took great delight.)

VI. No boy or woman to be allowed among men. If any man be found seducing any of the latter sex, and carried her to sea disguised, he was to suffer Death. (So that when any fell into their hands, as it chanced in the *Onslow*, they put a sentinel immediately over her to prevent ill consequences from so dangerous an instrument of division and quarrel. But then here lies the roguery; they contend who shall be sentinel, which happens generally to one of the greatest bullies who, to secure the lady's virtue, will let none lie with her but himself.)

VII. To desert their ship or their quarters in battle was punished with Death or Marooning.

VIII. No striking one another on board, but every man's quarrels to be ended on shore, at sword and pistol. (Thus, the quartermaster of the ship, when the parties will not come to any reconciliation, accompanies them on shore with what assistance he thinks proper, and turns the disputants back to back at so many paces distant. At the word of command they turn and fire immediately or else the piece is

Bartholomew Roberts with the two ships he commanded at the time of his death, from the General
History.

knocked out of their hands. If both miss they come to their cutlasses
and then he is declared victor who draws the first blood.)

IX. No man to talk of breaking up their way of living till each had a
share of £1,000. If, in order to do this, any man lost a limb or became
a cripple in their service, he was to have 800 dollars out of the public
stock, and for lesser hurts proportionately.

X. The Captain and the Quartermaster to receive two shares of a
prize; the master, boatswain and gunner, one share and a half, and
other officers one and a quarter.

XI. The musicians to have rest of the sabbath day, but on the other
six days and night none, without special favour.

The pirates tended to differ from the privateers in their insistence on the
most rigorous democracy. The powers of a captain, even one as successful
as Roberts, were extremely limited, except when the fighting began, when
they were absolute. Though the captain was generally allowed the use of
the ship's great cabin, any man aboard had the right to intrude upon him,
to use his punchbowl, plate and china, to swear at him and to seize his food
and drink. The interests of the crew *vis-à-vis* their captain were represented
by the powerful figure of the quartermaster, elected by the men

205

The General History's *depiction of a pirate mock court.*
BRITISH LIBRARY

themselves. It was he, not the captain, who was responsible for the ship's discipline; and it was he who was the first to go aboard any prize, to apportion shares. In addition to this, the captain often had to subject himself to the advice of a kind of privy council. There was also a custom on some ships of holding pirate courts, with a good deal of buffoonish ceremonial, to give judgment on prisoners.

But, in spite of, or perhaps even because of, the intricacy of the regulations which they made for themselves, life aboard a pirate ship was often chaotic: "for being almost always mad or drunk, their behaviour produced infinite disorders, every man being, in his own imagination, a captain, a prince, or a king." One source gives a most graphic description of piratical table-manners, which bears out the impression of chaos:

> They eat in a very disorderly manner, more like a kennel of hounds than like men, snatching and catching the victuals from one another. . . . It seemed one of their chief diversions and, they said, looked martial-like.

What attracted men to the pirate life was the prospect of freedom almost as much as the prospect of gain, and it is not surprising that they insisted on enjoying their liberty to the full, however brutishly they sometimes exercised it. Compared to the life aboard a man-of-war, or even life aboard a merchantman, existence aboard a pirate vessel was a kind of paradise, or at least could seem so in prospect. One of the difficulties faced by the authorities was that those whom they sent to hunt pirates would be tempted to turn pirate themselves. Kidd's crew, if not Captain Kidd himself, provide a case in point. And, at the same time as Kidd's voyage, the East India Company was gravely embarrassed by mutiny aboard two of its own ships, the frigate *Mocha* and the ketch *Josiah*, both of which turned pirate. The *Mocha*'s freebooting career lasted for three years under the new name *Resolution*. Privateering ventures could also be a bad risk in this respect. In 1703, when Governor Dudley of Massachusetts commissioned the eighty-eight-ton brigantine *Charles* as a privateer, the crew were no sooner at sea than they mutinied, threw their sick captain overboard, and turned to piracy.

Resistance to pirate attack was frequently half-hearted, especially if the black flag—a signal that no quarter would be given—was not hoisted. When the crew of a merchant ship fought well, it was often because the owner or captain had promised an immediate reward for successful resistance. Piratical attempts could be beaten off because the pirate crews of the early eighteenth century were by no means the berserkers who had

Captain Edward England, from the General History.

populated the Spanish Main at the time of the rise of the buccaneers. A handbook of the period, designed to tell the captains of merchantmen how to resist privateers and pirates, points out the relative strengths of the two sides:

> Merchant-ships and colliers are built for burthen, and accordingly have their strength proportioned to the use they are designed. On the contrary, privateers are built for sailing, which is the property of a weak ship, and consequently they are; otherwise they'd not answer the expectation of the adventurers.

According to the author the correct tactics, if the ship looked like being boarded, were for the crew to retire to what were called "close quarters"— that is, to barricade themselves in the forecastle and great cabin, from which places they could only be dislodged by heavy gunfire, or else by desperate hand-to-hand fighting. He estimated that a ship worth £8,000, and carrying a crew of eighty men, could easily be defended against a privateer or pirate of forty guns and 200 men.

It is perhaps significant that any instance of a strong defense being made against pirates caused a great stir, even when it was unsuccessful. In July 1720, for instance, the Indiaman *Cassandra*, a strong ship of 380 tons, was captured by the pirates Taylor and England at Johanna in the Comoro Islands, having been deserted by two consorts, one of them another Indiaman. Her captain, Macrae, put up a very strong fight, but was forced to run his ship ashore and take refuge with a native prince. He then successfully negotiated with the pirates for his release, partly through the good offices of "a man with a terrible pair of whiskers and a wooden leg, being stuck round with pistols, like the man in the Almanac with darts," who had once sailed with him. (He is supposed to have supplied Stevenson, when he read this description, with his inspiration for the character of Long John Silver.) Macrae, who was the son of a poor Ayrshire cottager and had worked himself up slowly to the command of a ship, made a heroic passage back to India in an ill-found vessel the pirates gave him, and then returned to England, where the directors of the East India Company received him with acclamation. He was made supervisor of the west coast of Sumatra, with the right to succeed to the Presidency of Madras, an event which took place within eighteen months. He was six years in office, and eventually left India with a fortune of £100,000.

What militated against the long continuation of piracy on the grand scale was not so much the success of the authorities in dealing with it as the inherent weakness of pirate society. Perhaps more pirates died of drink and

A shipwreck off the coast of Madagascar, from Robert Drury's Journal.

Madagascar: a nineteenth-century scene.
BRITISH LIBRARY

disease than were ever imprisoned or hanged. Syphilis was a great
scourge—we are told that when the *Cassandra* was taken "no part of the
cargo was so much valued by the robbers as the doctor's chest, for they
were all poxed to a great degree"—and the disease must have been spread
by the fact that homosexuality was so prevalent, just as it had been
among the buccaneers. Many ships were wrecked, rather than sunk or
captured, and keeping them in trim was always a serious problem, though
few seem to have been surprised while careening, which was the time when
they were at their most vulnerable.

What a pirate needed most of all was a secure base, but such regular
bases as the pirates possessed increasingly became closed to them during
the third decade of the eighteenth century. The large, sparsely inhabited
island of Madagascar was a favorite from the 1680s onwards. There were
several reasons why it suited them so well. Not only was there a number of
good harbors, but the widely dispersed tribes had little communication
with one another thanks to the wildness of the interior, and were thus not in
a position to put up much resistance to European incursions. The island
produced nothing which was coveted by the European powers.

For a while a number of pirate settlements existed there, often ruled over by self-appointed "kings." One of these was a mulatto called Abraham Samuel, who lorded it at Port Dauphin. He had been quartermaster and then captain of a pirate ship, and had been able to take advantage of the fact that a local chieftain's daughter, who had lost an infant many years previously, "recognized" him as her missing child. At Ranter Bay, the local ruler was a Jamaican called James Plantain:

> For his further state and recreation, he took a great many wives and servants, whom he kept in great subjection; and after the English manner called them Moll, Kate, Sue or Peggy. These women were dressed in the richest silks, and some of them had diamond necklaces.

But the pirates were not disciplined enough to maintain their foothold on the island. In 1711, Captain Woodes Rogers, coming home from the coast of South America by way of the Cape, was told that the pirates who had settled in Madagascar were now very poor, and were despised by the natives from among whom they had taken wives. In 1726 the captain of the Indiaman *Compton*, then newly arrived in Bombay, reported that the pirates established in Madagascar had so cruelly maltreated the natives that the latter had risen and massacred them: "Only a dozen remain, having taken refuge in the woods, where they are like to perish miserably."

Other havens were lost for rather different reasons. One was the gradual development of economic and political institutions which could make a colony much less friendly than it had once been to visiting freebooters. The Carolinas are a case in point. In the seventeenth century the settlements in North and South Carolina had been amongst the most isolated and vulnerable in North America, cut off by many miles of wilderness from their neighbors, and constantly threatened by Indian raids. Carolina was ruled by a trade corporation, the Proprietary Government, whose local representatives were often corrupt. The pirates brought in goods which would otherwise have been unobtainable, and did little damage to a maritime trade which was still feeble. What changed the situation was, first of all, that in the late seventeenth century the economy of South Carolina was transformed by the cultivation of rice. The prosperity of the planters now began to depend on safe access to English markets, and this altered their attitude to piracy. Large numbers of English Dissenters and French Huguenots arrived to change the social tone of an area which had once been described "as the common sanctuary of runaways," though North Carolina remained more primitive and inclined to lawlessness than the area round Charleston to the south. The last phase, which is the period when Blackbeard was at large and basing himself on the town of Bath, runs

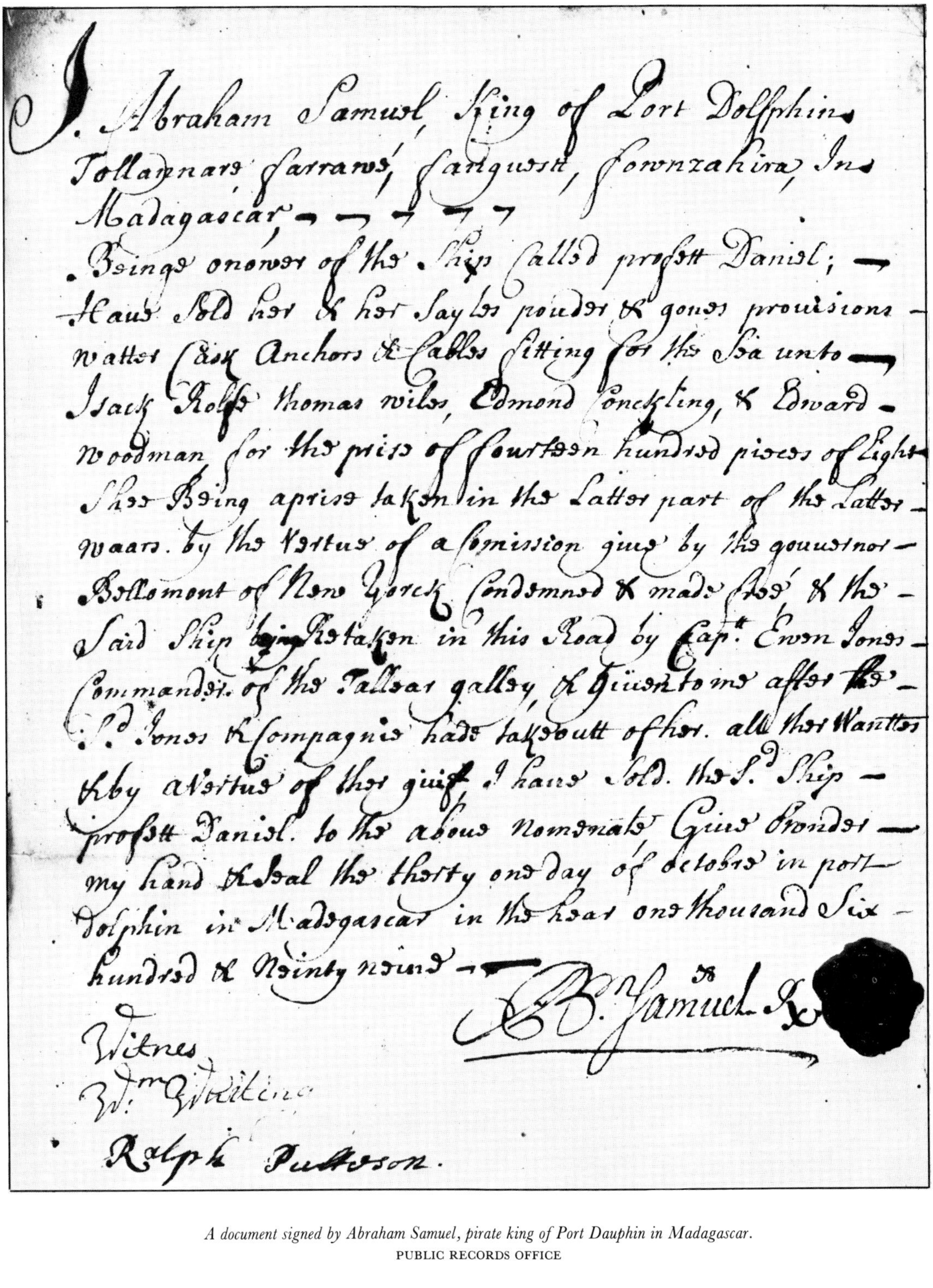

I. Abraham Samuel, King of Port Dolphin,
Tollanare Farrawe, Fanguest, Fownzahira, In
Madagascar, —
Beinge owner of the Ship Called prophett Daniel; —
Have Sold her & her Sayles powder & gons provisions —
watter Cask Anchors & Cables fitting for the Sea unto —
Isack Rolfe thomas wiles, Edmond Conckling, & Edward —
woodman for the prise of fourteen hundred pieces of Eight
Shee Being aprise taken in the Latter part of the Latter —
waars. by the Vertue of a Comission give by the gouvernor —
Bellomont of New Yorck Condemned & made free & the —
Said Ship being Retaken in this Road by Capt. Ewen Jones —
Commander of the Tallear galley, & given to me after the —
Sd Jones & Compagnie hade takeoutt of her. all ther Wantes
& by a Vertue of ther guift I have Sold. the Sd. Ship —
prophett Daniel. to the above Nominated Give Vnder —
my hand & Seal the thirty one day of october in port —
dolphin in Madagascar in the Year one thousand Six —
hundred & Ninety Nine —

A B. Samuel &

Witnes
Wm. Whiting
Ralph Patterson.

A document signed by Abraham Samuel, pirate king of Port Dauphin in Madagascar.
PUBLIC RECORDS OFFICE

from 1713 to 1719, that is from the Peace of Utrecht, which created an upsurge in piracy as privateersmen fell out of employment, until the abolition of the Proprietary Government. A Carolina ruled directly from Whitehall could not countenance the irregularities which had flourished in the past.

Almost the only pirate settlements to be extirpated by determined and successful official action were those at Mauritius and Bourbon, and that at New Providence in the Bahamas. Mauritius and its sister island were visited by a small English naval squadron in 1721, and thereafter were officially considered to be free of the taint of piracy, though on Bourbon at least amnestied ex-pirates continued to form a very considerable proportion of the population. The fact that New Providence ceased to be a pirate haven was due chiefly to the untiring efforts of one individual—the successful privateer Woodes Rogers, who now embarked on a new phase of his career. The base was of recent origin. The pirates first came to the island in 1716, under the leadership of Henry Jennings. Jennings was a former privateer who had been ordered by the governor to leave Jamaica because he had caused a major diplomatic crisis by robbing the salvors working on the Spanish plate fleet, wrecked by a gale on the coast of Florida in 1714. The community grew very rapidly after Jennings's arrival, until it had about 2,000 inhabitants, most of them pirates. There was even a sailmaker's widow in the township who made a living by creating Black Jack flags for pirate ships. She took part-payment in brandy, but never worked unless she was sober.

The place was at this time ruled by a council of captains and quartermasters, just as if it had been a very large pirate ship. And indeed it possessed almost every natural advantage such a body of men could desire—it was well-wooded, fertile, with numerous wells and cattle and hogs running wild. There was a safe natural harbor with difficult approaches because of coral reefs and rocks. Hills rising from the beach made good look-out points, and there was even a fort, though in bad repair, to guard the entrance to the harbor. The home government had good reason to be alarmed when they heard what was going on. Their reaction was to appoint Woodes Rogers Captain-General and Governor-in-Chief for the Crown, at a salary of £50 per annum for the first seven years, £100 per annum for the next seven, and £200 per annum thereafter.

To prepare for the new governor's arrival a warship, H.M.S. *Phoenix*, was dispatched from Bermuda to the Bahamas with a copy of the new royal proclamation of amnesty, which had been issued in September 1717. Captain Pearce read it twice to the assembled freebooters, on different

Woodes Rogers and his family, by William Hogarth—a picture perhaps paid for by the profits of Rogers's privateering voyage.

occasions, but each time was badly received. Yet when Rogers himself arrived at New Providence in June 1718, it was decided to admit him, after a special meeting called by Jennings, who said that he himself had decided to take the king's pardon, and advised the other captains who were present to do so. One of them, Captain Charles Vane, demanded that he be allowed to keep a French brigantine he had just taken. The message was relayed to Rogers, and, when the latter refused, Vane sent a fire-ship out to clear the harbor entrance, and got clean away with his prize. But he was almost the only dissenter. Rogers arrived to find some two hundred ships at anchor in the port, and a pirate guard of honor waiting to receive him. The pirates swore allegiance to the king, formally renounced piracy, and then fired a salute in the air with their muskets. Rogers offered every former freebooter 120 square feet of land provided that he cleared it and built a cabin for shelter. This was almost the end of the matter, though Rogers did have trouble with a few men who returned to their old trade. They were duly hanged, and at least one of their former colleagues sat among the judges. But the governor's woes, henceforth, were concerned more with the laziness of the inhabitants than their criminal tendencies. They were, he said in a letter written home the year after his arrival, "so indolent they are content to live on potatoes, yams and turtle." In another letter, written the same year to the Lords Commissioners of Trade, he complained:

> These wretches can't be kept on watch at night, and when they do come they are rarely sober and rarely awake all night, though our officers and soldiers often surprise their guard and carry off their arms and I punish, fine and confine them almost every day.

Yet, despite his anxieties, they were active enough under his leadership to beat off a Spanish attack in 1720.

The story of the transformation wrought by Rogers in New Providence has been told at some length because it seems to illustrate the change of mood which was making pirates into merchants again, or settlers, or at the worst smugglers. Some of the leaders, such as Bartholomew Roberts, had got their deserts—he was killed by a blast of grapeshot in the throat when resisting the assault of a king's ship on his own vessel. He made, we are told, "a gallant figure at the time of the engagement, being dressed in a rich crimson damask waistcoat and breeches, a red feather in his hat, a gold chain round his neck, with a diamond cross hanging to it, a sword in his hand and two pair of pistols, hanging at the end of a silk sling, flung over his shoulders." But others successfully made the transition back to some kind of civilian existence. One such was Taylor, who had fought Macrae to get possession of the *Cassandra*. He took the prize to the West Indies, and after fruitless negotiations with the English got a pardon from the King of Spain. He seems to have taken a Spanish naval commission, and to have commanded the man-of-war which in 1723 attacked the English logwood-cutters in the Bay of Campeche, taking eleven of their ships and murdering their crews. Edward Low, still pursuing his piratical career, is said to have made his appearance just as the massacre was completed, and to have retaliated by putting all the Spaniards to the sword. But Taylor evidently survived, and in 1744 there is some trace of him in Cuba, living with a wife and three children and engaged in a modest commerce among the islands. By this time West Indian piracy was again an almost purely local affair, and ironically enough had largely fallen into Spanish hands. Their *guarda costas*, being unpaid, now often turned to piracy, and the Spanish island of Puerto Rico was a nest of Spanish pirates of this kind.

One pirate's end: almost the only known representation of a hanging at Execution Dock, Wapping, London.
LONDON MUSEUM

8
The End of Piracy?

WHAT ONE MAY CALL THE post-Defoe era of piracy and privateering is considerably harder to write about than the age of the buccaneers and that of Avery, Bartholomew Roberts and Teach. Not only are the materials scattered, but there is a certain reluctance on the part of historians to call things by their real names. If the Peace of Utrecht in 1713 had brought about what seemed to be a general settlement, and if this, in turn, had turned into piracy what would simply have been privateering before, the new European system proved to be more fragile than its makers had hoped. By 1739 England was involved in a commercial war against Spain—the War of Jenkins' Ear—and this soon merged into a great European war, that of the Austrian Succession, which the American colonists dubbed "King George's War." The Treaty of Aix-le-Chapelle put an end to this in 1748, but the peace did not last for long. In 1756 the Seven Years War broke out, and this in turn was followed by the War of American Independence in 1776. In 1778 the French joined the conflict on the American side, and they were followed in 1779 by the Spanish and in 1780 by the Dutch. The American Revolution was followed by the Revolution in France, and the whole of Europe was embroiled in a conflict which lasted until Napoleon's defeat at Waterloo in 1815.

Lord George Graham in his cabin, by William Hogarth. Graham was a naval officer who made considerable sums in prize money from taking privateers.
NATIONAL MARITIME MUSEUM

At all times when a state of war existed, privateering became a legitimate activity, and letters of marque were issued. Certain ports— French, English and American—specialized in the privateering industry, and depended upon it for much of their prosperity. This was the case with Liverpool, for example, which began to expand very rapidly in the eighteenth century under the double impetus of privateering and slaving. The link between the two occupations of privateer and slaver was also to be found elsewhere, especially in the American colonies, and the same kind of vessel was found to be suitable for both kinds of activity. American shipbuilders began to evolve the special ship-types which eventually led, in the nineteenth century, to the invention of the tea-clipper, the fastest and most beautiful of all sailing vessels. Taking some hints from the Bermuda sloops which had always been popular with pirates, American yards began to turn out rakish topsail schooners which could show a clean pair of heels to almost anything else on the oceans. Though size increased both towards the end of the Revolutionary War and during the War of 1812, these were

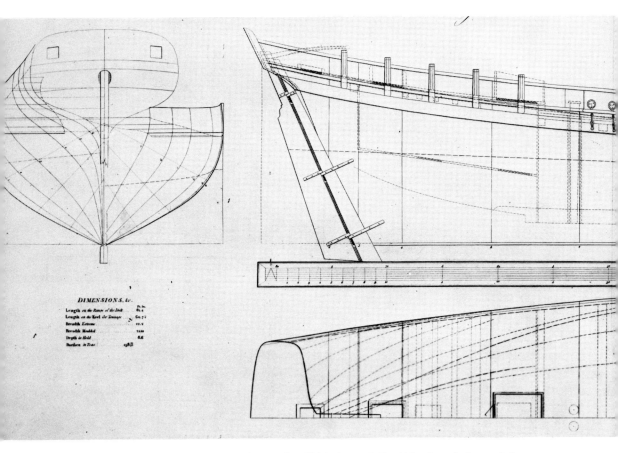

never really large ships. A typical example of the middle period of their development was the *American Tartan*, captured by the British in 1778. Her dimensions were 115 feet on the lower deck, 95 feet on the keel, with a beam of 33 feet 3 inches and a depth of hold of 15 feet. The one respect in which these beautiful sailing machines fell short of the ships produced in Europe was that they were usually made of badly seasoned wood, pine rather than oak, and therefore could not be expected to last for long.

The most active colony in the privateering business from 1740 onwards was perhaps not surprisingly Rhode Island, which had once been Tew's home port and an important place of call on the Pirate Round. In 1744, for instance, the colony had no less than twenty-one privateers at sea. The crews averaged more than 100 men per vessel. If one takes into consideration not only those who went to sea in these ships, but those on land who depended upon them for all or even part of their livelihood—the

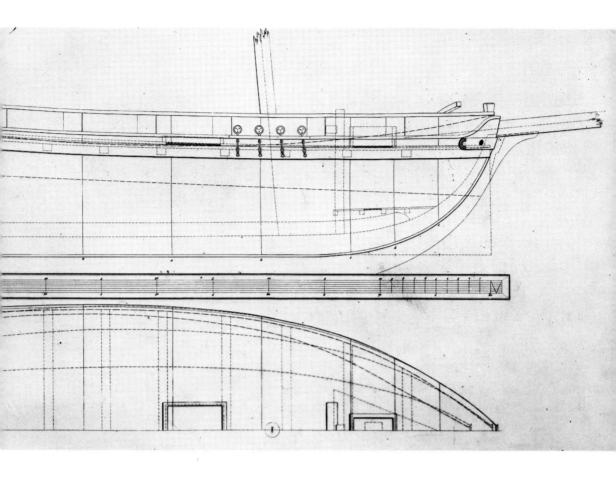

crewmen's families, dockyard employees, owners of ships, lawyers dealing with prize business, etc.—it is clear that privateering was a major industry. Indeed, throughout the period, the industrial and commercial aspect of American privateering invariably took precedence of any naval service it might do.

Yet there were limits to being businesslike—the Rhode Island privateers were as superstitious as most mariners. Their custom was to have the ship's horoscope cast, to find a suitable sailing date for a cruise. Unfortunately, the predictions made were not always as accurate as they should have been: two newly outfitted Rhode Island privateers sailed as their horoscopes commanded them on December 24, 1745, at the beginning of a violent northeast snowstorm. They were never heard of again.

At this period, privateering could be a very profitable business for

Privateer's prey: a contemporary model of a late eighteenth-century merchantman.

American owners. In 1748, for instance, the *Bethel* of Boston captured the Spanish merchantman *Jesus, Maria and Joseph*, a ship with a crew of 100 men and carrying twenty-six guns and a cargo valued at 300,000 dollars including 171,000 dollars in cash. Four years previously, four New York privateers had returned to their home port with a convoy of six prizes taken in the West Indies, the smallest being a ship of 180 tons. But these gains were not made without reprisals upon American commerce. In 1745 New York shipping was being so harassed by enemy privateers that the General Assembly offered to pay a special bounty for any of them taken and destroyed in the immediate vicinity of the port. Further afield, in the West Indies, a situation began to develop which closely resembled that which had been brought about by the age-old corsair war in the Mediterranean. Privateers from opposing sides pillaged the plantations and carried off the Negroes; and neutrals, especially the Dutch, found themselves persecuted by both parties. There was frequent changing of ships' names to conform with whatever papers the captain might happen to possess, and privateer ships could be found carrying two sets of papers of different nationalities. These bad customs persisted throughout the eighteenth century.

In European waters, one of the most interesting features of the conflict was the way in which French privateers became involved in the second Jacobite rebellion. Some of the leading fitters-out of privateers in France were in fact Irish Catholic exiles—they included a man called O'Heguerty, who had good court connections, Ruttledge of Dunkirk and Anthony Walsh of Nantes. These Irish Catholics supported the Young Pretender, Prince Charles Edward, with money, gave him an interest in their privateering and trading ventures, and made plans for his triumphant return to the throne. In July 1745 these plans were at last put into effect, and the ship on which the prince embarked for Scotland was a

Privateer actions in the Mediterranean: the French ship Intrepide *takes two English prizes, 1804.*
MUSÉE DE LA MARINE

English ketch-rigged sloop, 1756. Vessels of this kind were used for anti-privateer patrols.
SCIENCE MUSEUM

frigate called the *Du Teillay*, owned by Walsh and commanded by a well-known Nantais privateer captain called Charles Durbé. Off Belle-Isle she was joined by a larger ship, the *Elizabeth*, lent by Louis XV but fitted out by Ruttledge. The second-in-command of this vessel was Pierre Bart, cousin of Jean.

Later, when the prince had landed on Eriskay after an adventurous journey, it was privateers, chiefly from Dunkirk, who brought him troops and supplies. Following his defeat, it was again privateer vessels which were sent to try and rescue him. After numerous failures, the rescue was at last effected by a ship called the *Prince-de-Conti*, fitted out by a St. Malo ship-owner with the good Irish name of Butler. She was accompanied by a consort, the *Heureux*. To each of these corsair vessels the prince gave a hundred gold louis, fifty for the captain, and fifty to be divided among the crews. The captains, who belonged to leading St. Malo families, refused the gift; but their crews took it readily enough, and indeed thought it none too generous.

The most distinguished French corsair of the Seven Years War, François Thurot, was also concerned with a descent on British territory—the abortive attack on Carrickfergus in Ireland which cost him his life. He had begun his career as a surgeon aboard a small corsair vessel which was almost immediately captured. He used his captivity to perfect his knowledge of both surgery and navigation, and also apparently of the English language. When he escaped, as he eventually did, he put the second and third of these branches of knowledge to good use in daring corsair exploits, often running for shelter to Scottish or Irish ports, and frequently flying English colors. In 1759, he was given joint command of an invading force which was originally supposed either to burn Bristol or to ravage the Northumberland and Durham coalmines, but which had to change its objective when the plan became known to the English.

Thurot slipped out of Dunkirk in the autumn of 1759, evading the blockade thanks to a gale, and went first to Gothenberg, then to Thorshaven in the Faroes. The soldiers he had taken on board were commanded by M. de Flobert, an aristocrat who despised the naval commander for his humble origins. By the time they got to Ireland the two men were on the worst of terms, and, with de Flobert's encouragement, three of Thurot's five ships mutinied against him and turned for home. The mutiny was quelled with some difficulty, and it was decided to go ahead with the invasion plan, despite the news which reached the French at the Isle of Islay that the main French fleet under Conflans had just been disastrously defeated by Hawke at Quiberon. Carrickfergus was duly taken, despite the by now half-starved condition of the French troops, but a projected advance on Belfast had to be given up. The troops were re-embarked, but the French were intercepted at sea by a British squadron and disastrously defeated, thanks largely to the faintheartedness of those who had mutinied previously. Thurot was killed just as his flagship surrendered—the only one of the great French corsairs to die in action. The French government treated his widow, an Irish Protestant named Smith, with great shabbiness. The king would do nothing at all for her, and Madame de Pompadour was only prepared to grant her a small pension when she converted to Catholicism. Thurot's sad story perhaps illustrates why privateers on both sides preferred on the whole to stick strictly to business rather than to concern themselves with great affairs.

In the Seven Years War the balance of advantage for privateering may for once have been on the English side. The English blockade of French

225

ports was very effective; and the Americans, who could not be blockaded, made an immense number of captures from the enemy. It was in this war that a system of collusive captures grew up. A privateer would "by arrangement" take a vessel filled with enemy goods, and shepherd it to what was always its intended destination, thus providing a form of convoy. In the Revolutionary war which followed the French eventually found themselves allied with those who had harried them a decade and a half previously. But before the stage of alliance could be reached there was an uneasy period when American privateers operated out of French ports in defiance of French neutrality. Such conduct could be construed, at least technically, as piracy. Gustavus Cunningham, an American privateer captain, succeeded in capturing the Harwich to Helevoetsluis packet on a voyage out of Dunkirk in 1777. On his second voyage he got himself into so much hot water with the French authorities that he was forced to make for Bilbão instead of returning to his home port, and from here he escaped to America. The French shipowner who had backed him served a term in the Bastille.

In 1778, when the French openly allied themselves to the new republic, the situation entirely changed. The Americans, who had already nearly ruined the West Indian trade thanks to corsairs based on their own home ports (in six months 700 vessels worth nearly £2,000,000 had been taken) could now expect a free hand on the other side of the Atlantic. Even before the French were definitely at war with England ten percent insurance had to be paid on the voyage from Dover to Calais.

Once war was declared privateer ships sailed out of French ports under French rather than American colors, and the ship-owners were also French. The crews, however, were cosmopolitan, with a strong American element. Some captains refused to obey regulations about the flying of the French flag—one, called Joseph Margery, insisted on flying the harp of Ireland. Among these captains were a great number of rogues, and their conduct was often unscrupulous.

The situation can be illustrated by the case of the *Eclipse* and the *Emiliard*. The *Eclipse* was a privateer nominally commanded by Captain Nathaniel Fanning of Connecticut, but in fact largely directed by the mate, Thomas Potter, who was the stronger personality of the two. The *Emiliard* was a merchantman returning from the West Indies, and flying the Danish flag. She was thus a neutral vessel. Aboard her were three distinguished French passengers. She was stopped by the *Eclipse* in the Channel, and Potter took a boat and prize-crew over to her. He and his men robbed the passengers of considerable sums of money, and also of their

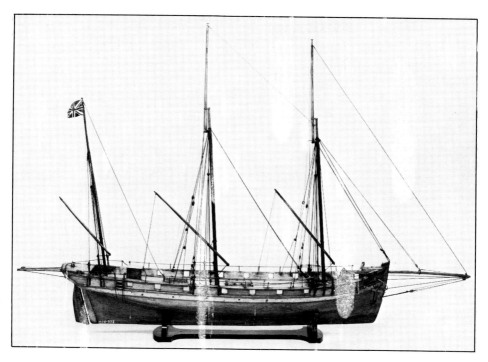

Armed lugger. Many eighteenth- and early nineteenth-century privateers preferred small ships of this type.

clothes. Fanning, who remained on his own vessel, made no protest when he heard what had happened, and having (as he said later) "perhaps drunk a little," was persuaded by the mate to try on some of the stolen finery, strutting up and down in it for the amusement of his men.

A subsequent inquiry revealed that the captain of the *Eclipse* kept two log-books, one of which was in cipher, and that he professed total ignorance of the rules which governed privateering.

Things were likely to go hard with Fanning and his like if they were captured by the British, not because they were piratical, but because of their nationality. In British eyes, American privateersmen were rebels, who could expect short shrift if taken prisoner. There was no regular system of exchange for redeeming them, such as existed in the case of Frenchmen. Benjamin Franklin, the American minister at the court of Versailles, became so concerned about this that he conceived the idea of backing privateering voyages whose chief purpose would be to take prisoners who could afterwards be exchanged for Americans. Unfortunately the scheme did not work as well as he had hoped.

The outbreak of the French Revolutionary War immediately enabled French privateers to do much damage to British shipping. In the first phase—the years 1793–7—the French took 2,266 ships, and the English took only 375. Among the French exploits of this period were the taking of most of the Jamaican fleet in 1795, and the breaking up of the Newfoundland fisheries. The privateer responsible for decimating the fleet from Jamaica was one Moultson, an American sailing under French colors. Many of the leading French corsairs of the period achieved their successes with tiny vessels. The Boulogne corsair Jean-Jacques Fourmentin, Baron de Bucaille, made his debut in 1795 by capturing a large schooner when using a sloop that had only four men in it, his three brothers and himself. From that date until 1814 he commanded eleven different corsairs and took at least 100 English ships. Another man with a preference for small rather than large craft was the Bayonnais Etienne Pellot, who had made his reputation initially in the American War of Independence. He considered that a boat mounting no more than eight guns, and with a crew of about forty, offered a greater possibility of profit for a good deal less risk than something larger and more impressive. In one cruise with a sloop of this size he took seventeen prizes. Because of his methods he was often captured—five times altogether—but showed a remarkably philosophical attitude about it, combined with an equally remarkable skill in escaping. He survived his adventures, and lived on till 1856, the year in which the Declaration of Paris was signed that officially abolished privateering.

Control of privateers naturally became laxer the further their bases were from the home country. The West Indies began to move toward a state of anarchy after the slave-revolt in Haiti. One consequence of this was that Point-à-Pitre, the capital of Guadeloupe, became the headquarters of "revolutionary" piracy under the leadership of Victor Hugues, a Marseillais who had once had a business in Port-au-Prince. At one stage he even declared war on the United States on his own initiative, accusing the Americans of supplying arms and ships to the English. "We shall have to remind this treacherous nation," he said, "that but for us, who squandered our blood and our money to give them their independence, George Washington would have been hanged as a traitor." In 1798 Congress was forced to retaliate by declaring war on France in American waters. Hugues's captains were a mixed batch—they included Antonio Fuët of Narbonne, who became a legendary figure when, lacking grapeshot, he bombarded a Portuguese ship with guns loaded with gold coins. His contemporaries christened him Captain Moëda (Moidore) because of this exploit.

The most famous privateering headquarters of the Revolutionary and Napoleonic period was, however, the island of Mauritius, together with its

A view of St. Malo by Garneray, Surcouf's companion on his adventures.
VICTORIA AND ALBERT MUSEUM

neighbor, the island of Bourbon. The decree announcing war between England and France was signed on February 8, 1793, and did not reach Bourbon until June 11. Yet in less than fifteen days, thirteen ships had already been armed and sent out as corsairs. The most famous of the French Indian Ocean corsairs, and perhaps the most daring privateer who ever existed, was Robert Surcouf of St. Malo. Surcouf arrived in Mauritius after early experience in the slave trade, which had been forbidden by the Revolutionary Convention. From the moment war was declared he was determined to get into the privateering game, but only succeeded in making his first cruise in 1795, in a small brig called the *Emilie*, with three guns and only forty men. Even then he left his starting-point of Réunion officially labeled as a trader, since the governor there had refused him letters of marque. Surcouf increased his crew in the Seychelles, and proceeded to make in leisurely fashion for the mouth of the Hooghly. His first prize was a three-master laden with wood. This was followed by two rice ships and a pilot-brig, to which he transferred himself, naming it the *Cartier*. In the *Cartier*, with a crew reduced to nineteen men, he managed to take the 800-ton Indiaman *Triton*, which was armed with twenty-six guns and had 150 men aboard. He arrived back in Mauritius to find that, since he had no letters of marque, his prizes had been adjudged to the French

An anonymous portrait of Robert Surcouf.
MUSÉE DE ST. MALO

230

Robert Surcouf, "perhaps the most daring privateer who ever existed."
BIBLIOTHEQUE NATIONALE

government, and that he himself was to get nothing. He was forced to carry the case to France to get the decision reversed. If the taking of a large Indiaman seemed an almost impossible feat, Surcouf was nevertheless able to repeat it on a later cruise. His victim this time was the *Kent*, a ship with no less than 437 soldiers aboard, in addition to her crew, since she was carrying as well as her own complement the men who had been aboard a ship called the *Queen* which had been lost in a fire. Such a loss naturally caused an immense stir in Calcutta, whither the *Kent* had been bound. William Hickey records in his *Memoirs* that most of those who made the assault were "intoxicated, according to the custom of Frenchmen when being about to proceed upon some desperate service," and that Surcouf himself was in the dress of a common seaman so as not to be recognized and picked off. But he adds that the privateer "behaved with the tenderest humanity to the wounded and with the utmost liberality to the British prisoners in general, especially the ladies, whom he treated with every possible degree of respect and generosity." The painter Louis Garneray sailed with Surcouf on the cruise during which the *Kent* was captured, and

231

he gives a vivid picture of the man: "His manners were frank and easy; but original enough to make one have to study his nature to understand his genius." Garneray also tells the story of an Englishman whom Surcouf had captured, who said to him that the French only fought for profit, while the English fought for honor and glory. Surcouf replied: "That only proves that each of us fights to acquire something that he does not possess." However, he was practical enough in managing his affairs to be able to retire to St. Malo with a considerable fortune.

Many other corsairs were operating out of Mauritius at the same time as Surcouf. One of the most successful, until he was captured by the English frigate *Concord* in 1804, was François Le Même. In one cruise in his ship *La Fortune* he took no less than twelve prizes, worth more than a million francs. The islanders became heavily dependent on what the privateers brought in, not only for wealth but also for basic foodstuffs. The two rice ships which Surcouf took in 1795 had relieved a food shortage which was beginning to become serious. In the circumstances, the authorities often tended to overlook the strict letter of the maritime law, especially when confronted with a personality as abrasive as that of Surcouf himself. He, like all the other privateer captains using the port, was forced to take good men where he could find them, and there was great rivalry for the best seamen. Surcouf's crews were of extremely mixed nationality (Hickey is not correct in calling them simply French), and even included Englishmen.

The irregularity of the privateers' proceedings was bound to worry some people, and it worried no one more than the British naval authorities. Lord Nelson had a particular dislike for those on his own side. In 1801 he wrote:

> Respecting privateers I own that I am decidedly of the opinion that with few exceptions they are a disgrace to our country; and it would be truly honourable never to permit them after this war. Such horrible robberies have been committed by those in all parts of the world, that it is really a disgrace to the country which tolerates them.

Surprisingly enough, one of the deputies to the French National Assembly had, in 1792, proposed that privateering be abolished. Benjamin Franklin, despite his experiments with privateers in the American War, had long been opposed to them, and wrote of "this odious usage of privateers, ancient relic of piracy." His influence may have had something to do with the proposal, which was nevertheless rejected on grounds of impracticality.

If the upheaval which was shaking Europe meant an immense growth of

An early nineteenth-century West Indiaman. French privateers seriously threatened trade with the West Indies in the Napoleonic Wars.
SCIENCE MUSEUM

privateering, some of it of dubious legality even by the lax standards of the time, it also meant the return of piracy, especially in the Americas. The most interesting pirate of the late period, and the one who possesses the most complex and intriguing history, is Jean Lafitte. Lafitte told a tangled tale about his own origins, most of which seems to have been untrue. He claimed to be French. By his own account he was born in Bordeaux, and had emigrated to Santo Domingo with his parents. In fact, he was born in Port-au-Prince, the son of a Frenchman who had married a Spanish Jewess. His date of birth seems to have been 1782. He himself married at eighteen, but his wife died soon afterwards of puerperal fever, after giving birth to a daughter. She and her husband were at sea at the time, but her death was not due to ill-treatment by Spanish privateers, as Lafitte afterwards claimed.

Lafitte's public career began with his appearance in New Orleans in 1804, in company with his brother Pierre. Pierre was the captain of a small privateer, equipped with letters of marque against the English. Accompanying Pierre's vessel, *La Soeur Chérie*, were two merchantmen, with Jean in charge of one of them. From the first the American authorities were suspicious, but they did not realize that the brothers were pirates until they had got clean away. Instead, they thought Pierre was an arms smuggler. In fact, the merchantmen were American prizes which the brothers had impudently brought to an American harbor.

Despite this unpromising beginning they managed to settle in New Orleans the next year as the proprietors of a smithy. They also began to deal in contraband slaves, until in 1806 they legalized to some extent their position by asking for an official license as slave-dealers, which they duly received. It is uncertain how soon they turned pirate again, but they were certainly quickly established as smugglers. From 1807 a community of smugglers began to grow up on the island of Barataria, at the mouth of a bay which communicated by a series of lakes and bayous with the city of New Orleans itself. Jean Lafitte became the chief of these men, and left his brother to manage their joint business affairs in town. In order to provide some cover for what he was doing, Jean got privateering commissions from the anti-Spanish authorities in Cartagena. Both brothers appeared regularly in good society in New Orleans, and Pierre married the daughter of a well-known local miniature-painter, a man who also happened to come from Santo Domingo.

By 1812 the scale of the Lafittes' operations had become so extensive that the authorities could not ignore what they were doing any longer, and both Jean and his brother were arrested for contraband activity. They were released on bail after a fortnight's imprisonment. When they were summoned to appear again it was found they had vanished. They had in fact simply decided to ignore the legal machinery of Louisiana, and had retired to their stronghold at Barataria. The community there continued to flourish. During a six-month period in 1814 probably no less than a million dollars' worth of pirated and contraband goods were brought there. Though there were no racial distinctions among the islanders, who may have numbered as many as a thousand, and though the form of government practiced there was "highly communistic," much of the trade continued to be in slaves. At least a tenth of the population of New Orleans was by this time involved in one way or another with the Lafittes, and the brothers' lines of communication with the city remained excellent. But the authorities were unforgiving, and in 1814 a New Orleans grand jury impeached Jean Lafitte for piracy and caught and imprisoned Pierre when the latter visited town.

A presumed portrait of Jean Lafitte (center) and his brother in a New Orleans tavern.
LOUISIANA STATE MUSEUM

235

This was the moment which the British, who had been at war with the United States since 1812, chose to approach Jean Lafitte for help in attacking New Orleans. The English envoys who arrived at the island were roughly treated by some of his subordinates, and he used this as an excuse to gain time. He sent to offer his services to the governor of Louisiana, and at the same moment his brother escaped from imprisonment. Heedless of the British menace, the Louisiana government decided to deal with Barataria first. On September 16 Commodore Patterson arrived with a naval force, took the island with little or no resistance, and recovered about 500,000 dollars worth of loot. Lafitte escaped, but some of his lieutenants were arrested. He nevertheless persisted with his offer to help repel a British invasion, and played a prominent part in the defence of New Orleans when the attack at last took place. After this the brothers found themselves free but virtually penniless and pursued by their creditors. They received a pardon from President Madison, but it soon became clear that nothing would be done to help them recover the goods they had lost at Barataria.

Jean Lafitte's reaction was to embark on another, and even more complex, series of adventures. He moved, after ordering some fast ships at Baltimore, to the island of Galveston off the coast of Texas. Galveston was not unoccupied. It was being used as a pirate base by the Frenchman Louis d'Avry, operating as a privateer with a commission from the republican government of Mexico. Lafitte managed to get rid of him and his force of 500 men by encouraging them all to go and help with the liberation of the mainland. He then assembled the remaining citizens of the place (to the number of about forty) and made them swear allegiance to the free republic of Mexico. The irony was that Lafitte was already employed as an agent, at an annual stipend of 18,000 dollars, by the Spanish government in Havana. He had been recruited by Père Antoine, curé of the cathedral of St. Louis at New Orleans, who was a Spanish spy, and had himself gone to Havana in February 1817 to report to the authorities there after a preliminary mission in Texas. What interested the Spanish was the possibility of reducing piracy in the Gulf of Mexico.

Instead, Lafitte proceeded to fortify Galveston, and to turn it into another Barataria. He built himself a comfortable house which he painted red, and exercised strict rule over those who had come to join him. Bachelors were separated from married men, and Lafitte threatened to hang any man who insulted a woman. The financial structure was as "communistic" as it had been earlier. The security of the base depended not only on the strength of the fortifications, and the good order that was kept, but on the peculiar legal position. If the Spanish authorities persuaded the United States (the only power equipped to do so) to mount a punitive expedition against the stronghold, this was tantamount to recognizing American sovereignty over Texas.

The magnitude of the problem the American authorities faced can be gauged from a statement made by the Collector of Customs at New Orleans:

> On the part of these pirates we have to contend with, we behold an extended and organized system of enterprise, of ingenuity, of indefatigability, and of audacity, favored by a variety of local advantages, and supported by force of arms; and unless they be met by corresponding species of resistance, the results of the contest are of very simple calculation.

Though the Americans demanded Lafitte's departure, the Mexicans made him official governor of Galveston, and (in his capacity as their agent) Lafitte had the audacity to demand that the Spanish in Havana should do the same. The situation might have continued for a long time had not the Galveston settlement been wrecked by a hurricane in the summer of 1818. Lafitte sold all the Negroes to keep the settlement alive, including some perhaps whom he already counted as freed, but it never recovered its former prosperity. By May 1821 he was willing to go of his own free will. He is described by an eyewitness to his departure, a young American officer, as being at this time:

> A stout, rather gentlemanly personage, some five feet ten inches in height, dressed very simply in a foraging cap and blue frock-coat of a most villainous fit; his complexion, like most Creoles, olive; his countenance full, mild and rather impassive, but for a small black eye, which now and then, as he grew animated, would flash in a way which impressed me with a notion that *Il Capitano* might be, when roused, a very ugly customer.

When Lafitte left Galveston, he was considered until very recently to have vanished from history, borne away by his "long black, clipper-built schooner, with low black hull and lofty fishing-rods of masts, the very beau-ideal of a pirate." It was considered that he might have died soon afterwards in southern Mexico. New evidence, on the other hand, suggests that by 1832 Lafitte was a respected citizen of Charleston, South Carolina, going under the name John Lafflin, and with business interests as a merchant and ship-owner. He married the daughter of Edward Mortimore, his business partner (both bride and father-in-law seem to have

237

been well aware of his true identity), and after the birth of a son the couple moved inland to Saint Louis.

In 1847 Lafitte-Lafflin went to Europe, going first to London, where he attended several revolutionary meetings; then going to Holland, Switzerland, Paris and Brussels. In the course of his travels he met Marx and Engels, and it seems possible that it was he who put up the money for the printing of the *Communist Manifesto*. When he returned to America, he brought specimens of Marx's and Engels's work with him, and these were passed through his partner and father-in-law Mortimore to Abraham Lincoln, then serving his single term as a Congressman. Lafitte, perhaps from a keen awareness of his own past, was unwilling to meet the politician. "I have no desire to show myself," he wrote to Mortimore, "nor to take anything whatsoever myself to Mr. Lincoln." On his return to the United States, Lafitte and his wife moved still further upriver, to Alton, Illinois, at the confluence of the Mississippi and the Missouri; and it was at this place that he died in 1854.

Lafitte's story has been told in detail for several reasons. First, though he was already the subject of romantic fictions in his own lifetime—he is the hero, for example of J. H. Ingraham's novel *The Pirate of the Gulf*, published in 1837—the true facts of his career have remained little known. It was a recent biographer who discovered the details of the payments made to him by the Spanish authorities, which were still preserved in the Havana archives, and who also unearthed the story of what became of Lafitte after he left Galveston. Secondly, he of all pirates best seems to fit the image of the corsair as leveler and pioneer democrat which had been propagated by many authors, from Defoe's time onward. When we consider Lafitte in comparison to equally famous predecessors such as Morgan, Blackbeard and Bartholomew Roberts, we see that he is a man who already belongs to a different epoch, no more immune than any of his contemporaries to the revolutionary currents of his time, and even, perhaps, endowed with a kind of Byronism which earlier pirates acquired only in retrospect.

The immense political and social upheaval brought about by the Revolutionary and Napoleonic Wars left predictable shock-waves behind it when those wars at last came to an end. Thousands of privateersmen were thrown out of employment by the conclusion of a European peace, and some were not slow to find a new occupation as pirates. The situation thus resembled those which had come about when James I's peace policy put an end to Elizabethan privateering, and when the conflicts of the seventeenth century had been resolved by the Peace of Utrecht. A new

The French privateer Courageuse *pursuing the English ship* Outram, *1797.*
MUSÉE DE LA MARINE

factor, however, was the continuation of the European war in a series of struggles for national independence, most conspicuously in Greece and in Central and South America. Information from the files of the New York Shipping and Commercial list shows that in the years 1824–32 the two black spots for piracy were off the shores of Central America and Cuba, and in the Greek archipelago.

In fact, the struggle for Greek freedom was largely led by men who had previously been outlaws, and in the Greece of the time the same word was in use to mean either a thief or a patriot. Acts of piracy were sometimes committed under the direct orders of the Greek provisional government. Among the leading corsairs were the Klepht Zakarios, who operated on the coast of Aegina and off Salamis; the Maniots and Epirots; and Jean Capsi of Melos, who at one time wrested this island entirely from the

239

Turks. The chief base of all, however, was Grabusa on the south coast of Crete, a nest of pirates who preyed on all the shipping passing through the Cerigo Channel and even raided as far west as Malta. The taking of Grabusa by the British navy brought about a very marked diminution of piracy in the Levant.

The situation in the Spanish Indies was even more serious, and continued to give ship-owners anxiety for a much longer period. In the late eighteenth century the Spanish Indies had experienced a very real economic revival; and to outside observers they then seemed stable, prosperous and orderly. Spanish involvement in the Napoleonic Wars brought this happy condition of affairs to an end. The new American republics, being unprovided with any kind of naval force, resorted to issuing privateering commissions which were frequently abused—Lafitte is a case in point. From 1815 onward corsairs based upon Buenos Aires were devastating Spanish commerce in the Caribbean. But in the period 1815–21 they ranged much further than this, making captures off Cape St. Vincent and cruising at the entrance to the Straits of Gibraltar. They penetrated the Mediterranean, and even got as far as the Black Sea. Throughout the year 1818 Corunna was almost completely blockaded by them. The corsairs from New Granada, later to be the republic of Colombia, acted in much the same way until the capture of Cartagena by royalist forces disrupted privateering activity.

Those who took privateering commissions from the new Spanish republics were men of many nationalities, but it is probable that the majority were American, just as the majority of their vessels, especially in the early period of their activity, were American-built. A stock of suitable privateering ships was left over in the United States from the War of 1812. One ex-American privateer, originally called the *Regent*, was rebaptized the *Tupac-Amarú*; in 1817 this ship was responsible for the capture at the Canaries of the Philippine Island Company vessel the *Tritón*, perhaps the most valuable prize made by any corsair based on Buenos Aires. The *Tritón* was not taken easily: she had twenty-two guns, and put up a fight lasting two and a half hours. Twenty of her crew of eighty-five were killed.

Some remarkable voyages were made at this period by captains equipped with "patriot" letters of marque. One was led by Guillermo (otherwise William) Brown, who had been born in County Mayo in 1779, and who came to Buenos Aires in 1811. In 1815, as soon as privateering commissions began to be issued from Buenos Aires, he departed on a voyage round the Horn and up the coast of Chile, where it was hoped to contact the inhabitants and promote a *levée en masse*. For a period, he succeeded in bringing about the cessation of trade between Lima and Guayaquil, and also completely cut lines of communication with Spain.

Hippolyte Bouchard, who had previously accompanied Brown as far as the Galapagos, was a French corsair who in July 1817 left the River Plate on an expedition which took him most of the way round the world. He sailed via the Cape of Good Hope, the Indian Ocean, Madagascar, Java and Malaya to trouble Spanish commerce in the Philippines. Off Manila he took sixteen small prizes, and in the Straits of Macassar he beat off a squadron of five Malayan pirate prahus, who had mistaken his vessel for a merchant ship. From the Philippines he went to Hawaii, where he was able to retake possession of a mutinous corsair ship he happened to find there. He then went via California, Mexico, Central America and the Galapagos to Valparaiso, where his voyage came to a disastrous conclusion, since he found himself accused of piracy and was detained by Admiral Cochrane as the representative of the Chilean authorities. From this accusation he was finally cleared by a tribunal. He never returned to Buenos Aires, but finished up as the commander of the Peruvian fleet.

By 1819 it had become difficult to tell the difference between a "patriot" and a pirate, and the American government was beginning to be alarmed. More than forty-four ships flying the United States flag were looted or captured in the West Indies in this year, in spite of the fact that the privateers often used American ports as their bases. Philadelphia, Baltimore and New Orleans were especially favored, and Baltimore captains were numerous. It was estimated, indeed, that as many as 3,500 Americans were now engaged in the privateering business. Unsigned letters of marque issued by many of the new republics were in circulation, and available to anyone at a price. The abuses of the privateers had become so flagrant that the Buenos Aires authorities realized that something had to be done about it, and on October 6, 1821, they issued a decree ordering that privateering under their flag should cease. It is perhaps no coincidence that this was the year in which Lafitte decided to abandon Galveston, since the attitude of the United States authorities was clearly hardening. In 1822 an act of Congress was passed giving an appropriation of 500,000 dollars to equip an expedition to wipe out the West Indian pirates. Commodore David Peter resigned his office as navy commissioner to take command of it, and it was he who organized what was dubbed the "Mosquito Fleet," which consisted of vessels suitable to the shallow waters of many Cuban harbors and bays. One of the vessels under his command was the *Sea Gull*, the U.S. Navy's second steamer.

To be taken by West Indian pirates at this period could certainly be an unpleasant experience. Captain Lincoln of the schooner *Exertion*, which was taken in 1821 off Cape Cruz reports that:

> It is impossible to give an account of the filthiness of this crew, and were it possible to would not be expedient. In their appearance they were terrific, wearing black whiskers and long beards, the receptacles of dirt and vermin. They used continually the most profane language; had frequent quarrels, and so great was their love of gambling that the captain would play cards with the meanest man on board.

Sometimes the pirates practiced cruelties worthy of Lolonnois and Low. One captain of a merchant ship, taken in the early 1820s, first had both his arms cut off at the elbows, and was then placed on a bed of oakum soaked with turpentine and had his mouth filled with the same material. After this he was set on fire.

The information we have about the pirates themselves is largely legendary—more so than that supplied by Exquemelin and Defoe about earlier freebooters in the West Indies. One called Domingo Mugnoz was said to have started life as a priest, and to have fallen in love, when serving at Quito, with a woman called Wanda, of great beauty but undetermined origin, whom her husband had brought back from the United States. After many adventures Mugnoz, who had turned pirate in the wake of Bolivar's victories, took Wanda prisoner, and kept her, half-slave, half-mistress, aboard his schooner *Emmanuel*, where the cabin was fitted with an altar for voodoo ceremonies.

One pirate about whom we do possess some solid facts is Benito de Soto, though he is often confused with his near-namesakes Benito Bonito and Bernando de Soto (the latter was the mate of the pirate ship *Panda*, and his fate will be described in a moment). Benito de Soto was born in Corunna of Portuguese parents, and in November 1827 shipped in the large brigantine *Defensor de Pedro* for the coast of Africa, where she was to load slaves. He seized the ship when the captain was absent, and killed his confederate the mate when the latter and the rest of the crew were drunk. The ship was renamed the *Black Joke*, and set out on a pirate cruise in the course of which Benito de Soto took the Indiaman *Morning Star* but failed in his attempt to scuttle her, a fact which brought his activities to the notice of the authorities. Later, having wrecked the *Black Joke* on the coast of Spain, and after narrowly missing arrest in Cadiz, where some of his crew were apprehended, he went to Gibraltar. There he was recognized by some invalid soldiers who had been passengers on the *Morning Star*, and when his quarters were searched items taken from the ship were found in his

The French privateer Bayonnaise *taking the English ship* Ambuscade, *1798. By Antoine Roux.*
MUSÉE DE LA MARINE

possession. He was subsequently tried before the Governor of Gibraltar, and executed, going to his death with an insouciance which amazed the spectators.

There are also few first-hand accounts of the pirate life from this epoch. One, disingenuous and clearly ghosted, is Aaron Smith's *The Atrocities of the Pirates*, published in London in 1824. The preceding year Smith had been an officer (he claimed that he was "forced" by his companions) aboard a ship which piratically attacked the British vessels *Vittoria* and *Industry* in the West Indies. Though he succeeded in saving his neck, Smith's reputation was heavily damaged, and he wrote the book to defend himself. He is heard of again, much later, in 1849, when he put up a vigorous defence of Rajah Brooke's extermination of the Borneo pirates.

The vigorous efforts made by three governments, those of the United States, Great Britain and Spain, to suppress piracy in the West Indies were eventually effective, and the affair of the brig *Mexican* was one of the last to attract widespread attention. The *Mexican* sailed for Rio de Janeiro from Salem on August 29, 1832, with 20,000 dollars in specie concealed aboard her. She was taken by the schooner *Panda* on September 20, her crew was driven below and she was then set on fire. Her men managed to escape from their confinement and put out the blaze, and were thus able to give information about what had happened to them. Subsequently the *Panda*, who was also a slaver (the roles of pirate and slaver were interchangeable at this time) was taken by a British brig-of-war off the West African coast, and her crew were sent for trial. Her mate, Bernardo de Soto, was pardoned by President Jackson and survived for many years. At the end of his life he was the captain of a steamer operating between Havana and Matanzas.

Some pirate activity was still taking place off the Cape of Good Hope as late as the early 1850s, and the pirate ships of this period often sailed under the Spanish flag, and seem in general to have been men of the same type as those who harassed West Indian shipping a little earlier. They too had close connections with the illicit slave trade.

Privateering, after an existence of more than 600 years, was at last brought officially to an end by the Declaration of Paris, signed in 1856. One of the last privateers was Giuseppe Garibaldi who, in what is perhaps the least-known episode of his career, served aboard the ship *Mazzini* in 1837–8, with a commission from the rebellious province (calling itself a "republic") of Rio Grande when the latter rose against the central Brazilian authority. The seven countries who signed the original declaration were soon joined by others, but they did not of course include the Confederate States in the American Civil War. These at once began to issue letters of marque, and Confederate privateers had considerable success before the blockade on their home ports was tightened. Their activity reached a peak in the months of July and August 1861, and during this period they took about sixty ships and caused a panic amongst northern ship-owners. President Lincoln threatened to treat the Confederate privateers as pirates, but this proposition was resisted by the neutral powers, and in the end the crews, if captured, were treated as ordinary prisoners of war.

One feature of the last age of piracy was the tendency of the pirates to massacre the crews of any vessels they took, so as to leave no evidence of their crime, since this was now so much more seriously regarded by the authorities. This is a feature we could expect to see repeated, if piracy were ever to revive. On October 31, 1976, the English newspaper the *Sunday Express* carried a report from a correspondent in New York which began: "American authorities are convinced that 200 people, reported missing at sea during the past two years, were coldly murdered—victims of a new upsurge of vicious piracy which has been steadily increasing in Caribbean waters." A Congressional sub-committee, investigating a wave of yacht-jacking, came to the conclusion that it was connected with drug-running, and that the yachts were seized to provide the constant change of boats which the drug-runners needed to avoid detection. It is significant that piracy, however brutal, now confines itself to small craft. What put an end, in its classic form, to a crime which had existed since history began, was chiefly the coming of steam. Mechanical propulsion, which meant that the men who traveled the oceans were no longer at the mercy of the winds, also removed much of the danger they had hitherto run from the man who made the wind his ally, and cast himself upon its mercy as the price of an irregular and ferocious independence.

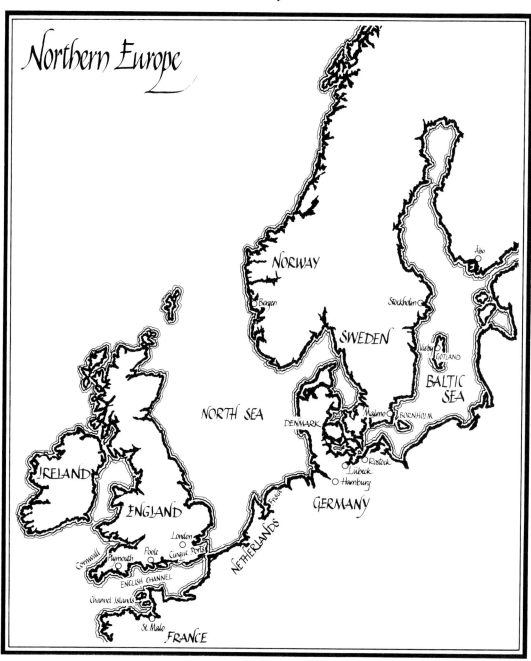

Northern Europe

NORWAY

Bergen

SWEDEN

Stockholm

Åbo

Visby GOTLAND

BALTIC SEA

NORTH SEA

IRELAND

ENGLAND

London

DENMARK

Malmo

BORNHOLM

Rostock

Lübeck

Hamburg

GERMANY

Cornwall Plymouth Poole Cinque Ports

NETHERLANDS

Frisia

ENGLISH CHANNEL

Channel Islands

St Malo FRANCE

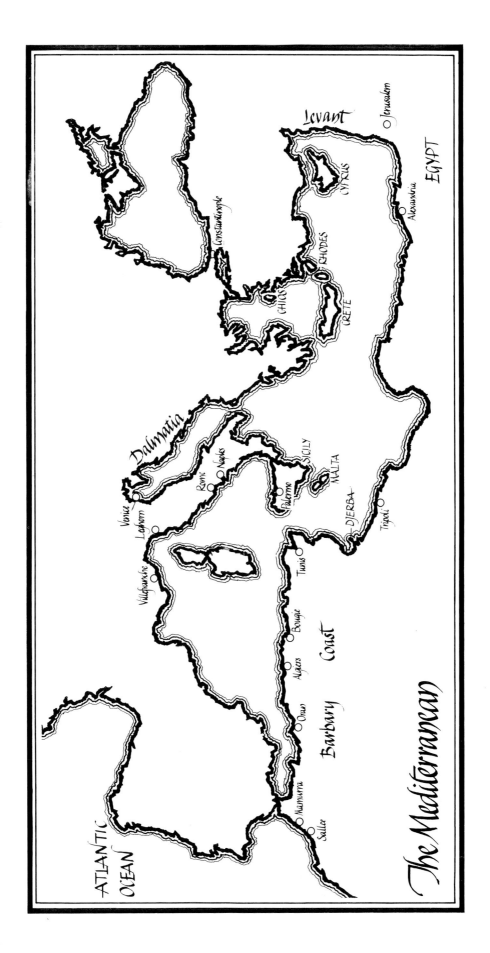

ATLANTIC OCEAN

Levant

Jerusalem

CYPRUS

EGYPT

Alexandria

Constantinople

RHODES

CHIOS

CRETE

Dalmatia

Venice

Leghorn

Rome

Naples

Palermo

SICILY

MALTA

DJERBA

Tripoli

Vilafranche

Tunis

Bougie

Algiers

Barbary Coast

Oran

Mamurra

Sallee

The Mediterranean

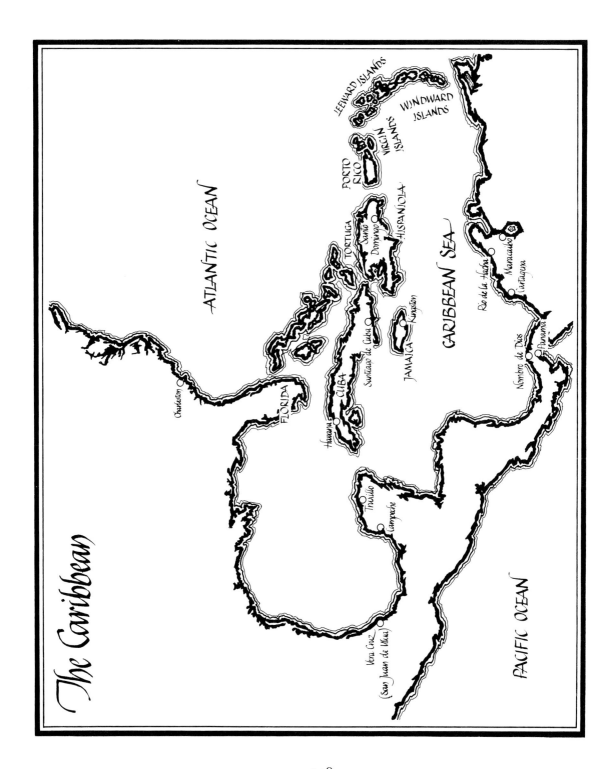

The Caribbean

ATLANTIC OCEAN

LEEWARD ISLANDS

WINDWARD ISLANDS

VIRGIN ISLANDS

PORTO RICO

TORTUGA

HISPANIOLA

Santo Domingo

CARIBBEAN SEA

Rio de la Hacha

Maracaibo

Cartagena

Santiago de Cuba

Kingston

JAMAICA

Nombre de Dios

Panama

FLORIDA

Charleston

CUBA

Havana

Trujillo

Campeche

Vera Cruz
(San Juan de Ulua)

PACIFIC OCEAN

Bibliography

Adams, P. G., *Travellers and Travel-Liars, 1660–1800*, Berkeley and Los Angeles, 1962.

Allen, Merritt Parmelee, *Sir Henry Morgan, Buccaneer*, New York and London, 1931.

Andrews, K. R. (ed.), "The Last Voyage of Drake and Hawkins," Hakluyt Society, 2nd series, vol. 142, Cambridge, 1972.

———, "English Privateering Voyages to the West Indies, 1588–1595," Hakluyt Society, 2nd series, vol. III, Cambridge, 1959.

———, *Drake's Voyages: A Re-assessment of their place in Elizabethan maritime expansion*, London, 1967.

———, *Elizabethan Privateering*, Cambridge, 1964.

Anglo-Saxon Chronicle, trans. and intro. by G. N. Garmonsway, London and New York, 1953.

Archenholz, J. W. von, *The History of the Pirates, Freebooters and Buccaneers of America*, London, 1807.

Armand, Jean, *Voyages d'Afrique*, Paris, 1631.

Austen, H. C. M., *Sea Fights and Corsairs of the Indian Ocean*, Port Louis, Mauritius, 1934.

Ayres, P., *Voyages and Adventures of Captain B. Sharp*, London, 1684.

Barker, Andrew, *A True and Certain Report*, London, 1609.

Barlow, Edward, ed. Basil Lubbock, *Journal*, London, 1924.

Barnard, John, *History of the Strange Adventures and Signal Deliverances of Mr Philip Ashton*, Boston, 1735.

Bartlett, H. M., *The Pirates of Trucial Oman*, London, 1966.

Bealer, Lewis Winkler, *Los Corsarios de Buenos Aires*, Buenos Aires, 1937.

Belgrave, Sir Charles, *The Pirate Coast*, London, 1966.

Bell, Herbert Clifford, and D. W. Parker, *Guide to West Indian Archive Materials*, Washington, 1926.

Besson, M., *Les Frères de la côte*, Paris, 1928.

Biddulph, Colonel J., *The Pirates of Malabar*, London, 1907.

Blond, Georges, *Histoire de la flibuste*, Paris, 1969.

Bonner, W. H., *Pirate Laureate*, New Brunswick, 1947.

———, *Captain William Dampier*, Stanford, California, 1934.

Bourdeille de Brantôme, *Les Vies des Hommes Illustres*, Leyden, 1699.

Bourdon, Léon, *Francisco Dias Mimoso*, Lisbon, 1956.

Bradlee, F. B. C., *Piracy in the West Indies and its Suppression*, Salem, Mass., 1923.

Breton, Raymond, *Les Caraïbes—La Guadeloupe, 1635–1656*, Paris, 1929.

Bridenbaugh, Carl and Roberta, *No Peace Beyond the Line: The English in the Caribbean, 1624–1690*, New York, 1972.

Brøndsted, Johannes, *The Vikings*, 2nd ed., Harmondsworth and Baltimore, 1973.

Burney, James, *History of the Buccaneers of America*, London, 1949.

Calendars of State Papers, Colonial, America and West Indies.

Calendars of State Papers, Venetian.

Candido, Salvatore, *Giuseppe Garibaldi, corsario riograndense*, Rome, 1964.

Castro y Bravo, Frederico de, *Las Nãos Españolas en la carrera de las Indias*, Madrid, 1927.

Chapelle, H. I., *The History of American Sailing Ships*, London, 1936.

Chapin, H. M., *Privateering in King George's War, 1729–1748*, Providence, R.I., 1928.

———, *Bermuda Privateers, 1739–1748*, Hamilton, Bermuda, 1923.

———, *Bermuda Privateers, 1625–1703*, Hamilton, Bermuda, 1925.

———, *Rhode Island Privateers in King George's War, 1740–1748*, Providence, R.I., 1926.

———, *Privateer Ships and Sailors*, Toulon, 1926.

Charlevoix, P. F. X. de, *Histoire de l'Ile Espagnole*, Paris, 1730.

Chaunu, H. and P., *Seville et l'Atlantique, 1504–1660*, 6 vols., Paris, 1955—.

Chetwood, William Rufus, *The Adventures of Captain Falconer*, London, 1720.

Clark, William Bell, *Ben Franklin's Privateers*, Baton Rouge, 1956.

Cleugh, James, *Prince Rupert*, London, 1934.

Coindreau, R., *Les Corsaires de Salé*, Paris, 1948.

Collis, Maurice, *The Grand Peregrination*, London, 1949.

Contreras, Alonso de, trans. Catherine Alison Phillips, *The Life . . . written by himself*, London, 1926.

Cooper, Gordon, *Treasure Trove, Pirates' Gold*, London, 1951.

Cotton, Sir Evan, *East Indiamen*, London, 1949.

Course, Alfred George, *A Seventeenth-Century Mariner*, London, 1965.

———, *Pirates of the Western Seas*, London, 1969.

Crouse, Nellis M., *French Pioneers in the West Indies, 1624–1664*, New York, 1940.

———, *The French Struggle for the West Indies, 1665–1713*, New York, 1943.

Cruikshank, E. A., *The Life of Sir Henry Morgan*, Toronto, 1935.

Currey, E. Hamilton, *Sea-Wolves of the Mediterranean*, London, 1910.

Dahlgren, *Les Relations commerciales et maritimes entre France et les côtes de l'Océan Pacifique*, Paris, 1909.

Dalton, Sir Cornelius N., *The Real Captain Kidd*, London, 1911.

Dampier, William, *Voyages Round the World*, London, 1729.

Dan, Pierre, *Histoire de Barbarie et de ses corsaires*, Paris, 1649.

D'Aranda, Emanuel, *Relation de la captivité et liberté du Sieur Emanuel d'Aranda, jadis esclave à Alger*, Brussels, 1662.

D'Arvieux, Chevalier Laurent, *Mémoires*, Paris, 1735.

Davidson-Houston, J. V., *The Piracy of the Nauchang*, London, 1961.

Dearden, Seaton, *A Nest of Corsairs*, London, 1976.

Defoe, Daniel, *The King of the Pirates and The Adventures of Captain John Gow* (Collected Works, Vol. 16), Cambridge, 1903.

———, *Captain Singleton* (Collected Works, Vol. 6), Cambridge, 1903.

———, *The Four Voyages of Capt. George Roberts . . . written by himself*, London, 1726.

———, (under pseudonynm "Captain Charles Johnson"), ed. Arthur L. Hayward, *A General History . . . of the most notorious pirates*, London, 1955.

Dekker, Thomas, *If this be not a Good Play, the Devil is in it*, London, 1612.

De Montmorency, Hervey, *On the Track of a Treasure*, London, 1904.

Deschamps, H. J., *Pirates et Flibustiers*, Paris, 1952.

———, *Les pirates à Madagascar*, 2nd ed., Paris, 1972.

Desmay, L., *Relation nouvelle et particulière du voyage des R.R.P.P. de la Mercy au Royaume de Fez*, Paris, 1682.

Dow, G. F. and J. H. Edwards, *The Pirates of the New England Coast, 1630–1730*, Salem, Mass., 1923.

Downing, Clement, *Compendious History of the Indian Wars*, London, 1737.

Driscoll, C. B., *Doubloons*, London, 1931.

Drury, Robert, *Journal*, London, 1729 (this book is often attributed to Defoe).

Duffy, James, *Shipwreck and Empire*, Cambridge, Mass., 1955.

Duguay-Trouin, ed. Henri Malo, *Sa Vie, écrite de sa main*, Paris, 1922.

Eagles, John, *The Journal of Llewellyn Penrose*, London, 1815.

Earle, Peter, *Corsairs of Malta and Barbary*, London and New York, 1970.

Ewen, Cecil L'Estrange, *The Golden Chalice*, Paignton, 1939.

———, *Captain John Ward*, Paignton, 1939.

Exquemelin, A. O., *The Buccaneers of America*, London, 1893.

Fernández Duro, Cesáreo, *Armada Espanola*, Vols. I to IX, Madrid, 1895–1903.

Filliot, J. M., *Pirates et corsaires dans l'Océan Indien*, Tanarive, 1971.

Fisher, Sir Godfrey, *Barbary Legend: War, Trade and Piracy in North Africa, 1415–1830*, London and New York, 1957.

Forester, C. S., *The Barbary Pirates*, London, 1956; New York, 1970.

Sir William Foster, ed., *The Voyages of Sir James Lancaster to Brazil and the East Indies, 1591–1603* (Hakluyt Society, 2nd series, volume 85), London, 1940.

Frézier, A. F., *Voyage to the South Sea*, London, 1717.

Fuller, B. and A. R. Melville, *Pirate Harbours and their Secrets*, London, 1935.

Funnell, William, *A Voyage Round the World*, London, 1707.

Gage, Thomas, *A New Survey of the West Indies*, London, 1648.

Garmonsway, G. N., *Canute and His Empire*, London, 1963.

Garneray, Louis, *Voyages, aventures et combats*, Paris, 1864(?).

Gebhardt, Victor, *Historia General de Espana y sus Indias*, Madrid, 1863–4.

Gerhard, Peter, *Pirates on the West Coast of New Spain*, Glendale, Calif., 1960.

Glasspole, R., *Mr. Glasspoole and the Chinese Pirates*, London, 1935.

Gordon Cooper, C., *Isles of Romance and Mystery*, London, 1949.

The Grand Pyrate, or the life and death of George Cusack, London, 1676.

Grandidier, Alfred and Guillaume, eds., *Collection des ouvrages anciens concernant Madagascar*, vols. III and V, Paris 1905, 1907.

Guarnieri, G., *I Cavalieri di Santo Stefano nella storia della Marine italiana (1562–1859)*, Pisa, 1960.

Guglielmotti, A., *La Guerra dei Pirati e la Marina Pontifica, 1500–1560*, Florence, 1895.

Hannay, David, *The Sea Trader*, London, 1912.

Haring, C. H., *The Buccaneers in the West Indies in the Seventeenth Century*, London, 1910.

———, *Trade and Navigation between Spain and the Indies in the Time of the Hapsburgs*, Cambridge, Mass., 1918.

Hawkins, Sir Richard, *The Observations*, London, 1622.

Hickey, William, *Memoirs*, London, 1925.

Hill, S. C., *Notes on Piracy in Eastern Waters*, Bombay, 1923.

Hinrichs, D. M., *The Fateful Voyage of Captain Kidd*, New York, 1955.

Hoppé, Emil Otto, *Pirates, Buccaneers and Gentlemen Adventurers*, New York and London, 1972.

Horner, Dave, *The Treasure Galleons*, New York, 1971; London, 1974.

Hughson, S. C., *The Carolina Pirates*, Baltimore, 1882.

Inchaustegui Cabral, J. M., *La gran expedición ingleses*, Mexico, 1958.

Jayne, K. G., *Vasco da Gama and His Successors*, London, 1970.

Johnson, Charles, *The Successful Pyrate*, London, 1713.

Jones, Charles G. P., *Piracy in the Levant, 1827–8* (Publications of the Naval Records Society, vol. 72), London, 1934.

Jonson, W. Branch, *Wolves of the Channel*, London, 1931.

Kelly, J., *A Full Discovery of all the Robberies of J. Kelly, with an Account of his Joining with Captain Kidd*, London, 1700.

Kemp, P. K. and Christopher Lloyd, *The Brethren of the Coast*, London, 1960.

Keppel, Capt. the Hon. Henry, *The Expedition to Borneo of H.M.S. "Dido,"* London, 1846.

Kidd, William, *A Full Account of the Proceedings*, London, 1701.

Knight, E. F., *The Cruise of the "Alerte,"* London, 1890.

Labat, Père Jean-Baptiste, *Memoirs 1693–1705*, London, 1970.

La Villestreux, A. E. E. de, *Deux Corsaires Malouins*, St. Malo, 1929.

Lediard, Thomas, *The Naval History of England*, London, 1735.

Le Golif, Louis, *Memoirs of a Buccaneer*, London, 1954.

Lepotier, Adolphe-Auguste-Marie, *Les Corsaires du Sud*, Paris, 1936.

Lewis, Michael, *The Hawkins Dynasty*, London, 1969.

Lilius, A. E., *I Sailed with Chinese Pirates*, London, 1930.

Lithgow, William, *The Rare Adventures*, 2nd ed., London, 1632.

Little, G. A., *The Ouzel Galley*, revised ed., Dublin, 1953.

Lloyd, Christopher, *Sir Francis Drake*, London, 1957; Mystic, Conn., 1966.

———, *William Dampier*, London, 1966; Hamden, Conn., 1967.

Lockhart, J. G., *Strange Adventures of the Sea*, London, 1925.

Lorrain, Paul, *The Ordinary of Newgate, his account of the behaviour . . .*, London, 1701.

Loviot, F., *A Lady's Captivity*, London, 1858.

MacLiesh, Fleming, *Fabulous Voyage*, New York, 1963.

Mainwaring, G. E. and W. G., Perrin, *The Life and Works of Sir Henry Mainwaring* (Publications of the Naval Records Society, Vol. 54 etc.), London, 1920.

Malo, Henri, *Eustache le Moine*, Paris, 1893.

Markham, A. H., ed., *The Voyages and Works of John Davis the Navigator* (Hakluyt Society, 1st series, volume 59), London, 1880.

Marx, Robert, *Naufragios in aguas Mexicanas*, Mexico, 1971.

———, *Port Royal Rediscovered*, London, 1973.

———, *They Dared the Deep*, London, 1968.

———, *Pirate Port*, London, 1968.

Masefield, John, *On the Spanish Main*, 2nd ed., London, 1922.

Mégroz, R. L., *The Real Robinson Crusoe*, London, 1939.

Medina, José Toribio, *La Expedicion de Corso de Commodoro Guillermo Brown*, Buenos Aires, 1928.

Mendes Pinto, Fernão, trans. Henry Cogan, *The Peregrination*, London, 1653.

Merrien, Jean, *La course et la flibuste*, Lausanne, 1970.

Miller, Harry, *Pirates of the Far East*, London, 1970.

Mitchell, David, *Pirates*, London, 1976.

Montero y Vidal, José, *Historia de la pirateria malayo-mahometana en Mindanao, Jolo y Borneo*, Madrid, 1888.

Moore, John Robert, *Defoe in the Pillory*, Bloomington, Indiana, 1939.

Morales, Ernesto, *Historia de la Aventura*, Buenos Aires, 1942.

Morel, Anne, *La Guerre de corse à Saint-Malo*, Rennes, 1957.

Moüette, Germain, *Relation de la captivité dans les royaumes de Fez et Maroc*, Paris, 1683.

Muri, Ramsay, *A History of Liverpool*, London, 1906.

Naldoni-Centenari, *La Guerra di Corsa in America, 1500–1700*, Rome, 1935.

Nambiar, O., *The Kunjalis*, London and Calcutta, 1963.

National Maritime Museum, *Piracy and Privateering*, London, 1972.

Newton, A. P., *European Nations in the West Indies, 1493–1688*, London, 1933.

Nicoll, Allardyce, *A History of the English Drama*, vols. IV–VI, Cambridge, 1960.

Norman, C. B., *The Corsairs of France*, London, 1887.

Novak, M. E., *Economics and the Fiction of Daniel Defoe*, Berkeley and Los Angeles, 1962.

Nuttall, Zelia ed., *New Light on Drake: a Collection of Documents relating to his voyages of Circumnavigation, 1577–80* (Hakluyt Society, 2nd series, volume 34), London, 1914.

Ólafsson, Jón, *The Life of the Icelander Jón Ólafsson, Traveller to India, Written by Himself* (Hakluyt Society, 2nd series, volumes 67 and 68), London, 1932.

Oppenheim, Michael, *Naval Tracts of Sir William Monson* (Publications of the Naval Records Society, vol. 22), London, 1902–14.

Ormerod, Henry, *Piracy in the Ancient World*, Liverpool and London, 1924.

Pananti, Filippo, *Avventure e osservazioni sopra le coste di Barbaria*, Florence, 1817.

Pares, Richard, *Yankees and Creoles*, London, 1956.

———, *War and Trade in the West Indies, 1739–1763*, Oxford, 1936.

Paris, Matthew, *Chronicle* (Rolls Series), London, 1866.

Park, Robert, *The Art of Sea-fighting*, London, 1706.

Parry, J. H., *The Spanish Theory of Empire*, Cambridge, 1940.
———, *The Spanish Seaborne Empire*, London, 1966.
———, and Sherlock, P. M., *A Short History of the West Indies*, London and New York, 1956.
Pena Battle, Manuel Arturo, *La Isla de la Tortuga*, Madrid, 1951.
Perez Martinez, Héctor, *Piraterias en Campeche*, siglos XVI–XVIII, Mexico, 1937.
Pitman, F. W., *The Development of the British West Indies, 1700–1763*, New Haven, Conn., 1912.
Playfair, R. L., *Scourge of Christendom*, London, 1884.
———, *Bibliography of the Barbary States*, Part 1, London, 1889.
Potter, John S., *The Treasure Diver's Guide*, London, 1973.
Pringle, Patrick, *Jolly Roger: The Story of the Great Age of Piracy*, London and New York, 1953.
Pyrard, François, *Travels etc.* (Hakluyt Society, 1st series, volumes 76, 77, 80, London, 1887–90.
Ragatz, L. J., *A Guide for the Study of British Caribbean History, 1763–1834*, Washington, 1932.
Raveneau de Lussan, *Journal of a Voyage to the Great South Sea*, Cleveland, 1930.
Real, Cristóbal, *El Corsario Drake y el Imperio Espanol*, Madrid, 1942.
Rectoran, P., *Corsaires Basques et Bayonnaises*, Bayonne, 1946.
Regnard, Jean-François, *La Provençale*, Paris, 1920.
Richards, Stanley, *Black Bart*, Llandybie, 1966.
Richetti, John J., *Defoe's Narratives*, Oxford, 1975.
———, *Popular Fiction before Richardson*, Oxford, 1969.
Roberts, W. A., *The French in the West Indies*, Indianapolis and New York, 1942.
Rogers, Woodes, *A Cruising Voyage Round the World* (intro. and notes G. E. Mainwaring), London, 1928.
Rosenthal, E., *Cutlass and Yardarm*, Cape Town, 1957.
Rouard de Card, E., *Livres français des XVIIe et XVIIIe siècles concernants les Etats barbaresques*, Paris 1911 (supplement, Paris, 1917).
Rowse, A. L., *Sir Richard Grenville of the Revenge*, London, 1937.
Rumeu de Armas, Antonio, *Los Viajes de Sir John Hawkins a América, 1562–1595*, Seville, 1947.
Russell, Edward F. L., *The French Corsairs*, London, 1970.
Rutter, Owen, *The Pirate Wind: Tales of the Sea Robbers of Malaya*, London, 1930.
Sandre, T., *Le Corsaire Pellot*, Paris, 1932.
Savary de Brèves, *Relation des voyages*, Paris, 1628.
Saxon, L., *Lafitte the Pirate*, New York and London, 1930.
Schurz, William L., *The Manilla Galleon*, New York, 1939.
Secord, Arthur W., *Robert Drury's Journal and Other Studies*, Urbana, Illinois, 1961.
Shelvocke, George, *A Voyage Round the World* (intro. W. G. Perrin), London, 1928.
Shipman, Joseph C., *William Dampier*, Laurence, Kansas, 1962.
Smith, Aaron, *The Atrocities of the Pirates*, London, 1824.
Smith, John, *True Travels and Adventures*, London, 1630.
Snelgrave, Capt. W., *A New Account of New Guinea*, London, 1734.
Snow, E. R., *Pirates and Buccaneers of the Atlantic Coast*, Boston, 1944.

Somerville, H. B. T., *Will Mariner*, London, 1936.
Spratt, Devereux, *The Autobiography*, London, 1886.
Stark, Francis R., *The Abolition of Privateering and the Declaration of Paris*, New York, 1891.
State Trials, compiled by T. B. Howells, vols XIII and XV, London, 1812, etc.
Stockton, F. R., *Buccaneers and Pirates of Our Coasts*, New York, 1898.
Sullivan, T. D., *Bantry, Berehaven and the O'Sullivan Sept*, Dublin, 1908.
Surcouf, Robert, *Un Capitaine corsaire*, Paris, 1925.
Tenenti, Alberto, *Naufrages, corsaires et assurances maritimes à Venise, 1592–1609*, Paris, 1959.
Thomazi, A., *Les Flottes d'Or*, Paris, 1937.
Thomson, George Malcolm, *Sir Francis Drake*, London, 1972.
Thornbury, G. W., *Monarchs of the Main*, London, 1855.
Thornton, Archibald Paton, *West India Policy under the Restoration*, Oxford, 1956.
Trelawney, Edward John, *Adventures of a Younger Son*, London, 1831.
Unwin, Rayner, *The Defeat of Sir John Hawkins*, London, 1960.
Uring, Nathaniel, *Voyages and Travels*, London, 1725–7.
Verney, Lady Frances, *Memoirs of the Verney Family*, London and New York, 1892.
Vignols, L., *La Piraterie sur L'Atlantique au XVIIIe siècle*, Rennes, 1886.
Westergaard, W., *The Danish West Indies under Company Rule, 1671–1754*, New York, 1917.
Wilkins, H. T., *Captain Kidd and his Skeleton Island*, London, 1935.
Williams, Eric, *From Columbus to Castro: the History of the Caribbean, 1492–1969*, London, 1970; New York, 1971.
Williams, Gomer, *History of the Liverpool Privateers and Letters of Marque*, Liverpool, 1897.
Williams, Neville, *Francis Drake*, London, 1973.
———, *Captains Outrageous*, London, 1961; New York, 1962.
———, *The Sea Dogs*, London, 1975.
Williamson, G. C., *George, Third Earl of Cumberland*, London, 1920.
Williamson, J. A., *Maritime Enterprise, 1485–1558*, Oxford, 1913.
———, *The Caribbee Islands under the Proprietary Patents*, London, 1926.
———, *Hawkins of Plymouth*, 2nd ed., London, 1926.
Wiseman, H. V., *A Short History of the British West Indies*, London, 1950.
Woodburn, G., *The Great Days of Piracy*, New York, 1954.
Wright, Edward, *Certaine Errors in Navigation*, London, 1599.
Wright, Irene A., ed., *Documents concerning English Voyages to the Spanish Main, 1569–80* (Hakluyt Society, 2nd series, vol. 71), London, 1932.
———, ed., *Spanish Documents concerning English Voyages to the Caribbean, 1527–68* (Hakluyt Society, 2nd series, vol. 62), London, 1928.
———, ed., *Further English Voyages to Spanish America* (Hakluyt Society, 2nd series, vol. 99), London, 1951.
Yung-lun-Yuen, *History of the Pirates who infested the China Sea* (1807), trans. Carl Friedrich Newman, London, 1831.

Index

253

254

255

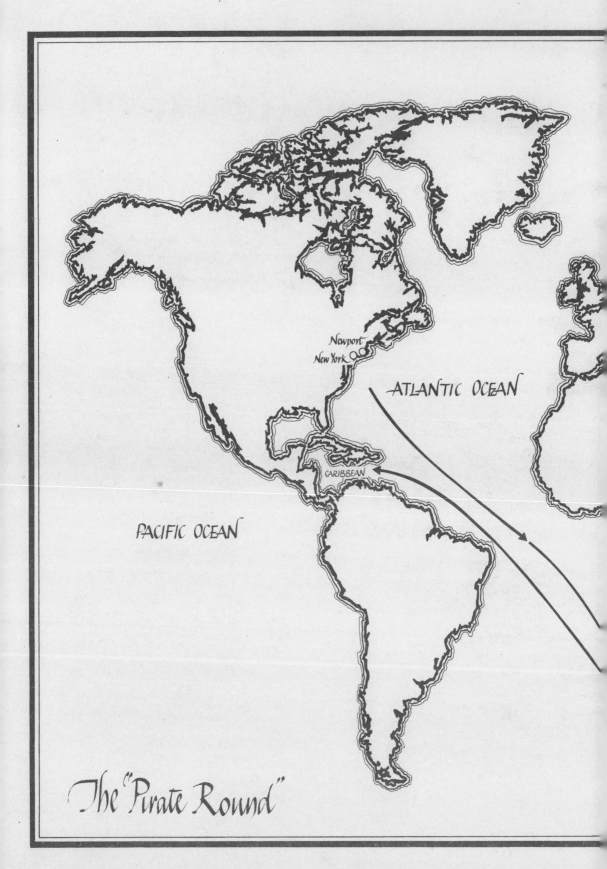

ATLANTIC OCEAN

Newport
New York

CARIBBEAN

PACIFIC OCEAN

The "Pirate Round"